新编英汉汉英翻译教程：
翻译技巧与误译评析

李　青　编著

北 京 大 学 出 版 社

北　京

图书在版编目(CIP)数据

新编英汉汉英翻译教程:翻译技巧与误译评析/李青编著.—北京:
北京大学出版社,2003.6
ISBN 978-7-301-06225-8

Ⅰ.新… Ⅱ.李… Ⅲ.英语－翻译－教材 Ⅳ.H315.9

中国版本图书馆 CIP 数据核字(2003)第 016475 号

书　　　名：新编英汉汉英翻译教程:翻译技巧与误译评析
著作责任者：李　青　编著
责 任 编 辑：汪晓丹
标 准 书 号：ISBN 978-7-301-06225-8/H · 0836
出 版 发 行：北京大学出版社
地　　　址：北京市海淀区成府路 205 号　100871
网　　　址：http//www. pup. cn　电子邮箱：zpup@pup. pku. edu. cn
电　　　话：邮购部 62752015　发行部 62750672　编辑部 62759634
　　　　　　出版部 62754962
印　刷　者：北京飞达印刷有限责任公司
经　销　者：新华书店
　　　　　　890×1240　A5 开本　9 印张　250 千字
　　　　　　2003 年 6 月第 1 版　2017 年 5 月第 7 次印刷
定　　　价：22.00 元

内 容 简 介

　　本书分汉译英、英译汉两部分。对翻译中常见的错误,分门别类,归纳分析;举例典型,内涵丰富,辐射广阔;深浅兼顾,简繁恰当,讲解透彻。善于学习者可通过他人的错误,举一反三,提高自己的能力和水平。

前　言

　　学习一些翻译理论与别人的翻译经验能使人在认识上得到提高，要把理论应用于实践，把别人的经验化为己有，从而提高自己的翻译能力，却非一朝一夕之功。而误译评析在提高翻译水平方面的作用则更有效、更实在，它能使人看到一种原文理解或表达方面的错误，从而引以为戒。有一句名言："聪明的方法是从别人的错误中吸取教训"就是这个道理。对误译进行总结不失是翻译学习中吸取他人教训的一种聪明的方法。刊物上虽有一些误译评析的文章，谈论翻译的书籍中也都有一些误译评析的例句。但数量不多，且较零散。集结成册者很少，且往往只是众多例句的罗列堆积，缺乏系统条理。而要对误译进行总结，不仅应有大量的、各种各样有代表性的典型译例，而且应对这些译例进行综合分析，按照一定方法组成一个有机的整体，从中得出一定的经验教训，使读者不仅能从一个个单个例句得到启发，学会如何正确地思考，准确地理解，灵活而又贴切地表达，以避免类似的误译，而且能从这一整体中系统地学到有关翻译的基础知识、原则与方法以及翻译中应注意的各个方面，即成为一份理论与实践相结合的翻译学习材料。

　　本书在写作过程中力图以英汉对比、错误分析和语言理论这三方面为出发点，对翻译技巧及例句进行综合评述。本书的突出特点是包含大量例句、译文和分析，笔者通过[误译]、[正译]、[评析]三方面把翻译中的错误进行整理和分类，通过分析，结合翻译理论，总结出一些有规律的东西，供读者借鉴。每个例子包括原文、误译和正译，最后对错误所在作出评析。旨在帮助读者切实提高英汉互译水平。书中所用材料包含丰富的译例和详尽的评析。它既能作为高校英语翻译课教材，也非常适合水平相当的众多英语学习者自学使用。为适应各层次读者，所选例句深浅兼顾。以简短、浅易、具有一定代表性，能说明问题者为主。讲解材料循序渐进地介绍翻译的基本知识和方法,努力做到深入浅出、明白易懂。按词法、句法来分类,贯穿一线,从简到繁。全书分上、下两篇,分别叙述汉译英和英译汉。本书收集了英汉互译常见的错误,进行归纳和分析,使读者通过正误译文的比较,举一反三,提高英汉互译的能力。

这部书稿取材广泛,多为本人在教学中搜集整理的材料。增删修改,数易其稿。其中引用的例句,几乎全部都是直接从近年来国内外书刊摘录的,在此特向原作者表示感谢。

汉语和英语是当今世界上使用人数最多的语言,源远流长,兼收并蓄,词汇丰富,且极富于表达力。两种语言的异同远非一本书所能包罗。在此衷心希望借此抛砖引玉,求教于专家。

李青

2003 年 6 月于北京

目　　录

第一部分　汉译英

第二部分　英译汉

第一部分　汉译英

第一章　汉译英概说

第一节　汉译英的翻译过程

汉语转换成英语的机制应该不同于英语转换成汉语的机制。汉语是中国人的母语，中国人从出生之日起就开始学习汉语，在讲汉语的环境中生活，受汉文化的影响，具备重形象、重直觉、重整体的思维方式。英语是中国人的外语，是具备重理性、重逻辑、重个体的思维方式的英美等西方人的母语。中国人运用英语的能力一般低于运用汉语的能力。一般来说，中国人学习汉译英时，是分析理解用母语写成的原文，按与习惯的思维方式相对立的较陌生的思维方式，以较母语能力差的外语能力写成一篇与原文意义相符、功能相似的英语作文。所以，在翻译之前，先要看明白材料是关于什么方面的，是否需要以及如何寻找相应的工具书和背景材料。如果文章专业性很强或者文字艰深，就要先认真把它读懂，然后再开始翻译。这样译者才能有把握使其译文通畅连贯，而不至于牵强附会，断章取义。每当看到一个句子，先要弄明白它说的究竟是什么意思，然后根据这个意思，找到相应的英语表达法。

要翻译好一个汉语句子，除了全面完整地理解它的含义之外，重要的一点就是为句中的关键词语找到适当的英译法。对于一个汉语词，先要准确理解，然后才能准确翻译。虽然我们能熟练地应用自己的母语，但有时要说出一个常用语的确切含义，还得借助于各类词典。所以，在汉英翻译过程中，必要时要查阅汉语和英语工具书，切忌生搬硬套和望文生义。

翻译是用译语语篇传达原语语篇的信息，再现原语语篇及译者的交际目的。一篇文章是由一个个段落组成，而段落又是由句子组成，句子又可以由若干个分句组成，分句里又有一个个的词组和词。因此，我们不能忽视文章语言的层次性，而在不同层次上的翻译处理的侧重点也是不一样的。在词和词组层次上主要是解决语义理解，选择恰当的词汇以及搭配；在分句与句子层次上主要是解决原文信息的解析、组合以及译文句子的结构问题；在段落和篇章层次上则需解决分句、句子之间的衔接和连贯问题。同时我们应注意，原文的语体特征，风格是贯穿于各个层次之中的。

汉英两种语言由于用词造句的规律不同，因而在表达同一个思想时，文字处理就有区别。汉译英时，既有为保证语法结构完整和行文流畅而需要增补词语的现象，也有为避免文理不通或词义重复而需要省略词语的现象。对于这一点，有些译者往往不能把握好。

第二节　汉译英的标准

汉译英的标准同英译汉的标准应当是一致的，无论是"信、达、雅"标准，还是"形似与神似"说，无论是"准确、通顺、易懂"三原则，还是"形合、意合"两要素，仍然要以"忠实于原文"为至高准则。汉译英的标准可以通过"忠于原文，译文通顺，保持风格"等要求具体地用两个字来表示，即"信"与"顺"。信是指忠实于原文的内容、思想、感情、风格等，即把原文完整而准确地表达于译文中。顺，是指用词正确得体，行文流畅通顺，符合英语习惯。信与顺是辩证的统一关系，是相辅相成的。忠实原文并不等于逐字、逐句、逐段死译和硬译。译文通顺，并不能随意增删，歪曲原作内容。要达到这两条标准，译者就要不断提高汉英语言水平，要进行大量的翻译实践。除此之外，还必须了解英语国家的文化背景和风土人情，掌握相关专业的技术知识，只有这样才能真正做好翻译工作。

汉译英是看来容易做来难，要做得好，更不容易。译者不但必须正确理解汉语原文的内容，而且还要掌握原文的句子和词语的意思，才能把英译文处理好，可以直译的地方，尽量直译；不能直译时，便要运用适当的技巧，把原意表达出来。这样的翻译才能既忠实又通畅，这样的翻译，才算是好的翻译。

第三节 汉译英水平的培养

一、要提高英语表达能力

汉译英的基本要求是汉语和英语的语言能力。具体而言,主要是汉语的理解能力和英语的表达能力。语言的表达往往比理解要困难,对汉译英来说更是如此。所以汉译英的最大难点是英语的表达能力。表达是语言能力的最高层次,只有整体英语水平提高了,英语的表达能力才能相应增强。如果没有足够的中英文水平,尤其是要有一定的英文基础,无论对汉译英的原则理解多么透彻,学了多少翻译技巧,都是纸上谈兵。原则可以很快地理解,技巧可以通过机械的训练得以速成,语言表达能力则要靠多年的学习积累,无捷径可寻。所以,一切有助于提高自己英语水平的听说读写练习都不要间断,只有这样才有希望提高汉译英水平。要真正搞好汉译英,对英语水平提出较高的要求,但并非英语水平达到很高的人才能开始学习汉译英,因为汉译英本身既是对已经获得的语言能力的一种运用,也能作为培养英语语言能力的一种有效手段。

二、进行有针对性的翻译实践

翻译是一门与实践紧密相关的学问。如上所述,汉译英本身既是对已经获得的语言能力的一种运用,也能作为培养英语语言能力的一种有效手段。所以要想提高汉译英水平,除了不断加强自己的语言能力之外,还必须进行广泛的汉译英实践。这种实践不应是盲目的,而应有针对性,要在指导下进行。检查译文是否正确地传达了原文的意思,对误译加以更正,检查译文本身是否流利通顺、是否符合英语的习惯表达,在不改变意思的前提下对文理或者措辞进行修正。

三、精读各类英语读物,提高总体英语水平

有效增强英语表达能力的主要途径是精读。具体到汉译英,我们可以有针对性地选择英语国家出版的介绍中国的高质量英文书籍

和文章来仔细阅读,从语言和文化两方面进行学习和吸收。否则,译文能够做到语法基本正确,大致表达原文的意思,但是语言不够地道,不够自然,比较生硬。精读英语国家出版的关于中国的高水平英文书籍是彻底摆脱中国式英语,达到汉译英最高境界的必经之路。

第四节　汉译英的必要条件

一、要有较高的汉语水平

要精通原作,才能开始翻译。精通原作是搞好翻译的前提。要精通原作,必须学好原作所用的语言。对于汉英翻译来说,就是必须较好地掌握汉语,因为原文的思想感情等是通过语言体现出来的。因此,学好汉语是翻译中必不可少的条件之一。

二、要有较高的英语水平

无论英译汉或汉译英,都必须有较高的英语水平,汉英翻译尤为如此。对汉英翻译来说,中国人对原作的理解一般不会有问题的,主要问题在于译者的英文水平。英文水平的高低是汉译英翻译的关键。要做好汉译英,就必须在英语方面打好基础。要学会英语的各种表达方法,要广泛地阅读,经常做英语写作的练习,要熟悉不同文体所使用的各种不同的表达方法。做汉英翻译决不能只靠字典和语法。不能完全字对字、词对词、句对句的翻译。理解了原文的意思之后,要忘掉汉语,用英语去思维,然后用英文的惯用法表达出来。译文要准确、生动,还要传神,这就需要平时刻苦学习,经常进行汉译英训练,努力提高我们的英语水平。

三、要有一定的专业知识和丰富的文化知识

要搞好翻译,还必须有一定的专业知识。不了解所译文章,所涉及的专业,就搞不清汉语原文的意义,也就谈不上翻译。即使大致理解了所译的汉语文章,但是如果不知道英文中的专业词汇及其习惯用法,译出来的东西就不准确,读者要么看不懂,要么引起误解。

在进行汉英翻译过程中,有时会碰到不少汉语意义相同的词,但

这些词在不同的搭配中和特定的上下文中,是有明显区别的,译者一定要注意语言的逻辑性,勤查专业工具书。例如:"草签文本"和"草签合同",这两个术语中的"草签"的含义是不同的,前者是指"缩写签字",草签时,当事人只签其姓名的第一个字母(如:James King 草签为 "J.K."),因此"草签文本"这条术语应译成,"initialed text",而后者的"草签"是指构成对合同条款的认证,但尚不具有法律效力,所以"草签合同"应译成"referendum contract"。再如:"正式协议"和"正式声明",这两条术语中的"正式"就不能盲目地套用,必须弄清它们之间的不同含义。第一个"正式"是指"符合规定的";第二个"正式"是表示"官方权威性的",因此,"正式协议"应译作"formal agreement"而"正式声明"则译成"official statement"。

以上例子说明翻译有些文章时要有一定的专业知识,如果欠缺者方面的知识,就要勤查字典、工具书,必要时还需咨询懂行的人,充分理解原文之后,才有可能以出准确的英译文。

四、要有一定的英语为母语国家的背景知识

除了要有一定的专业知识和丰富的文化知识外,还要了解英美等说英语国家的历史、地理、风土人情、文化等等。否则,一些英译文虽然符合英语语法,但不符合英语表达习惯,甚至影响到跨文化交际。只有具备一定的说英语国家的背景知识,才能在翻译中具有灵活性,才能使译文容易被读者接受,才能缩短译文与读者的距离,使译文准确、通顺、明白无误。例如:

【例1】请到休息室去喝杯咖啡。

[误译] Please go to the restroom to have a cup of coffee.

[正译] Please go to the lobby to have a cup of coffee.

[评析] "restroom"与汉语不对应,并非表示"休息室",而是"厕所"。在美国,restroom、bathroom、washroom 都是"厕所"的意思,是一种委婉的说法,如果对此文化现象不了解,又不去查字典,就会闹出笑话来。"休息室"可根据语境用 crush-room, drawing room, foyer, lobby, retiring room 等。

【例2】红眼

[误译] red eye

[正译] pink eye

[正译] to be green-eyed

[评析] 汉语里的"红眼"与 red eye 没有任何关系。red eye 在英语里是"廉价的威士忌酒"的意思。pink eye 是汉语里所称的"红眼病",指流行性结膜炎或急性传染性结膜炎的俗称;而 to be green-eyed 是 envy 的意思,喻指眼红、忌妒别人的富裕或成功。所以原文应根据语境译为 pink eye 或者 to be green-eyed。

【例3】日本以温泉驰名。

[误译] Japan boasts warm springs.

[正译] Japan boasts hot springs.

[评析] "温泉"在英语中不说 warm spring,而说 hot spring 或 thermal spring。这和上下几例一样从某个侧面反映了两种语言看事物的不同视角。

【例4】我通常睡得很晚。

[误译] I usually sleep very late.

[正译] I usually go to sleep very late.

[评析] 汉语的"迟睡"英语须说 go to sleep late 或 go to bed late。而 sleep late 意为"晚起",即 get up late。文化的不同,看问题的视角不同,表达的角度也不同,应多了解异国文化。

【例5】我们是 1997 级的学生。

[误译] We are students of the 1997 grade.

[正译] We are students of the 1997 enrolment.

[评析] 表示上几年级的"级"须用 grade。例如:她是二年级的学生。应译为:She is a student in the second grade. 所谓 1997 级、1998 级等的"级"是指在该年份注册入学的意思,应译为 enrolment。如果要表示某某年毕业,可以用 to graduate 或 graduate。例如:

我们是 1997 届的学生。We are graduates of the 1997.

他是牛津大学 1998 届毕业生。He was (has been) graduated from Oxford in the class of 1998.

【例6】凶宅

[误译] fearful mansion

[正译] haunted house

[评析] 汉语说"凶宅",英语要说闹鬼的屋子。如果译为 fearful mansion,英美人就不太能理解。

　　翻译应不单是语言的转换,在某种程度上,是文化的转换。汉英两种语言在语系、文字系统、语音、词汇、语法、篇章、语用诸方面均有较大差异,这些差异是它们在物质文化与制度文化不相同的社会中产生和发展、被具有不同心理文化的人长期使用而形成的。由于这两种语言具备不同的特征,反映不同的文化,所以具备一定的说英语国家的背景知识对于汉译英时很重要的。

第五节　汉译英错误分析概说

　　对英译文的典型错误进行分析,既是检验汉译英水平的最佳方法,也是提高汉译英水平的最有效途径,所以它贯穿本书始终。本书充分展示错误分析的方法和作用。下面列举普遍出现的、具有代表性的翻译错误。应仔细对照原文,努力挑出其中的错误,并且学会改正它们。在这个过程中,可以把找出的错误分门别类,然后根据自己容易犯的错误类型,有针对性地进行深入的英语学习和翻译训练。

　　单句翻译是翻译的基本功,也是本书的主要内容。在一个句子中,每个词语都和其它词语发生关系,互为语境,而句子本身则处于孤立状态。所以当我们翻译各个词语时,要做到相互协调,前后一致,逻辑严谨;而当我们对句子做整体处理时,就享有一定灵活性,也许能够给出多种恰当的译法,而这些译法适用于不同的段落或篇章语境。无论在词语的选择还是句子结构的处理上,我们对其适用范围都要做到心中有数。

　　成年人学习外语与幼儿学习母语不同。幼儿学习母语时,客观事物在他们的头脑中尚未与任何一种语言体系建立起联系。他们学习母语的过程就是发展思维能力的过程,当他们成年后学习外语时,固定的文化习惯及思想意识已融入了民族化的语言形式,所用母语的系统已固定,其影响根深蒂固。因此,成年人在学习外语尚未能熟练自如的情况下，自然会在外语与母语之间寻求等值的词、等值的句法表达手段，甚至寻求民族文化的交换。这种不顾英语和汉语在语法及用词方面的差异而进行等值交换就是误译的根源。

第二章　与语法有关的误译

汉译英要求我们把汉语原文的意思理解之后用英语表达出来。一般地说,理解原文相对比较容易,难处在于使英译文所用的表达方式符合英语习惯。为了保证英译文是通顺地道的英语,首先要做到把句子的总体结构安排合理,然后才能讲求句子各组成部分的细节处理。由此说来,汉译英最基本的功夫就是对英语基本句型的掌握和运用了。

英语句子的主要成分是主语和谓语,有时再加上宾语,形成主—谓—宾的基本句式。主语是句子所要述说的对象,而且谓语则表明主语的动作、性质或者状态等。英语是注重主语的语言,而主语几乎离不开谓语动词。主语和谓语动词一旦确定,句子大体框架就相应地固定下来了。所以谓语动词是构建英语句子的关键成分之一。

第一节　不及物与及物动词的误译

英语动词可分为两大类:不及物动词和及物动词。不及物动词基本能够独立使用,后面不接宾语,依然表达完整的意思;而及物动词不能单独使用,后面必须接宾语才能做到语义完整。进行汉译英时,我们需要随时注意汉英在语法方面的差异。英语不及物动词的使用,要随时避免受汉语句子结构的影响,不要错把英语的不及物动词当作及物动词。例如:

【例 7】敲门

[误译] knock the door

[正译] knock on the door(或者 knock at the door)

[评析] 因为 knock 是不及物动词,需加介词后才能接宾语。

【例 8】靠墙

[误译] lean the wall

［正译］lean against the wall

【例9】笑话她

［误译］laugh her

［正译］laugh at her（或者 mock her）

【例10】想你

［误译］think you

［正译］think of you（或者 miss you）

【例11】考虑问题

［误译］think the problem

［正译］think of the problem（或者 consider the problem）

　　另一方面,把句子的谓语用及物动词译出时,需要正确运用单宾语、双宾语和复合宾语的结构,尤其要注意动词与宾语的搭配。由于汉英词语用法的差别,当把原文动宾结构里的动词和名词分别译出后,这一对英语词语不见得搭配得当。也就是说,翻译及物动词时,我们需要把动词和宾语作为一个整体来考虑。中文里的同一个动词,英语里却需要译成不同的动词。比如汉语动词"打"与各种名词搭配时,其译法不尽相同。例如:

打电话 make a phone call, 　打仗 fight a battle

打麻将 play mah jong 　　　打太极拳 practice Taijiquan

打毛衣 knit a sweater 　　　打榧子 snap one's fingers

打文件 type the document。

　　另外,我们还需要尽力摆脱原文形式的束缚,比如原文的动宾结构常常可以用不及物动词翻译,即有时英译文并非是动宾结构。例如:

打喷嚏 sneeze　　　打冷战 shiver　　　打瞌睡 nod

　　有些译者在翻译时容易犯语法错误不外乎有两个原因,一是语言基本功不扎实;二是对中英文句子结构的了解不够,语言转换时生搬硬套。中英文句法结构差异较大,汉译英时,受母语影响,有些译者在表达英语句子时不按照英语的语法规则,而是套用汉语的句式,常常犯一些语法错误。例如:

【例12】因此在这个问题上我重复了这么多遍以后,我今天实在不想再讲了。

[误译] But after repeating so many times on the question, I'm really very reluctant to talk about it any more today.

[正译] But after repeating my answer so many times on the question, I'm really very reluctant to talk about it any more today.

[评析] 汉语中不及物动词较多,这句中的"重复"没有宾语;但英语中及物动词较多, repeat 是及物动词, 应补译宾语：after repeating my answers so many times..., 如果不想补宾语, 就要改用名词短语 after so many repetitions...。

【例 13】如果今年再提出来, 我想也不会有别的结果。

[误译] If they insist on re-submitting this year, I don't see any different outcome.

[正译] If they insist on re-submitting the draft this year, I don't see any different outcome.

[评析] "再提出来"没有宾语, 而 re-submit 是及物动词, 受汉语原文的影响, 原译文 re-submit 后没有宾语, 但是根据英语语法, 这里必须要有宾语。英译时要补上宾语, 译成 re-submit a draft(前文提到一个提案)。

【例 14】在亚洲的金融风暴当中, 对香港的影响在今年已经陆续显现了, 尤其是在今年的上半年。

[误译] The effect on Hong Kong of the financial crisis in Southeast Asia has begun to show, especially in the first half of this year.

[正译] The effect on Hong Kong of the financial crisis in Southeast Asia has begun to be shown, especially in the first half of this year.

[评析] 汉语的不少动词很灵活, 既可当及物动词, 也可当不及物动词;而使用英语动词时限制较多, 一定要弄清楚是及物还是不及物动词。汉语中不及物动词多, 英语中不及物动词少, 所以将汉语不及物动词译成英语不及物动词有时会出问题。如果将"显现", 译为 show, 不合乎英语语法, 可译为不及物的 appear。但是还应注意使用及物动词 be shown 和 manifest itself 等等。

　　还有另外一种形式的不及物动词和及物动词的误译, 也同样是到受汉语句子结构的影响,错把英语的不及物动词当作及物动词。例如:"吃饭"、"读书"、"唱歌"、"付钱"等汉语词组均属于动宾结构,但是这些词组在英语中由于动词本身已经含有宾语所表达的意思,所以宾语的意思在动词本身已不言自明,其宾语一般在句中都可以省略。但有些译者习惯于将宾语说出来,这完全是中国式英语,不符合英语的表达习惯,应当戒除。

【例 15】 咱们去吃饭吧。

[误译] Let's go and eat our meal.

[正译] Let's go and eat.

【例 16】 他们在读书。

[误译] They're reading books.

[正译] They're reading.

【例 17】 我们要在音乐会上唱歌。

[误译] We're going to sing songs at the concert.

[正译] We're going to sing at the concert.

【例 18】 你付钱了吗?

[误译] Have you paid the money?

[正译] Have you paid yet?

以上这些误译的句子从语法上看,似乎没什么问题,但是从表达方式上看,英语没有这样的表达习惯,实际上仍是属于是犯了语法错误:没有分清及物与非及物动词的用法。在汉译英时要十分注意逻辑严密,因为英语比汉语更讲究逻辑结构的严密。

第二节 时态的误译

汉英语句转换的首要问题是句中动词时态含义的理解和表达。把动词时态含义表达好,就是在英译文中把动作的时间和方式说清楚。时态是汉译英时出现误译的另一个多发点。

【例 19】 到 2000 年,这个比例将达到 92%。

[误译] By 2000, the percentage will reach 92%.

[正译] By 2000, the percentage will have reached 92%。

[评析] 这个句子应该用将来完成时,以表示到将来的某个时刻已经完成的动作。

【例20】我妹妹今天没去上学。她得了重感冒,她头痛、发烧。

[误译] My sister doesn't go to school today. She has got a bad cold. She has got a headache and a fever.

[正译] My sister didn't go to school today. She had (has got) a bad cold, a headache and a fever.

[评析] 如把"没去上学"理解为今天早晨"未曾发生过去上学这一行为",应该译为 My sister doesn't go to school today. She has got a bad cold. She has got a headache and a fever. 如果把"没去上学"理解为"在家不在学校这一状态",原文还可译为:My sister hasn't gone to school today. She has got a bad cold, a headache and a fever. today 一词可以和表示状态、情态和感觉等一类动词的一般现在时用在一个句子里,例如:He isn't at school today. He can't go to school today. He feels better today. 但不可以为用了 today 就可以随意用一般现在时。

【例21】你没有迟到,还有三分钟。

[误译] You are not late. You still have three minutes. (There are still three minutes.)

[正译] You are not late. You've got three minutes. (There are three minutes left.)

[评析] still,"(还)是,仍然"的意思,说以前怎样现在还是怎样,可以用 still,例如:天还在下雨。It's still raining. /我们面前仍然有困难。We still have difficulties before us. /There are still difficulties before us. 而"还有三分钟"是还余下、还剩下三分钟的意思,应该用 left 修饰 minutes。

【例22】——你今天下午有空吗?
——我四点以后才有空。

[误译] ——Will you be free this afternoon?
——I'll be free till half past four. (或者 I won't be free after half past four.)

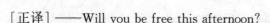

〔正译〕——Will you be free this afternoon?

　　　　——I won't be free till half past four.

〔评析〕A till B,指 B 一发生 A 就停止。例如:他做功课一直到十点
钟。He did his lessons till ten o'clock.(到十点钟就停止做功课
了。) not A till B,指 B 发生 A 才开始。例如:他到十点钟才开始
做功课。He didn't do his lessons till ten o'clock.

　　I'll be free till half past four. 四点半以前我有空。/到四点半我
就没有空了。I won't be free after half past four. 四点半以后我没有
空。这两句都不符合原文的意思。

【例 23】我们一出发,天就下起雨来了。

〔误译〕It rained as soon as we started.

〔正译〕It began to rain as soon as we started out.

〔评析〕as soon as 刚一…马上就,表示某一时刻(a point of time)两个
动作紧接着发生,不宜和表示延续性动作的动词(durative verb)和
表示状态的动词连用。rain 是延续性动词,可以说:It rained all
day yesterday. (昨天下了一天雨。)却不能说:It rained at six
o'clock. 而要说:It began to rain at six o'clock. 或 It was raining at
six o'clock。所以原文一定要改为 It began to rain 才能和 as soon
as 所表达的"某一时刻"不相矛盾。

【例 24】如果她更用功些,她就会学得更好。

〔误译〕She is going to do better in her studies if she works harder.

〔正译〕She will do better in her studies if she works harder.

〔评析〕will(shall)和 be going to 在许多句子里是可以通用的。但如
果将要发生的事受条件(condition)或环境(circumstances)所制约
时,一般宜用"will"(shall)。例如:你要是到法国去,你会喜爱那里
的食品的。If you ever go to France, you will like (不能用 are going to) the food there. 找到了一套房间的话,他们将迁居巴黎。
They will move to Paris when they have found a flat.

【例 25】——他入党多久了?

　　　　——他入党二十多年了。

〔误译〕—— How long has he joined the Party?.

── He has joined the Party for over twenty years.

[正译] ── How long has he been a Party member?

　　　　　── He has been a Party member for over twenty years.

[评析] join 是瞬间动词,表示短时间就结束的动作,不能和表示一
　　段时间的状语连用。join the Party (入党)是不能延续进行的行
　　为,be a Party member(是或当党员)是可以延续存在的状态。汉
　　语可以说"入党二十多年了",英语却要说"当了二十多年的党员"。
　　这种区别,要注意。

【例 26】电影已经开始十分钟了。

[误译] The film has begun for ten minutes.

[正译] The film has been on for ten minutes.

【例 27】已经上课十分钟了。

[误译] The class has begun for ten minutes.

[正译] The class has been going on for ten minutes.

【例 28】那本英语书他已丢了三天了。

[误译] He has lost his English book for three days.

[正译] He lost his English book three days ago.

[评析] lost 是瞬间动词不能与表示一段时间的 for three days 搭配使
　　用。原译文不符合英语语法。

【例 29】图书馆已经开门半小时了。

[误译] The library has(been) opened for half an hour.

[正译] The library has been open for half an hour.

[评析] open 是形容词,表示开放的。

【例 30】托马斯·爱迪生去世已经六十五年了。

[误译] Thomas Edison has died for 65 years.

[正译] Thomas Edison has been dead for 65 years.

[评析] die 是一个表示瞬间的动词不能与表示能延续一段时间的介
　　词 for 连用,所以这里用完成时加表示状态的形容词 dead 就可以
　　表达句中的意思。原文也可以这样翻译:Thomas Edison died 65
　　years ago。

【例 31】20 年来,中国的科学家们为祖国做出了贡献。

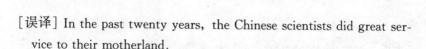

[误译] In the past twenty years, the Chinese scientists did great service to their motherland.

[正译] In the past twenty years, the Chinese scientists have done great service to their motherland.

[评析] in the past + 时间段，要求主句用现在完成时。因此，句中的 did 应改为 have done。

【例 32】等我们的老师从国外回来，我们就要做完我们的工作了。

[误译] We shall finish our work by the time our teacher returns from abroad.

[正译] We shall have finished our work by the time our teacher returns from abroad.

[评析] by + 将来的时间，要求主句使用将来完成时。所以句中的 shall finish 应改为 shall have finished。

【例 33】中国人民不用多久就会变得富裕起来。

[误译] It won't be long before the Chinese people will become well off.

[正译] It won't be long before the Chinese people become well off.

[评析] 一般将来时态，用于主句时，从句不再用将来时表示，而应用一般现在时。所以，句中的 will 要去掉。

【例 34】一般人要到失去他们所拥有的一切时，才会珍惜他们所拥有的一切。

[误译] People at large do not appreciate what they have after they lose it.

[正译] People at large do not appreciate what they have until they lose it.

[评析] "直到……才……"应译为 not... until...。句中的 after 改为 until。

【例 35】我们某些产品应该说已经达到先进水平。

[误译] Some of our products ought to be said to reach advanced levels.

[正译] Some of our products ought to be said to have reached advanced levels.

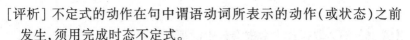

[评析] 不定式的动作在句中谓语动词所表示的动作(或状态)之前发生,须用完成时态不定式。

【例36】你记得她的名字吗? 我忘了。

[误译] Do you remember her name. I forgot.

[正译] Do you remember her name? No, I forget.

[评析] forget, remember 都是表示现在的一种心理状态, forget her name＝don't remember her name (想不起她的名字了)。原译的含义是 I forgot her name before, but l remember it now. (我过去忘记了她的名字,但现在想起来了。) 和"我忘了"的含义相反了。我们绝不可以为汉语里有个"了"字,英语就要用过去时。例如:我明白了。I see. /我知道了。I know. /我懂得了。I understand.

第三节 比较句型的误译

汉语注重总体效果,不太要求细节上的准确性;但英语则比较刻板,逻辑思维严密,要求语言的准确性。

【例37】今年的产量比去年高。

[误译] This year's output is greater than last year.

[正译] This year's output is greater than that of last year.

[评析] 在汉语中可以说"今年的产量比去年高",我们可以理解全句的意思,而不必吹毛求疵地说:"今年的产量比去年的产量高"。可以不对应"产量"与"去年"这两个不同类的词组进行比较。但是英语就一定要准确地表述,原文还可以译为: This year's output is greater than last year's.

【例38】中国的人均农业土地面积比不上世界上其他许多国家。

[误译] China's per Capita agricultural land cannot compare with many other countries in the world.

[正译] China's per Capita agricultural land cannot compare with that of many other countries in the world.

[评析] 就本句而言,"土地面积"与"国家"之间没有可比性。翻译时如果选择"土地面积"作为主语,表达一定要严谨,拿来与之相比较

的应该是其他国家的"土地面积",需要添加"that"来表示。

【例39】不会取得过去七次会议上的那种结果。

[误译] The outcome would not be different from the previous seven times.

[正译] The outcomes would not be different from those of the previous seven times.

[评析] 英语比较讲究逻辑上的准确性。在这句译文中, the outcome 与 seven times 不属同类, 不应进行比较。译文可改为 the outcomes will be different from those (the outcomes) of the previous seven times。

【例40】学习外语的方法和学习游泳的方法一样,必须把实践放到第一位。

[误译] The way of learning foreign languages is the same as learning swimming. Practice must be put first.

[正译] The way of learning foreign languages is the same as that of learning swimming. Practice must be put first.

[评析] 原文相比较的双方是将(学习外语的)方法和(学习游泳的)方法相比, 而误译的意思却是将学习外语的方法和学习游泳相比, 英译文不符合语法规则,意思不清晰。

第四节 冠词的误译

由于汉语没有冠词,汉译英很容易在这方面出现语法错误。

【例41】他们三人主修物理学。

[误译] Three of them major in physics.

[正译] The three of them major in physics.

[评析] the three of them 意为"他们三人", 而 three of them 意为"他们当中三人", 例如:他们当中三人会讲德语。Three of them speak German.

【例42】我的热度已经退了,但仍旧咳嗽和头疼。

[误译] My fever is gone, but I still have cough and headache.

[正译] My fever is gone, but I still have a cough and a headache.

[评析] 英语疾病名称之前习惯上不加冠词,但是少数常用表示病痛的词须加不定冠词,例如:我的背痛。I've got a pain in my back. 她患上感冒并发高烧。She had a cold and a high fever.

【例 43】这项工程由一位有经验的工程师负责。

[误译] This project is in charge of an experienced engineer.

[正译] This project is in the charge of an experienced engineer.

[评析] in the charge of sb 作"由…负责管理"解。例如:医院这间病房由史密斯医生管理。This ward of the hospital is in the charge of Dr Smith. in charge of sb(or sth)意为负责照看。例如:格林先生负责这个班级。Mr Green is in charge of the class.

第五节　逐词对译与语法问题

有时有些译者逐词死译,导致一些虽然似乎符合英语语法,但是不符合英语表达习惯的误译,影响到跨文化交际。这也是汉译英常见的误译类型之一。例如:

【例 44】欢迎你参观我们商品交易会。

[误译] Welcome you to visit our trade fair!

[正译] Welcome to our trade fair!

[评析] "欢迎某人做某事"英译时,welcome 用的句型是 welcome + to + 名词,例如:欢迎你到中国来! Welcome to China! 不能译为 Welcome you to come to China。

【例 45】店主让我父亲一天干 16 小时的活。

[误译] The shop-owner let father work 16 hours a day.

[正译] The shop-owner made father work 16 hours a day.

[评析] 误译文全句表达的意思成了"店主同意我父亲每天工作 16 小时"。let 在此表示同意,而不是迫使。汉语原文的"让"的其中一个英语对应词是 let,但是原文虽然用了"让",其在原句的内涵是"迫使",因此,应使用 make(迫使,促使)。

【例 46】作为一个世界贸易组织,缺乏中国, 没有中国的参加,我看它也很难发挥作为一个世界贸易组织的应有作用。

[误译] As a world trade organization, I think, WTO without China will be hard to play its due role.

[正译] As a world trade organization, I think, WTO without the participation of China will find it hard to play its due role.

[评析] 由于受汉语结构的影响,"很难"一词很容易被误译成(the organization) will be hard (to play its role),这就犯了语法错误,应改译为"(the organization) will find it hard (difficult) (to play its role)"。

【例47】错误和挫折教训了我们,使我们比较地聪明起来了,我们的事情就办得比较好一些。

[误译] The mistakes we committed and the setbacks we experienced have taught us lessons and made us wiser, therefore we can handle our affairs better.

[正译] Taught by mistakes and setbacks, we have become wiser and handle our affairs better.

[评析] 译文没有抓住原文的精神实质。原文强调的是"我们变得聪明起来了……"。而原译文强调的是"使我们聪明起来了……"把原文主动的意思变为被动了。所以这句不能按汉语原文顺序翻译。

【例48】他使用长句、难句和大量词汇有时使他的书很难读。

[误译] His use of long sentences, difficult syntax, and large vocabulary sometimes make his books hard to be read.

[正译] His use of long sentences, difficult syntax, and large vocabulary sometimes make his books hard to read.

[评析] 形容词 hard 和 difficult 之后所跟的不定式一般用主动形式,例如:中国古文很难理解。Ancient Chinese prose is hard to understand

【例49】他把肘子靠在桌子上。

[误译] His elbows were leaned on the table.

[正译] He leaned his elbows on the table.

[评析] 当动宾关系十分密切时, 表示动作的工具、方式或结果的名词不能作为被动式的主语。

【例50】 因为一连几天在下雨, 他只得待在家里。

[误译] Having rained for successive days, he had to stay at home.

[正译] As it had rained for successive days, he had to stay at home.

[评析] 原译文分词的逻辑主语与句子主语不一致, 有语法错误。

【例51】 一到北京, 我的朋友就在机场等着接我。

[误译] On arriving at Beijing, my friend was waiting for me at the airport.

[正译] On arriving at Beijing, I found my friend waiting for me at the airport.

[评析] On arriving...和主句的主语 my friend 不一致, 因此这种译法不符合英语语法。

第六节　无语法概念的误译

逐词死译, 没有英语语法概念导致误译, 由于汉语是一种没有形态变化的语言, 有些汉译英误译的错误类型是对英语的词形不注意而造成的:

【例52】 他有两个颇有说服力的理由。

[误译] He has two quite convinced reasons.

[正译] He has two quite convincing reasons

[评析] 弄混现在分词与过去分词用法, 是常见错误。convinced 是过去分词, 具有"被说服"、"信服"的意思。应改为现在分词 convincing, 即"有说服力"的意思。

【例53】 写作的技巧比起其他艺术的技巧来相当困难。

[误译] The technique of writing is rather difficult comparing with that of the other arts.

[正译] The technique of writing is rather difficult compared with that of the other arts.

[评析] 用 compare with 翻译"和……对比"这样的汉语句型时, 一般

应译为过去分词结构来表示被动的意味。

【例 54】录音机为学习外语提供了方便。

[误译] Learning foreign languages has been facilitated by recording machines.

[正译] Recording machines facilitate learning foreign languages.

[评析] facilitate 这个词要求名词或动名词作宾语,而且几乎不用被动语态。

【例 55】随着现代化发明的出现简化了家务事。

[误译] Housework is facilitated with the advent of modem inventions.

[正译] Modern inventions facilitate housework.

[评析] facilitate 的意思是"使容易"、"使便利",它不以人作主语,不用于被动语态,因为它本身已包含被动的意思。像这种本身内含被动意味的词组还很多,例如:

to abide by 遵守, to abound with (in) 充满, to accord with 符合, to add up to 总起来意味着, to brim over with 充满, come in for 受到, to come to light 被发现, to consist in 存在于, to date back to 要追溯到。

【例 56】高举邓小平理论的伟大旗帜是这次大会的灵魂,把邓小平理论确立为我们党的指导思想是这次大会的最主要成果。

[误译] Hold high the great banner of Deng Xiaoping Theory has been the soul of this conference and identifying Deng Xiaoping Theory as a guiding ideology of the whole Party is the most important outcome of this congress.

[正译] Holding high the great banner of Deng Xiaoping Theory has been the soul of this conference and identifying Deng Xiaoping Theory as a guiding ideology of the whole Party is the most important outcome of this congress.

[评析] 汉语中有一些动词,如原文中的"高举",看似没有主语,有些译者很可能译成英语动词原型 Hold high。这就成了祈使句,因为动词原型常被理解成"命令式",即请大家高举,应当避免这种译法。汉语有相当多的无主句,而英语一般要求主谓宾要全,对汉译

英转换时的句子结构的把握是确保不出现语法错误的关键。

第七节　固定用法的误译

【例 57】在看到李伟的杀人行为时我感到十分震惊。

[误译] I was very much shocked at the sight of Li Wei's killing.

[正译] I was very much shocked at the sight of Li Wei's killing a person

[评析] Li Wei's killing 可做"李伟杀人"解,也可做"李伟被杀"解。读者很难从上下文关系中看懂这句话的真正含义。如果译为 Li Wei's killing a person,就没有歧义了。又如:

　　Liu's education(是教育刘还是刘教育别人?),Zhang's release (是释放张还是张释放别人?),等均有两种解释。在名词的使用过程中,名词的所有格如果使用不当,可能造成意思模糊,因为名词所有格可以表示动作的执行者,也可表示动作的承受者。所以用名词所有格有时可能引起误解。

【例 58】世界范围内的人均木材积蓄量将下降 47％。

[误译] On the world-wide scale, the per capita timber reserve will drop 47％.

[正译] On the world-wide scale, the per capita timber reserve will drop by 47％.

[评析] 当表示"降低多少"(减少多少)时,英语可用 to decrease, reduce, be reduced, go down, fall, drop, dwindle 等表示。这些动词后面都要跟介词 by 来表示"减少(了)"。例如:减少了三十人次 to decrease (reduce; be reduced) by thirty person-times /减少四万公顷 to go down (fall; drop; dwindle) by forty thousand hectares

【例 59】昨天他从一辆卡车上跳下来,伤了胳臂。

[误译] Yesterday he jumped down a truck and hurt his arm.

[正译] He jumped down from a truck and hurt his arm yesterday. 或者 He jumped off a truck and hurt his arm yesterday.

[评析] down 作介词用是"沿着……往下"的意思,例如:他从那山上

走下来。He walked down the hill. /眼泪顺着她的面孔流下。The tears ran down her face. 从卡车上跳下来只能用 jump off（跳离）或 jump down from（从…跳下，down 是副词），例如：一只猫从梯子上一蹬一蹬地跳下来。A cat jumped down the ladder.（沿着梯子一跳一跳地下来）一只猫从梯子上跳下来。A cat jumped down from the ladder.（一瞬间的动作）

【例 60】夜里下过一场雷阵雨。

[误译] There was a thunder shower at night.

[正译] There was a thunder shower in the night.

[评析] in the night 指在某个特定的夜晚，意为在晚上某个时间。例如：她夜间醒过两次。She woke up twice in the night.

　　　at night 指在任何一个夜晚。是"在夜里"的意思，例如：夜间这里灯要开着。A light should be kept on here at night.

【例 61】这水可以饮用吗？

[误译] Is this water good to be drunk？

[正译] Is this water good to drink？

[评析] 形容词 good 作"有益的"解时，其后所跟动词不定式须用主动态。例如：这种药睡前服有益。This medicine is good to take before going to bed.

【例 62】安娜想明年结婚。

[误译] Mary wants to be married next year.

[正译] Mary wants to get married next year.

[评析]"结婚"作为一种行为，英语须说 get married。例如：他是1990 年结婚的。He got married in 1990. be married 表示一种状态，例如：你结婚了吗？Are you married?

【例 63】我不怀疑你有科研工作的能力。

[误译] I do not doubt your ability of making scientific research.

[正译] I do not doubt your ability to make scientific research.

[评析] 名词 ability 常用不定式作定语，习惯上不用"of ＋动词 ing"的结构。

　　　以上这些误译的句子也都是受到母语干扰的不纯正的英语，是有些译者在跨文化交际过程中硬套母语规则和习惯的不规则英语，也是在学习过程中出现的"过渡语"。人们认为，过渡语是指在整个外语学习的心理语言过程中所体现的语言体系，其特点是涉及大量的母语干扰和语言迁移现象，它是一个独立的语言系统，它出于试图掌握第二语言所做出的努力。该语言系统是在英语学习和使用过程中对英语的理解与验证的结果，它在不断的验证中发展，应该使之越来越接近英语的语言系统。

第三章 词汇的误译

第一节 机械对应

汉英两种语言中有不少词汇看似对应,但在口译中可能造成译文拖沓或不准确。译者应事先熟悉这些假对应现象,并掌握适当的译法。无论在英语学习还是翻译过程中,机械对应都是一种普遍存在的错误倾向,它严重阻碍着我们提高翻译水平和整体英语水平。所谓机械对应,就是英语学习者在头脑里自觉或不自觉地把某个汉语词和某个英语词划上了等号。比如不少人见到"可能"就想到 possible,见到不大可能就想到 impossible。其实 possible 更接近于汉语的并非不可能,而 impossible 的意思是"完全不可能"。如前所述,表示可能性的大小,英语最常用的词是 chance,但是这个词在许多译者心中的对应词却是"机会"。

机械对应的另一个坏处是误导我们把某些英语词语使用得过于频繁。比如说,"水平"一词译成英语,不一定都是 level,要根据句子的含义确定译法。但是如果我们认定"水平"就是 level,那么就会在汉译英时滥用 level 这个词,例如把"英语水平"译为 English level,把"生活水平"译为 living level,把"游泳水平"译为 swimming level 等等。其实在上面那些词语中,"水平"更恰当的译法分别是:

英语水平 English proficiency

生活水平 living standard

游泳水平 swimming skill

或者根据上下文灵活处理,例如:

【例 64】他的游泳水平还挺高。

[误译] His swimming level is very high.

[正译] He has become quite good at swimming.

[评析] 本句英译文完全不同于原文句型,但是正确地完成了预言的

转换。所以,汉英词语间的对应不是绝对的、死板的,而是相对的、灵活的,要受具体语境的影响。明白了这一点,英语学习才能够深入,汉译英水平才能够不断提高。

【例65】他的英语水平比我的高。

[误译] The level of his English is higher than that of mine.

[正译] He knows more English than I.

[评析] 这句里的汉语"水平"一词虽未译出,但其意已含在句子中。若按照汉语字面生硬译成:The level of his English is higher than that of mine. 就不符合英语表达习惯。

【例66】要奋发图强,把我军的军政素质提高到一个新的水平。

[误译] We must work hard to raise to a new level the military and political quality of our army.

[正译] We must work hard to raise to a new height the military and political quality of our army.

[评析] 这里原文的"水平"指的是高度,所以译为 height, 和动词 raise 的搭配也比较好。

【例67】各级领导干部必须提高领导水平。

[误译] Cadres at all levels should improve their level of leadership.

[正译] Cadres at all levels should improve their art of leadership.

[评析] 这里的"领导水平",实际上指领导能力、领导艺术,故译作 art of leadership。

又如"关心"一词的英译:

【例68】关心人民生活

[误译] to be concerned about the living of the people

[正译] to care about the well-being of the people

[评析] 有些译者经常把"关心"译成 to be concerned about, 但是它的内涵是"挂念"、"担心"。care about 用在这儿很贴切原文的意思。"生活"翻译成 living (生活, 生计)没有译成 well-being(康乐, 安宁, 福利, 幸福)意思到位。

【例69】关心局势发展

[误译] to be concerned about the developments of the situation

［正译］to follow the developments closely

［评析］to be concerned about 有"担心"的含义，而原文的"关心"意思是追踪事态的发展，因而译为 to follow ... closely。另外，由于本句的"发展"（developments）就是指局势（situation）的发展，situation 可以省去不译。

【例 70】共同关心的问题

［误译］issues of common concern（或者 common interest）

［正译］issues of mutual interest

［评析］"共同关心的"在这儿的含义是共同感兴趣的。mutual interest 译出了其神，而 common concern 逐字死译，只是译出了其形。mutual interest 的译法要高出 common concern 一筹。

【例 71】我们关心中国是否能保持持续发展。

［误译］We are concerned about whether China will be able to maintain a sustainable development.

［正译］We would like to know whether China will be able to achieve a sustainable development.

［评析］本句用 would like to know 表示"关心"看似偏离原意，实际上用 would like to know 在本句要比 to be concerned about 更为传神。

【例 72】领导人对两国关系非常关心。

［误译］Our leaders have been much concerned about our bilateral relations.

［正译］Our leaders have taken interest in the development of our bilateral relations.

［评析］对两国关系非常关心的实质意义是关心两国关系的状况及其走向。原译文只表达了原文所没有的担心之意，而没表示出原文的关切之意。

　　要摆脱这种词对词翻译的机械对应，根本上还要尽量培养对词、词组、习语等有正确理解的能力，要大幅度增加阅读量、加强语感和用外语思维，以便能深切体会和着重吸收英语的习惯表达方式。在具体的翻译实践活动中注意学习和掌握英译文词语的搭配是有效解决机械对应问题的良好途径。从另一个角度来看,语言所表达的内容毕竟不能完全脱离语言的形式而独立存在,完全摆脱原文字句结构的束缚仅是一种理想状况,在翻译实践中不容易达到。我们应对汉英两种语言进行对比,分析它们的共同点和主要差异,以此作为线索,对翻译实践中所用的语言转换的方法和技巧加以总结。这么做即使创造不出严格的理论体系,至少能归纳出一些经验之谈,再用这些理论或者经验之谈来指导翻译实践。如果充分领略和利用前人已经总结出来的汉英语言转换理论与技巧,就在一定程度上有助于尽快提高自己的翻译水平。

词义的正确选择首先取决于对原文词义的确切理解,而对原文词义的确切理解又取决于对原文上下文的推敲。有些词看起来很简单,翻译时一下子就会想到常用的对应词。但有时最常用的对应词却不能准确地表达原作的意思。

【例 73】当前在农业生产中要狠抓施肥。

[误译] At present, we should resolutely grasp manure in agricultural production.

[正译] Attention should be paid to the question of manure in agricultural production.

[评析] "抓"在这句里的实质意义是"重视",如果按字面翻译,英译文让人感到不知所云,并荒唐可笑。翻译"抓",必须根据语境确定其的内涵。例如:他主要抓生产。He is mainly in charge of production. / 抓苗头 watch out for the first signs / 抓重点 stress the essentials / 他抓紧时间进行技术训练。He lost no time in technical training. / 这部电影抓住了许多观众。The movie appealed to a lot of audience.

【例 74】这家工厂只有几年的历史,可是产品已经进入国际市场。

[误译] The factory has a history of only a few years, but its products have already got into the international market.

[正译] The factory was set up only a few years ago, yet its products have found their way into the international market.

[评析] 在中国话里,"历史"两字用得很广,在不同句中有不同的语

境意义,译成英文未必都是 history。本例句里"几年的历史",无非是说"才建厂几年",但是不能译为 a history of only a few years。因为 a history 不能与 only a few years 搭配。类似的例子是很多的,如:"历史经验"译成 past experience。

【例 75】 还要努力读一点历史和小说。

[误译] We should also make efforts to read some history books and novels.

[正译] We should also find time to read some history books and novels.

[评析] 这里"努力"一词理解为"挤出时间"是对的,如译为 make efforts,则会让人产生误解,以为文化水平低,读历史和小说很费力。

有些常用词看起来简单,但在不同的上下文却有不同的含义,因而译法也不一样。译者应该对此保持警惕。例如:问题的关键是外国军队撤出柬埔寨。The key to the problem is the withdrawal of foreign troops from Kampuchea。但是:

【例 76】 问题的关键是外国军队占领阿富汗。

[误译] The key to the problem is the occupation of Afghanistan by foreign troops.

[正译] The crux of the problem is the occupation of Afghanistan by foreign troops.

[评析] 本句"关键"的内涵不同了,意为"症结",译文应为 crux 或 root cause;若不小心,就会将意思译反,变成:The key to the problem is the occupation of Afghanistan by foreign troops. 而该句的意思是"解决问题的关键是让外国军队占领阿富汗"。

【例 77】 食言

[误译] eat one's words

[正译] break one's promise (或者 break one's word)

[评析] eat one's words 从形式上与"食言"对应,但其实际意义是"承认说错了话"。

【例 78】 他在一所高校学习。

[误译] He is studying in a high school.

[正译] He is studying in a university.

[评析] 这是望文生义而产生了误译，high school 并非"高校"，其汉语的对应词是"中学"，是 middle school 的另一种说法。

【例 79】 这里住房紧张。

[误译] There is housing tension.

[正译] There is housing shortage.

[评析] 把"住房紧张"死译为 housing tension，没有考虑到此处的"紧张"实际意义是供应不足，所以应译为 housing shortage。同样：

【例 80】 去年防汛能力不足。

[误译] There was flood combating shortage last year.

[正译] There was insufficient flood combating capability last year.

[评析] 由于原文中的"不足"用来修饰能力，就不能对应地套用 shortage，只能译为 insufficient flood combating capability。

【例 81】 罪行法定原则

[误译] principle of crime by law

[正译] the principle of a legally prescribed punishment for a specified crime

[评析] 原译文 principle of crime by law 实际的意思是"依法犯罪"。汉译英应注意两种语言之间的词义差异。某个汉语意义译成英文，可能会有好些选择，译者应在这些选择中挑出最符合汉语原意的那个词来，否则有可能造成误译，甚至闹出笑话来。

　　以上的例子说明一个词的具体含义往往要结合全句才能确定，在翻译的时候有时只有结合上下文来考虑怎样处理这个词，才能译得准确。上下文在这里不仅指一个句子中各部分之间的关系，还指一句话、一段话的前后关系。当然，句子表达的是一个多数情况下，读者或译者不必依靠句子以外的上下文便能弄懂全句的含义。但是也有非看上下文才能准确理解句子意思的情况。这主要有三种情况：(1) 一个句子由极简单的词语构成，读者必须进一步了解与它有关的语言环境才能弄懂其完整的思想；(2) 句子的语法结构不严密或比较复杂，也常常需要结合上文来弄明白；(3) 必须具有一定的背景知识并了解文章的思路和风格，才能确切了解句子的含义。

第二节 词义理解

汉语过去使用单个字的词就能表达意思,后来多习惯于用两个字构成一个词。加了一个字,这个词就可以表达各种各样微妙的意思,所以汉语的词汇非常丰富,改动一个字,意思就不同。单个字的词易译,"轻"可译成 light,基本上不会错,如果是"轻快",不能译成 light and fast 而要译成 brisk 或者 light-hearted 或者 lively。"轻柔"不一定译成 light and soft,可译成 soft 或 gentle;比较抽象的"轻盈"要译成 lithe 或 graceful,因为两个字已构成一个整体,意思也有所不同。

【例 82】盟友

[误译] allied friend

[正译] ally

[评析] 重心在"盟","友"帮助构成词组。

【例 83】高寒地区

[误译] highly cold district

[正译] alpine district

[评析] 重心在"高","寒"帮助构成词组。

【例 84】垂钓

[误译] vertical fishing

[正译] whiff (fishing)

[评析] 重心在"钓","垂"帮助构成词组。

【例 85】雅座

[误译] elegant seat

[正译] best (comfortable or private) room(corner)

[评析] 重心在"雅","座"帮助完成词义。

从以上例句可以看出,汉英两种语言的词汇,其含义和用法有相同之处,但有更多不同的地方。如果翻译时不注意这一点,没有领会此意的真实含义,逐词死译,译文势必会貌合神离,似是而非,有时甚至会与原意大相径庭。

【例86】从伦敦到巴黎,一种名为"空中公共汽车"的飞机,载客二百五十一人,每小时一班。

[误译] There is an hourly shift from London to Paris by a plane known as the Airbus capable of seating 251 passengers.

[正译] There is an hourly flight from London to Paris by a plane known as the Airbus capable of seating 251 passengers.

[评析] 把"每小时一班"译为 hourly shift, 可以说是让人不知所云。原文的"每小时一班",意思是每小时飞行一次,而 shift 是"轮班"的意思,如工厂里的日班(day shift)和夜班(night shift)。误译的错误是由于对 shift 这个词的意义没有很好掌握。

【例87】形成了体育文化热。

[误译] There has arisen a fever about physical culture.

[正译] There has arisen an intense popular interest in physical culture.

[评析] fever 是发高烧的"热"。而"体育文化热"是"体育文化受到人们普遍热烈欢迎"的意思,应译为 an intense popular interest in physical culture。

【例88】市教育局为我校选派了校长。

[误译] The Municipal Educational Bureau selected and sent a headmaster for our school.

[正译] The Municipal Educational Bureau appointed a headmaster for our school.

[评析] 在这里"选派"不应按字面翻译,其实质意义是"任命"。

【例89】她可以独立为人看病了。

[误译] She can treat patients independently.

[正译] She is now eligible to treat patients independently.

[评析] 原文的"可以"既不表示能力,也不表示可能性,不可译为can。根据西方国家的情况,"可以"在此应理解为"有资格"(即有处方权)。这句话的意思是"她有资格独立为人看病了。"

【例90】我被挑选为中国艺术教育考察小组成员。

[误译] I was chosen as a member of China's Art and Education Study

Group.

[正译] I was chosen as a member of China's Art Education Study Group.

[评析] "艺术教育"有两种理解：一是并列结构，即艺术与教育(art and education)；二是偏正结构，即艺术方面的教育(education for art; artistic education; art education)。根据上下文，这里应是后一种情况。

【例91】我们能否谈得来？

[误译] Can we talk with each other?

[正译] I'd like to know whether we can get along well.

[评析] "Can we talk with each other?" 的意思是"我们可以谈一谈吗？""谈得来"不是指具体"谈话"动作，而是指相处关系好，彼此有话可谈。应译为：to get along well。

【例92】也不会影响中国的金融保险事业对外的开放政策。

[误译] Nor will it affect China's policy of opening its banking and insurance causes.

[正译] Nor will it affect China's policy of opening its banking and insurance sectors.

[评析] "事业"常译为 cause, undertaking，但是国民经济的一个部门最好译为 sector。这句的汉语原文还可译为 Nor will it affect China's open policy in the field of fianance and insurance sectors.

汉语的许多词汇所要传达的信息都具有潜在性和隐蔽性，有的有深层含义，有的有言外之义，有的有语用意义或比喻意义。因此，汉译英时如不弄清汉语词汇所要传达的真实信息而机械地对等翻译，往往会造成机械对应。在翻译实践中这是一个很大的误区。不少初学翻译的人可能会以为，只有字对字、句对句地照着原文译，译文的保险系数才大。殊不知，恰恰与他们的愿望相反，在许多情况下，"绝对对等"的译文会成为机械对应而歪曲了原文的意思。有时会出现这样的情况：译文的外形与原文的外形越亦步亦趋，它所表达的信息离原文的实际意思却越远。当然，这样说并不是一概排斥"外形对等"，而是提醒译者不能以"外形对等"破坏"信息对等"。翻译的中心任务是从语义到文体都要再现原语的信息,而且要力争最贴切的再现。否则,翻译就失去了其自身的意义。

【例93】他有很强的事业心。

[误译] He has a strong heart of career.

[正译] He is self-motivated and result-oriented.

[评译] 此处不能望文生义,将"事业心"译为 heart of career,这样翻译虽然看起来对应,实际上根本不对应,完全歪曲了原文的意思。

【例94】庭院经济是很得人心的。

[误译] The courtyard economy has won the hearts of the people.

[正译] The courtyard economy has the great support of the people.

[评析] "人心"在这里不能按照字面逐词译为 hearts of the people,因为这样翻译歪曲了原文的意思。"得人心"就是得到人民的支持。原文也可译为 to enjoy popular sympathy。

【例95】美国内部对中国政策究竟怎么样,我们还要观察。

[误译] What China policies are to be pursued after all within the US, we still have to wait and see.

[正译] The American authorities have to decide among themselves what China policy to pursue, and so we still have to wait and see.

[评析] 但是,"美国内部"并非指美国国内这样的概念,而是指美国的领导层要对中国采取什么样的政策。因为决策者是高层领导而不是平民百姓,因此 within the US 不足于表达这样的意思。

【例96】夜已很深了。

[误译] Then night is deep.

[正译] The night is well advanced.

[评析] 有些译者一看到这个汉语句子,可能马上会想到 deep 这个对应词。但这不是英文的表达方式。

【例97】我想南水北调的问题总不能够无限期地拖下去吧!

[误译] The south-north water transfer, in my view, is an issue that cannot be delayed indefinitely.

[正译] The south-north water transfer, in my view, should (must) not be delayed indefinitely.

[评析] 有些译者常常将"不能够"译成 cannot, 但是在一般情况下 cannot 的意思是无此能力。例如：盲人认不了颜色。A blind man cannot judge colours. 本文的"不能够"的含义是不允许, 应改译为 should not 或者 must not。

【例 98】 现在有许多人在提倡民族化、科学化、大众化。

[正译] Many people nowadays are calling for a nationalization, scientification and massilization.

[正译] Many people nowadays are calling for a transformation to a national, scientific and mass style.

[评析] 现代汉语使用"化"的例子很多, 但不都意味着要译成后缀 "-ization"的对应词, 许多情况下需要变通处理。变通的根据是上下语境的要求及惯用法, 不能自造词汇。如"科学化"就不能自造为 scientification。此外, 像"国产化"、"良种化"、"老龄化"、"年轻化"、"知识化"、"沙漠化"、"汉化"、"淡化"等等都没有英语对应词, 加后缀"-ization"自造也行不通。译时只能根据上下文灵活解决, 即利用其他词、词组或句子译出这些词的内涵意义。如"国产化"可译为 China-made 或根据上下文译为 home-made。

【例 99】 外向型经济

[正译] external economy

[正译] external-oriented economy

[评析] 汉语中的"型"近年来也是颇时髦的语言。一般以-oriented 组成词组, 如：export-oriented enterprise（产品出口型产业）, 但也有其他翻译方法：技术密集、知识密集型项目 technology-and-knowledge intensive project/劳动密集型产业 labour-intensive enterprise/粗放型产业 extensive enterprise, 等等。

【例100】 "小天鹅"牌洗衣机

[误译] the Little Swan Brand washer

[正译] the Little Swan washer

[评析] 我国商标英译时有一个通病, 不少都喜欢加上 brand 一词, 例如：Sunflower Brand, Diamond Brand Wrist Watch 等等, 实际上显得文字累赘。外国名牌商标 SONY, MOTOROLA, SIMENS

等都不带 brand 这个词。

有些汉语词语比较笼统,表意模糊,英译时应突破重直觉、重表象的思维模式,寻求词语的确切含义。

【例 101】 昨天看电影我没有买到好票。

[误译] I did not buy a good ticket for yesterday's film.

[正译] I did not buy a good seat for yesterday's film.

[评析] "好票"在这里比较笼统,实际上是指"好座位"。

【例 102】 我校目前尚未设博士点。

[正译] Our university hasn't yet had any doctoral point.

[正译] Our university hasn't yet had any doctoral programs.

[评析] "博士点"中的这个"点"字,看似明确,实际上是模糊的。这里译为 program,译得相当成功。如果译成 point,将会使读者不知所云。

【例 103】 这所全国重点大学为社会输送了大批的人才。

[误译] The national key university has sent batches of qualified talents for the society.

[正译] The national key university has prepared batches of qualified graduates for the society.

[评析] 在这里"输送"是一个笼统模糊的词,具体说来是指"培养出"。"人才"也是一个比较笼统的词,这里译为 graduates 是恰当的。

【例 104】 我们相信用不了多久我们的家用电器产品就会走向世界。

[误译] We believe that it will not be long before our house-hold electrical appliances products go to the world.

[正译] We believe that it will not be long before our house-hold electrical appliances products go global.

[评析] "走向世界"虽字义明确,但英译表达却必须地道而且有分寸。有人译为 go to the world, 就不太合乎逻辑,因为仿佛使人觉得,中国好像不属于这个世界似的。表达同样的含义使用 go global 这个短语,分寸把握得很好。也可译为 products will find their way into world market, 当然还有其他一些译法。

【例105】他们省吃俭用,为的是攒钱买房子。

[误译] They save food and expenses to accumulate more funds to buy an apartment.

[正译] They live frugally to accumulate more funds to buy an apartment.

[评析] 问题出在机械对译。"省吃俭用"译为 save food and expenses,字面意思对应了,但实质内容不对应。因为 save food 是把食物放起来的意思。应挖掘"省吃俭用"的深层意思,即生活节俭。

第三节　词语搭配

词是最小的语言单位,词的翻译是文章翻译的不可缺少的最基本构件。英语中有一谚语: Words have no meanings; people have meanings for words. 也就是说,一个词的意义取决于说话人或文章作者的立场、观点和感情,取决于一个词所用的场合,上下文等,取决于一个词的词典意义、联想意义、感情意义等。因此,译词需要锤炼。在句子层面上汉译英翻译错误的类型主要在词汇和语法两方面。词汇方面的错误又主要是对汉语原文词汇的理解以及随后的英译文词汇选择上,另一个主要问题是英译文中的词汇搭配问题,而词汇的选择和词义的搭配问题是很难截然分开的。

词义可以分为六种主要类型,即概念意义、内涵意义、风格意义、情感意义、搭配意义和主题意义。其中适合用在某一个上下文中的意义称为"搭配意义"。这就导致有些具有共同基本意义的词义搭配能力不同,意义也有所不同。这在任何语言中都有,各有特点,但用词有时就大相径庭了。英汉两种语言中对应词的搭配关系存在着较大差异。比如:汉语用"浓"字时,可以说浓茶、浓墨、浓烟、浓眉、浓缩、浓郁,但在英文中表达就并非用其对等词:

浓茶 strong tea　　浓云 thick cloud　　浓雾 dense fog

浓眉 heavy eyebrows　浓缩 concentrate　　浓郁 rich

如果从字典上生搬硬套了一些词汇,不顾搭配意义,就会导致译文生硬,不地道。

　　汉语里同一个字或词在不同场合应该有不同的译法。我们先要理解该词在汉语原句中的确切含义,然后再去考虑相对应的英文词语;绝不能知道了一种最常用的译法之后,见到该词就不顾场合,一律套用这种译法。例如:汉语"部"通常译为 department,如"培训部"译为 training department;但"部"与其他词语搭配时,译法很可能不同:

编辑部 editorial office　　　　指挥部 command post
师部 division headquarters　　外交部 Ministry of Foreign Affairs
南部 the southern part

　　英语词语不少都是有固定搭配的,译者往往不注意英语的这个特点,受汉语影响乱点鸳鸯谱,造成英译文的语言错误。而英语词语的固定搭配属于惯用法的范畴,并没有什么道理可讲,而只能死记硬背。搭配不当应是逻辑上的问题,但大多数还是语言习惯问题。我们要有意识地去熟悉哪些词经常连用,哪些词不能连用,否则就必然会出现想当然和任意搭配之类的错误。

　　有些译者刚接触到一个词儿时,便会很自然地联想到自己母语中与这个词语相对应的某个词语,进而将两者等同起来,造成理解和使用上的偏差。如"开"这个动词,所给的英语对应词是 open,而这时学过的能与"开"搭配的词有:开门、开灯、开车、开夜车、开会、开机器、开工、开花、开绿灯、开业、开玩笑。有些译者往往会误认为"开"与该词的概念外延里的其他意义也相对应,于是就出现了 "He is opening a machine." 之类的错句。实际上,"开"在英语中的对应词不只是 open。比如:

开门 open a door　　　　　　　开灯 turn on a light
开车 drive a car　　　　　　　　开夜车 burn the midnight oil
开飞机 pilot a plane/fly a plane　开关 swich
开会 hold a meeting　　　　　　开机器 operate a machine
开工 go into operation　　　　　开花 blossom
开绿灯 give free rein to　　　　　开业 start business
开玩笑 make a joke

　　母语中某个词的一个意义与目的语某个词的一个或几个意义相

对应,原因之一是汉语是无形态或少形态变化的语言,而英语则是有形态变化的语言。学英语的中国学生常常把母语中(无形态变化)的某个词套用于目的语中与其他词搭配关系(有词形变化)的对应词上。错误产生的原因很多,除了母语干扰目的语外,学习策略偏差,学习动机不强,所学知识不牢固等也可能造成错误。

一、主谓搭配

主谓搭配是指主语和谓语动词的搭配。英汉两种语言的主谓搭配,在大多数情况下是相通的。英语里一个主谓搭配,译成汉语后,可以保持原来的搭配。但有时却不行,汉译英时也是这样。一般说来,汉语的主谓关系没有英语那么密切。英语对于主语能否做后面的动作考虑较多。因此,译文以什么作主语,怎样和谓语搭配,是汉译英时经常需要斟酌的一个问题。这里主要是指译文以什么作主语,也就是考虑主谓怎样搭配的问题。有时为了突出重点,译文需要保留原文的主语,那就需要考虑选用合适的动词了。抓住这个要点,可能避免许多中国式英语。

【例 106】中国水域、草原、山地资源丰富,开发潜力巨大。

[误译] China's water, grassland and sloping land resources are rich and they have great potential for exploitation.

[正译] China has rich water, grassland and sloping land resources which have great potential for exploitation.

[评析] 本句以中国作主语,而没有依照原文,以"水域"、"草原"、"山地"为主语。改正译文以 China 作主语,管住全句,比较合乎英语的习惯。

【例 107】中国的发展与进步,有利于人类文明。

[误译] The developing and progressing of China are favorable to the civilization of mankind.

[正译] A developing and progressing China is favorable to the civilization of mankind.

[评析] 原译文以"发展与进步"作主语,而改正译文以"发展与进步的中国"(China)作主语,这样后面比较好安排,所考虑的主要就是

主谓搭配的问题。

【例108】在少数民族聚居的地方实行了区域自治。民族地区的经济社会获得不断的发展。

[误译] The places where there is a high concentration of ethnic minorities practices regional autonomy. These regions' economic and social development have continued.

[正译] In places where there is a high concentration of ethnic minorities regional autonomy is in practice. These regions have witnessed continued economic and social development.

[评析] 原文的两个句子分别以"地方"和"经济社会"为主语,原译文也以它们为主语,但是出现了主谓搭配不当的问题。改正译文变换了主语,并用相应地改动了谓语。

【例109】我们进行改革开放的方向是正确的,信念是坚定的,步骤是稳妥的,方式是渐进的,取得的成就是巨大的。

[误译] The direction of our reform and opening is right, our conviction is firm, our steps are steady and our approach is gradual, therefore we have achieved tremendous successes.

[正译] We are going in the right direction, firm in conviction, steady in our steps and gradual in our approach when carrying out the reform and opening-up and that we have achieved tremendous successes.

[评析] 原文用了一连串并列的主谓结构,主语不断变换,而这是英语所不喜欢的。改正译文后的译文以 we 作主语,统管全句,符合英语的表达习惯。

【例110】合营企业的一切活动应遵守中华人民共和国法律、法令和有关条例规定。

[误译] All activities of a joint venture shall abide by the provisions of the laws, decrees and pertinent regulations of the People's Republic of China.

[正译] All activities of a joint venture shall comply with the provisions of the laws, decrees and pertinent regulations of the People's Republic of China.

[评析] 译文与原文一致,以 activities 为主语,关键是怎样选一个合适的动词和它搭配。"遵守"可译为 abide by 和 observe,可是 abide by 和 observe 都只能用于人或机构作主语的句子。在这种情况下"遵守"可译为 comply,这个动词的应用范围比较广。

【例 111】掌握针灸不是件容易的事情,非下苦功夫不可。

[误译] To master acupuncture, one must make strenuous effort because it is not easy to learn it well.

[正译] The mastery of acupuncture is not easy and requires painstaking effort.

[评析] 误译的译法显得有些累赘,改正译文的译法保持同一个主语,既符合英语的表达习惯,主谓搭配也合适,意思清晰,并忠实地表达出了原文的真正涵义。

【例 112】蹲在苇丛中的青蛙叫得很起劲。

[误译] The frogs that sat among the reeds were shouting enthusiastically.

[正译] The frogs that crouched among the reeds were shouting enthusiastically.

[评析] 原译文中的动词 sat, shouting 与主语不是一个合理的搭配。

【例 113】这二十年的经验告诉我:熟能生巧。

[误译] My working experience in the 20 years tells me that practice makes perfect.

[正译] My working experience in the 20 years teaches that practice makes perfect.

[评析] "经验"后面接"告诉",但在英语里 experience 可以 teach,可以 show,可以 demonstrate,可以 indicate,若让它与 tell 搭配使用,就显得勉强。本文是主语和谓语搭配的问题。

【例 114】目标确定了,从何处着手呢?就要尊重社会经济发展规律,搞两个开放,一个对外开放,一个对内开放。

[误译] How are we to go about achieving these goals? We must respect the laws governing social-economic development and follow an open policy both internationally and domestically.

[正译] How are we to go about achieving these goals? We must observe the laws governing social-economic development and follow an open policy both internationally and domestically.

[评析] 本句主要说明动词和宾语搭配的问题。汉语可以说"尊重……规律",但是英译文却不能那样表达,"尊重"在本句的实质意义是注意、留意,而且在英语中 respect 不能与 laws 搭配使用。

在保证传译信息内容的前提下,译者必须尽可能地保留原文的结构形式。但在不少情况下,结构形式是无法保留的。过分讲究形式倒会使译文晦涩别扭。因而,往往需要在不改变原文意义的基础上,对句子结构和词汇结构等进行必要的调整,重新组织信息。

二、动宾搭配

汉英翻译中搭配是个大问题。有的学者指出:用外国语写作或翻译最容易出毛病的地方就是搭配。在许多场合,汉语中词与词之间不发生搭配不当的情况,可是到了英语中却行不通,这是常常出现的问题。而动词在英语里,可以说是最活跃的一个词类。名词和形容词相对固定,而动词往往可以表示各种不同的含义,用法也特别多。因此,汉译英时,动词处理起来弹性特别大,需要考虑的往往是怎样选择一个能够很好地与主语搭配的动词。

汉英翻译中,英译文中动宾搭配受汉语原文字面影响的因素很多。例如:

【例 115】每晚我都要花一小时学习政治理论和企业管理知识。

[误译] I would spend one hour every evening on studying political theories and knowledge concerning business management.

[正译] I would spend one hour every evening on studying political theories and acquiring knowledge concerning business, management.

[评析] to study 有学习与研究两层意思。英语可以说 to study political theories,但不可以说 to study knowledge,而要说 to acquire knowledge。

【例 116】他们意识到学习知识的重要性。

[误译] They are aware of the importance of learning knowledge.

[正译] They are aware of the importance of acquiring knowledg

[评析] 汉语可以说"学习知识",但是,to learn 有两层意思:一是获得信息,例如:获悉他生病 to learn of his illness 二是获得知识或学会技能,强调结果。英语没有 to learn knowledge 这个搭配。学习知识是个过程,按照英语的习惯表达方法,只能用获得知识,可以译为 to acquire knowledge 或者 attain knowledge。

【例117】把中国建设成为社会主义现代化强国。

[误译] We will build China into a modern strong socilaist country.

[正译] We will turn (or transform) China into a modern strong socilaist country.

[评析] "建设成为"的实质意思是"使变成",turn (or transform)表示使变成、改变、使改变性质,英语中没有 build . . . into 这样的说法。再举一例:

【例118】几年来,为了培养学生,我牺牲了许多节假日。

[误译] In the past few years, I sacrificed many of my holiday to the training of my pupils.

[正译] In the past few years, I devoted many of my holidays to the training of my pupils.

[评析] sacrifice 是个大字眼。"牺牲生命"相当于英语的 to sacrifice one's life,但在英语中没有 to sacrifice one's holidays 这样的搭配,因此可以说 to devote one's holidays。

【例119】低洼地带的许多房屋都被洪水损坏了。

[误译] Many houses in the low-lying area were harmed by the floods

[正译] Many houses in the low-lying area were damaged by the floods.

[评析] 误译文的谓语动词 harmed 和主语 houses 不能搭配,harm 一般表示精神方面等受到损伤或者伤害。

【例120】这就给你机会运用你的知识和经验。

[误译] This will give you an opportunity to exercise your knowledge and experience.

[正译] This will give you an opportunity to use(make use of)your knowledge and experience.

[评析] 误译文有搭配的问题,其中的宾语 knowledge 和 experience 与其动词 exercise 不能搭配在一起。

【例 121】 他的眼睛被浓烟熏得满眼是泪。

[误译] Upset by the thick smoke, his eyes were filled with tears.

[正译] Irritated by the thick smoke, his eyes were filled with tears.

[评析] 修饰语 upset 和被修饰的名词 eyes 很不相称。把它们改译之后,词语间的搭配就很顺畅了。

【例 122】 中国的经济吸引着世界各国人民,中国的社会主义现代化建设,也得到世界各国人民的关注和支持。

[误译] China's economy attracted all the world's people. Similarly, our socialist modernization is winning interest and support.

[正译] China's economy is being watched by people all over the world. Similarly, our socialist modernization is attracting their attention and gaining their support.

[评析] 原译文的动宾 to win interest 不能搭配在一起,改正译文从全局的角度调整几个动词,使得动宾搭配合适。

【例 123】 那位教师介绍了他教物理的宝贵经验。

[误译] The teacher introduced his valuable experience in teaching physics.

[正译] The teacher passed on his valuable experience in teaching physics.

[评析] 英语中 introduce 不与 experience 搭配,作介绍解时,只用于人,例如:让我自我介绍,我的名字叫约翰逊。Let me introduce myself, my name is Johnson.

【例 124】 她掌握了大量英语词汇。

[误译] She masters lots of English words.

[正译] She possesses a wide vocabulary of English words.

[评析] 汉语既可说掌握某种外语,也可以说掌握多少词汇;而英语中"掌握"必须是某种具体的语言。例如:她掌握了英语。She masters the English language. 她精通英语。She has a good command of the English language. 她掌握大量英语词汇。She has (possesses) a wide (extensive) vocabulary of English words.

【例 125】电力公司的职员每月来抄表。

[误译] The clerk from Electricity Board comes to copy the meter every month.

[正译] The clerk from Electricity Board comes to read the meter every month.

[评析] read 有标明、记录的意思。read the meter 即汉语中"抄表"之意。例如：温度表标明摄氏 20 度。The thermometer reads 20℃. copy 意为抄写、仿制。

【例 126】史密斯接受了朋友的忠告。

[误译] Smith received his friend's advice.

[正译] Smith took his friend's advice.

[评析] "接受忠告"常用 take sb's advice, accept sb's advice, adopt sb's advice。

【例 127】当时教会对伽利略施加了压力,他不敢讲真话。

[误译] The Church brought pressure to bear on Galileo, so he didn't dare to say the truth.

[正译] The Church brought pressure to bear on Galileo, so he didn't dare to tell the truth.

[评析] tell the truth 说真话, tell a lie 或 tell lies 说谎话是固定搭配, 动词 tell 不能用 say 来替换, "讲真话"也可说 speak the truth。

【例 128】错误的结果必然得出错误的结论。

[误译] A wrong result is bound to get a false conclusion.

[正译] A wrong result is bound to come to a false conclusion.

[评析] "得出结论"常用下列词组:reach (arrive at, draw, make) a conclusion, 例如:你得出什么结论? What conclusion do you reach?

【例 129】她没能赴约,因为她病了。

[误译] She couldn't go to the appointment because she was sick.

[正译] She couldn't keep the appointment because she was sick.

[评析] keep an appointment 赴约, make（have）an appointment 订约, cancel an appointment 取消约会, change an appointment 改变约会……都是固定搭配。

　　句子理解之后,紧接着就是表达问题。汉英翻译不同于英汉翻译的是理解汉语,表达英语,这难免要受汉语习惯的影响,在选词、造句中总会有点中国式英文的味道。这是汉译英过程中的通病,但我们在汉英翻译中应尽量避免受汉语思维习惯的影响,要多注意两种语言的差异,使译文准确、流畅。但是如果流畅和准确发生矛盾时,应选择后者。

三、形名搭配

　　形容词在英语里是一个十分活跃的词类。其词义往往随前后搭配而变化,其用法也特别灵活。英语形容词的用法、搭配和词义有时和汉语是一致的。但是在许多场合下,汉语中形容词与名词之间不会产生搭配不当的情形,可是译成英语时却出现了问题。受到汉语字面影响而英译文搭配不当的例子经常碰到,例如:

【例 130】他们想问题做事情的方法,他们的历史习惯跟我们不同。

[误译] The way they think, the way they do things and their historical habits are different from ours.

[正译] The way they think, the way they do things and their traditional habits are different from ours.

[评析] 英语中无 historical habits 这种说法,所以应把"历史习惯"译为 traditional habits。

【例 131】这种型号的车床价格便宜。

[误译] The price of the lathe of this type is cheap.

[正译] The price of the lathe of this type is low.

[评析] 主语是 price(价格)时,"便宜"用 low,"贵"用 high。例如:这种新型计算机价格贵。The price of the new-type computer is high. 如果说某物"便宜"用 cheap,说某物"贵"用 dear 或 expensive。例如:彩色电视机从前贵,现在便宜多了。The color TV set used to be expensive, but now is much cheaper.

【例132】傍晚他要去参加一个化装舞会。

[误译] She would be going to a make-up party in the evening.

[正译] She would be going to a fancy dress party in the evening.

[评析] make(dress)up 意为"化妆",指妇女打扮自己,或演员化装。"化装舞会"指穿着奇装异服,带面具的舞会。可以说:fancy dress party, fancy dress ball, fancy ball 等。

【例133】你的帽子真好看。

[误译] You have a good-looking cap.

[正译] You have an attractive cap.

[评析] attractive (= having the power to attract)意为好看的、有吸引力的,既可修饰人,又可修饰物。例如:I think you have very attractive kids. 我认为你的小孩子很讨人喜欢。good-looking 意为美貌的、好看的,主要修饰人。例如:她是一个漂亮的女孩。She is a good-looking girl.

　　类似的例子还有:

【例134】强硬政策

[误译] strong policy

[正译] tough policy

【例135】战火扩大

[误译] the flames of war expand

[正译] the flames of war spread

【例136】实现了自给自足

[误译] realise self-sufficiency

[正译] reach self-sufficiency

【例137】严密控制

[误译] close control

[正译] strict (or rigid) control

【例138】违反他的意图

[误译] violate his intention

[正译] go against his intention

　　我们要有意识地去熟悉哪些词经常连用,哪些词不能连用,否则就必然会出现想当然和任意乱套之类的错误。不过,语言在发展,有些原来不能搭配的,现在可以了,因为有人在创新。创新如果站得住脚,久而久之使用的人多了,就成为惯用的语言现象。

四、副动搭配

主语与谓语、主语与表语、主语与宾语、谓语与状语、动词与其后的介词短语、系动词与表语、谓语与宾语、修饰语与中心词介词与介词宾语、形容词与介词,在这些词之间汉语和英语的副词和其后的动词的搭配都各有其特定的搭配习惯,如果搭配关系不当,英译文就不会地道,读起来自然就感到不流畅。英译文中的副词和其所修饰的动词搭配不当的问题相当普遍,副词和其后的动词的搭配不仅是逻辑上的问题,大多数还是语言的习惯问题。

【例 139】　结果我们采取了一种比较适合情况的政策。

[误译] In the end we adopted the policy comparatively (relatively) suited to the prevailing conditions.

[正译] In the end we adopted the policy best suited to the prevailing conditions.

[评析] 英文中没有 comparatively suited 或者 relatively suited 之类的表述,comparatively 还是 relatively 都不能与 suited 搭配。按照英语的逻辑,适合就是适合,不适合就是不适合,不能说比较适合。

第四节　中国式英语

搭配不当的其中一个结果是形成中国式英语。当我们进行汉译英时,译文与原文在句子结构上,尤其是在主语、谓语、宾语等重要成分的位置处理上,在某些情况下,应当能做到大致相同,我们能够直接把原文的主语作为译文的主语。然而,也有许多情况下,这种对应的结果却使译文成为中国式英语。理想的汉译英过程是充分理解汉语原文的意思,然后完全摆脱汉语句子结构的束缚,用英语思考,把原文的意思用英语表达出来。但是想要这么做,对英语水平的要求很高,有些译者往往难以企及,因为他们有意无意地按照汉语的形式去找对应的英语表达。在有些译者中常见的"中国式英语"，起因就在于译文与原文在用词和句子结构上的机械对应所形成的中国式英语。

在词汇表达方面，英汉两种文化的词语存在很大差异，各自的表达方式当然也无法对等。但有些译者经常会习惯性地按汉语的表达方式，生搬硬套到英语词汇中去。形成中国式英语。例如：

【例 140】注意身体。

[误译] Notice your body.

[正译] Pay attention to your health.

[评析] 虽然没有语法错误，但不符合英语的习惯表达法，并且显得有些失礼，因为 body 一词在英语中含义有多种，其中还有遗体之意。因此，正确的表达法应当是 pay attention to your health。

【例 141】那位科学家已经年迈，但身体健康。

[误译] The scientist is growing old, but his body is healthy.

[正译] The scientist is growing old, but he is healthy.

[评析] 汉语中"身体好"，英语中不用 His body is healthy. 而是说：He is healthy./He is in good health./His health is good.

【例 142】今天早晨我发生一件怪事。

[误译] I happened a strange thing this morning.

[正译] A strange thing happened to me this morning.

[评析] "发生某事"，汉语习惯主语在前，英语颠倒过来，以物作主语，再加介词 to。

【例 143】那个人眼睛瞎了。

[误译] The man's eyes are blind.

[正译] The man is blind.

[评析] "blind"(＝ not able to see) 意为"看不见的"、"盲的"、"瞎的"，作表语时须以人为主语。如：她左眼瞎了。She is blind in the left eye.

【例 144】他左腿跛了。

[误译] His left leg is lame.

[正译] He is lame in the left leg.

[评析] 形容词 lame 意为"跛的"、"瘸的",作表语时,按习惯的表达
方式以人为主语。

【例 145】我一点也不敢放松自己。

[误译] I daren't loosen myself.

[正译] I daren't relax my efforts.

[评析] 这里的意思是丝毫不敢怠慢。如果英译为 I daren't loosen
myself,那么意思就是我不敢松开某东西,有些词不达意。规范的
英语应当是:I daren't relax my efforts。

【例 146】他去广场北边的公共厕所了。

[误译] He went to the common toilet(或者 public toilet) to the north
side of the square.

[正译] He went to the toilet to the north side of the square.

[评析] 英语中没有 common toilet 或者 public toilet 这种表达方式,
即便是公共厕所,用 toilet 就足够了。在公共场合,公共厕所上只
标有 toilet,或是 men's, ladies'。

　　中国式英语作为一种特殊的语言现象越来越受到关注。由于英
语学习者在学习英语过程中不可避免地有时甚至积极地和母语进行
对比,因此广泛地受到母语的影响并造成母语成分的迁移。如果形
成正迁移,会对学习起到积极的促进作用;如果形成负迁移,就会对
学习起到干扰作用。下列的中国式英语既不符合英语表达习惯也不
符合语法。

【例 147】他的名字叫汤姆。

[误译] His name is called Tom.

[正译] His name is Tom.

[评析] 误译句有语法错误,为中国式英语。按照英语的表达习惯,
name 不与 to call 一起用。但是可以说:He is called Tom.

【例 148】他父亲死了。

[误译] His father was dead.

[正译] His father is dead.

[评析] 说某某人死了用现在时,表示现在的状态。误译的译文是这
样的意思:他过去死了,而现在还活着。was dead 只用于表示过

去的从句中。例如:那位登山者在人们发现他时已经死了。The
alpinist was dead when he was found.

【例 149】 天正在下雨。

[误译] The sky is raining.

[正译] It is raining.

[评析] 在表达天气情况时,英语的习惯表达法是用 it 作主语。例
如:今天风挺大。It is rather windy today.

【例 150】 上海的交通很拥挤。

[误译] Shanghai's traffic is very crowded.

[正译] The traffic is very heavy in Shanghai.

[评析] "交通拥挤"英语习惯的表达方法是 The traffic is heavy。不
能用 crowded 一词。

　　有时中国式英语虽然符合语法,也不影响跨文化交际,但是不符
合英语的表达习惯:

【例 151】 昨天我遇到了一位老朋友。

[误译] Yesterday I met an old friend.

[正译] I met an old friend yesterday.

[评析] 英语的习惯表达方式是把时间状语 yesterday 放到句末。例
如:请明天来。Come tomorrow, please.

【例 152】 我想他不会成功。

[误译] I think he will not succeed.

[正译] I don't think he will succeed.

[评析] 英语的惯常表达方式是把否定词放在主句而不是从句的动
词前面。例如:实际上,我觉得他的决定并不明智。I don't think
his decision is wise in reality. /我想我八点前回不来。I don't
think I shall be back until eight o'clock.

【例 153】 要和他相处非常容易。

[误译] To get along with him is very easy.

[正译] It is very easy to get along with him.

[评析] 英语通常不用不定式作主语,而是用 it 作形式主语,把动词
不定式后置。例如:处理这件事情是我们的责任。It is our duty

to attend to this matter.

【例 154】你仅凭眼睛不可能观察到火星的卫星。

[误译] You are not possible to observe the moons of Mars with the naked eye.

[正译] It is not possible for you to observe the moons of Mars with the naked eye.

[评析] possible (= that can be done; that can exist or happen)做表语时,不以表示人的人称代词或名词作主语,例如:现在医生有可能治愈癌症。It is possible for doctors to cure cancer.

【例 155】该研究所每个科学家都参加了这项工程的考察。

[误译] Every scientist of the institute took part in investigating the project.

[正译] Each scientist of the institute took part in investigating the project.

[评析] 形容词 every (= all) 意为"所有的",说话人着眼于整体。例如:这本词典里所有的词都重要。Every word in this dictionary is important. each(= every one separately) 意为"每一个",说话人着眼于个体。例如:每个工作人员都有一台电脑。Each worker has a computer. 误译的汉语意思是:该研究所全体科学家都参加这项工程的考察。

【例 156】你花的每分钱都值得。

[误译] It is worth every penny you cost.

[正译] It is worth every penny you spend.

[评析] 误译的 cost 是用来对应汉语中的"花钱"一词。但事实上,这完全不符合英语的表达习惯。这个句子中要用英语 spend 或 pay 才能确切地表达"花钱"这层汉语意思。cost 的意思是"(使)花费(金钱、时间、劳力等)"。例如:那个书包要多少钱? How much did that bag cost? / 在城市居住要付出更多东西。It costs more to live in the city.

【例 157】新学期已经过去一个月了。

[误译] Our new term has passed one month.

[正译] One month has passed since the new term began.

[评析] 误译的英语似乎符合英语语法规则,但是不符合英语的表达习惯。完全是套用汉语的句式,是汉语的思维方式。再看几个例子:我们在那儿已呆了三年。It was three years since we had been there.／我们到这儿刚刚一个星期。A week has just passed since we arrived here.／我已有很多年没有像昨晚那么痛快了。It's been years since I enjoyed myself so much as last night.

当然,上述所举之例都是为了表明母语(汉语)的干扰作用,事实上,中国式英语的出现还存在其他许多原因,如学习策略、交际策略等。总之,中国英语和中国式英语都是因母语、汉语干扰而形成的英语变异体。中国人介绍中国的情况,写出来的英文有中文的味道也许是不可避免的。但至少应该做到两点:一是不要让外国读者产生误解,二是不要违反英语的词法句法,也就是不要把汉语的词法句法强加在英语身上。在这种情况下,看上下文实际上就是看逻辑关系。作为译者,也就要清楚、准确地传达出作者所表达出来的符合逻辑的语言。要做到这一点,光讲语法是不够的,还要看上下文,讲求逻辑,使每一句话都做到文从字顺。汉译英的质量在很大程度上取决于词语翻译的准确性。虽然译文是否忠实于原文要看句子、段落或篇章的整体效果,但关键词语的准确处理依然是保证译文质量的决定性因素之一。翻译好汉语词语需要勤查汉英词典和英语词典,也需要在平时的学习中不断积累,加强对英语词汇丰富含义和用法的掌握。

第五节 中国特色词汇

要提高翻译质量,还需要研究自己民族特有的一些词汇。这是因为每一个国家有其自己的文化、传统、意识形态、制度、经济体制等,自然会有一些独特的表达方式,对这类词汇要翻译得既贴切,又符合所译语言的习惯说法,是不容易的。其中词的搭配和选择是翻译的一个基本技巧,也是翻译的难点之一。这些具有中国特色的词汇,稍不留心就会翻译成中国式英语。

【例 158】分配不公的问题

[误译] the question of unequal distribution

[正译] the question of unfair distribution

[评析] "分配不公"的内涵应是分配不公平。而误译译文的意思却是"不平均的分配", the question of unfair distribution 才忠实地翻译了"分配不公平的问题"。根据不同的上下文,"分配不公"还可以译为 income disparities, unfair distribution of wealth, unfairness as shown by income disparities。

【例 159】压力很大的工作

[误译] a stressful job

[正译] a demanding job

[评析] 通常意义上的"压力很大的工作"是指在工作中因达不到或害怕达不到期望值而焦虑的意思。a demanding job 即表示期望值高而感到压力大的工作;而 a stressful job 表示由紧张而感到压力大的工作。

【例 160】街道妇女

[误译] street women

[正译] housewives of the neighborhood

[评析] street women 与 street walker 意思相同,表示:(街头的)拉客妓女,曾在外国读者中造成了极大的误会。

【例 161】宣传

[误译] propaganda

[正译] publicity

[评析] propaganda 一词贬义的成分较多,易与吹牛、说谎、怀有政治目的等负面含义系起来,现在已改成了中性词 publicity。

【例 162】个体经济

[误译] individual economy

[正译] the family business

[评析] 原译是逐词死译的译文,"个体经济"这一短语要根据不同的文体,不同的场合选词翻译为 the family business 或者 the self-employed 等等。

【例 163】精神文明

[误译] spiritual civilization

[正译] ethical and cultural progress

[评析]"精神文明"这一词,广义上涵盖思想道德、文化科学、体育卫生、哲学伦理、民主法制等上层建筑的东西,狭义上主要指伦理道德。"精神文明"曾经被译为 spiritual civilization, 在外国人的心目中含有宗教色彩,现在已根据不同的场合、文体等不同的语境因素,译成 ethical and cultural progress 以及 ideological and cultural advancement 等其他词语。例如:建设社会主义物质文明和精神文明 to build a socialist society with both high material standards and high ethical and cultural standards 或者 to build socialist civilization with a high cultural level and moral standards/精神文明单位 a model unit in moral standards/搞精神文明 to promote ethical progress/文明礼貌月 the virtues and ethics month/讲文明礼貌 to behave civilly/文明经商 to conduct ourselves honorably in commercial transactions

【例 164】他的理念成为激励中国人民变革创新、努力奋斗的精神力量。

[误译] His idea has become an important spiritual force spurring the Chinese people to work hard for change and innovation.

[正译] His idea has become an important moral force spurring the Chinese people to work hard for change and innovation.

[评析]"精神力量"最好译为 moral force, 因为 spiritual 这个词还表示:of, concerned with, or affecting the soul(灵魂的,与灵魂相关的,影响灵魂的),以及 of, from, or relating to God(来自上帝的,与上帝有关的)之意,有较强的宗教色彩。用 spiritual 不能正确地传达原意。

【例 165】他还多次强调,要大胆吸收和借鉴人类社会创造的一切文明成果,包括资本主义发达国家的一切反映现代化社会生产规律的先进经营方式、管理方式。

[误译] He also emphasized time and again that we should boldly absorb and utilize all civilization achievements created by human society, including all advanced operation and management methods that reflect the law of socialized modern production in the developed capitalist countries.

[正译] He also emphasized time and again that we should boldly absorb and utilize all advanced achievements created by human society, including all advanced operation and management methods that reflect the law of socialized modern production in the developed capitalist countries.

[评析] 将"文明成果"译作 civilization achievements, 都用很长的名词作定语,修饰另一个很长的名词,这样的搭配使英译文不太顺畅。

【例 166】 邓小平是中国改革开放和现代化建设的总设计师。

[误译] Deng Xiaoping is the chief architect of China's reform, opening-up and modernization construction.

[正译] Deng Xiaoping is the chief architect of China's reform, opening-up and modernization.

[评析] 将"现代化建设"译作 modernization construction, 不太符合英语的表达习惯。"现代化建设"可以只用 modernization 一个词, 也可以译作 modernization drive。

【例 167】 总起来说,就是要把中国建设成富强文明的现代化国家。

[误译] In a word, it is to build China into a prosperous, strong, and civilized modern country.

[正译] In a word, it is to build China into a prosperous, strong, and culturally advanced modern country.

[评析] "精神文明"常译作 cultural and ethical progress。"文明的"常译作 culturally advanced, 而不译作 civilized。

【例 168】 运动员争取运动成绩与精神文明双丰收。

[误译] The athletes strive for a good harvest both in sports and morals.

[正译] The athletes strive for better (athletic) records and sportsmanship.

[评析] 把"丰收"译成 a good harvest, 是逐字死译;"精神文明"译成

morals 不太贴切，morals 还有别的含义。尽管误译的译文在语法上是完全站得住脚的，但是 morals 却给人的印象是东道主十分担心男女运动员之间会发生越轨行为。这样的译文可能让人误解，背离原文的意思。"运动成绩与精神文明双丰收"是个比喻的说法，只需译出其实质意义。

【例 169】也就是说，我们要把中国建成民主文明的现代化强国。

[误译] In other word, we shall build China into a strong, democratic and civilized modern country.

[正译] In other words, we shall build China into a strong, democratic and culturally advanced modern country.

[评析] civilized 的意思是 showing evidence of moral and intellectual advancement; humane, ethical, and reasonable，即文明的、表现出道德与知识上先进的、人道的、伦理的和讲道理的，但是，其常用的意思是"伦理的和讲道理的"，culturally advanced 用在这儿更能传达其实质含义。将"文明"译作 civilization，也还是常见的，问题在于如何搭配。例如：一切进步文明成果 all fruits of human progress and civilization/世界一切先进的文明成果 fruits of advanced world civilization/先进文明成果 advanced results of civilization

　　从以上的例子可以看出。"文明"一词可译作 culture，也可译作 civilization，但不能将"文明成果"直译成 civilization achievements。

　　这样的译文，从语法角度看没有什么错误，但外国人看不懂，毛病就出在不符合英语的习惯表达，所以不是地道的英语，而是中国式英语。许多学过多年英语的人也很难摆脱这种母语干扰的阴影，有时也会犯同样性质的错误。

【例170】这些原则一直是我们民族的精神支柱。

[误译] These principles have been our spiritual pillar.

[正译] These principles have nourished our souls.

[评析] 把"精神支柱"译成 spiritual pillar 是逐词死译，这两个字，一个是抽象的概念，一个是具体的，搭配不当，而且是一种典型的中国式英语。采用原英文表达方式，"给民族的灵魂提供营养"，也就把"精神支柱"的内涵意译出来了。spiritual pillar 不如 nourish the soul 用词恰当。

【例 171】这种论点目前还有一定的市场。

［误译］This argument has some market at present.

［正译］This argument has some appeal at present.

［评析］argument 不能与 market 搭配，误译文让人感到不知所云。改正译文没有用 market，而用 appeal，生动而意思到位地表达了原意。

【例 172】我们要做一个完全的创新者。

［误译］We should be a complete innovator.

［正译］We should be a true innovator.

［评析］这里使用的形容词属于典型的死译，complete 不能与 innovator，reformer 等一起使用，应改为 true。此处"完全的"的确切含义是"真正的"。

【例 173】好汉做事好汉当。

［误译］A good man has the courage to accept the consequences of his own actions.

［正译］A true man has the courage to accept the consequences of his own actions.

［评析］本句中的"好汉"不能按照字面理解，不能译成 good，而应根据上下文选用贴切的词。

【例 174】总之，几年的实践证明，我们搞实物债券的路子是走对了。

［误译］In short, our practice in the last few years has proved the correctness of our policies of unregistered bonds.

［正译］In short, our achievements in the last few years have proved the correctness of our policies of unregistered bonds.

［评析］"……证明，我们搞实物债券的路子是走对了"，实际上是证明实物债券已经取得了成绩，所以 achievements 用在本句反而比按字面翻译，用 practice 更传神，改正后的译文领会了原文的精神实质。

某些带有中国特色的语汇，很难在英文中找到对应的词或词组。译者应根据实际情况创造一些新的说法。

【例 175】加强科研是该研究所今年工作的基本立足点。

[误译] To strengthen its scientific research is a basic point of departure of this year's work in the search institute.

[正译] To strengthen its scientific research is a basic principle underlying this year's work in the research institute.

[评析] 如果把"基本立足点"译成 a basic point of departure(基本出发点)或者 a cornerstone (奠基石),这两种译法的意思都不够贴切,而 a basic principle underlying 则比较确切地表达了"立足"的原意。

【例 176】要敢于在公众面前讲话。这是一个关,这个关必须过。

[误译] We should have the courage to speak before public. This is a pass we must go through.

[正译] We should not be afraid of speaking before public. This is a key process we must go through.

[评析] 中文里经常谈到"过关","关"究竟怎么译,要看具体情况而定。在这句话里,"关"不是指 pass, juncture 或 checkpoint,也不是指 ordeal 或 barrier,而是指必须经过的一个重要的过程。

【例 177】可以鼓励、劝说台湾首先跟我们搞"三通":通商、通航、通邮。

[误译] They can encourage and persuade Taiwan first to have "three exchanges" with us, namely, the exchange of mails, trade and air and shipping services.

[正译] They can encourage and persuade Taiwan first to have "three links": link of trade, travel and post.

[评析] "三通"是个概括的说法,严格说来 trade 本身就是双向的,译成 exchange of trade 是不恰当的。况且 exchange 的意思是交换、交流,"通"字的含义不明显。"三通"的新的译法是 three links: link of trade, travel and post,这样就把"通"字连在一起的味道译出来了。

【例 178】过去实行"闭关自守"政策,结果搞得"民穷财困"。

[误译] They pursued the policy of "self-seclusion", and its people

62

were reduced to destitution and its financial resources were exhausted.

[正译] They pursued the policy of "self-seclusion", resulting in "the destitution of its people and exhaustion of its financial resources.

[评析] 把"民穷财困"翻译为 its people were reduced to destitution and its financial resources were exhausted, 这个译文意思虽然对, 但比较罗嗦, 不符原文风格。中文只有四个字, 因此英译文也应简练。

汉英翻译, 必须不断积累英语词汇和表达方式, 以便根据不同的情况从中选择更准确的译法。

第六节 拟 人 化

中国有人数最多的英语学习者。以中国文化为背景、以汉语为母语的学习者在习得英语时所呈现出中国式英语, 很值得研究, 对中国式英语持何种态度也十分重要。我们学习英语的目的是要进行跨文化交际, 不管此种交际是口头形式的, 还是书面形式的。要成功进行跨文化交际, 我们所使用的英语越接近地道英语越好。

中国式英语的其中一个标志是大量使用拟人化的手法。中文的拟人化程度较高, 拟人化现象在汉语中常见, 就是非人物性名词词组常可充当主语和行为的发出者, 在英语中, 多数情况下, 被视为是修辞上的一种病句。因此在汉英翻译中要注意这个区别, 英译时应注意将其转换为人物性的名词或与人类活动有密切关系的团体组织, 以避免受汉语影响而出现误译。例如:

【例 179】我也成了一个受害者, 因为在这个杂志的封面上面登了我的照片, 看起来像个死人。

[误译] I have been a victim too, because on the cover of that magazine my photo, my picture looks like a dead man.

[正译] I have been a victim too, because on the cover of that magazine my photo, my picture makes me look like a dead man.

[评析] 在原文中, 非人物性名词"照片"充当了"看起来像个死人"的

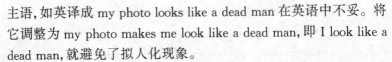

主语,如英译成 my photo looks like a dead man 在英语中不妥。将它调整为 my photo makes me look like a dead man,即 I look like a dead man,就避免了拟人化现象。

【例 180】 已经有一个美国的基金组织到中国来,准备投资。

[误译] One of the US foundations came to China to make some investment.

[正译] One of the US foundations once organized a mission to China to make some investment.

[评析] 本句汉语中拟人化程度较高,非人物性名词 foundations 与动作性动词 came 搭配使用。在英语中如说 a foundation came to China 不容易被人接受,所以在 one of the US foundations 后面补译 organized a mission (代表团) to China。

【例 181】 我国的高科技事业,需要尽可能多的知识分子为它服务。

[误译] The cause of our country's high technology industry needs as many intellectuals as possible to serve it.

[正译] China (Our country) needs the services of as many intellectuals as possible for the task of high technology industry.

[评析] 原译文的主要问题是主语没有用对,使原译文有拟人化的倾向。如果译文不能使主语和谓语动词搭配,那就应改变主语或改变谓语动词,不可逐词死译。"事业"在本句中是范畴词,是虚指,没有什么实质意义,可省去不译。

【例 182】 我国的经济建设,需要一个和平的国际环境,需要一个国内安定团结、天下大治的局面。

[误译] China's economic construction needs an international environment of peace and a domestic situation of stability, unity and great order.

[正译] For its economic construction, China needs an international environment of peace and a domestic stability, unity and great order.

[评析] 如果把"建设"译为主语,就有了拟人化倾向,不是英语的习惯表达方式。翻译这句话时,应设法把主语确定为 China 或 our country,这样才能抓住原文的精神实质,而且也与谓语搭配得合

适。

【例 183】 这篇文章十分特别,它认为该公司已经面临着灾难和破产,好像已经大祸临头了。

[误译] This article is very special. The article believes that it seems that the company is about to encounter a big calamity or bankruptcy and seems that a big disaster is looming near.

[正译] This article is very special. According to that article, it seems that the company is about to encounter a big calamity or bankruptcy and seems that a big disaster is looming near.

[评析] "它认为"也是汉语非人物性主语拟人化的用法,这在英语中不宜多用。不要译成 The article believes,而是调整为 According to the article。

【例 184】 二十年来,我国的航天事业从胜利走向新的胜利。

[误译] In the past twenty years, our aeronautics cause has won victories one after another.

[正译] In the past twenty years, we have won a series of victories for our aeronautics technology.

[评析] 汉语可以说"事业从胜利走向新的胜利",在英语中,事业本身是不能赢得胜利的。cause 与 win victory 不能搭配,因为 cause 是没有生命的,而 win victories 的主语一般是人,二者用在一起,就把 cause 拟人化了。英译文虽然在语法上站得住脚,但不符合英语习惯用法,不是地道的英语。改正译文把原文的主语"事业"译为 we,因为位于动词 have won 的主语一般需要人来充当。原文还可以改用被动语态,A series of victories have been won for aeronautics technology。

【例 185】 西部的矿产很丰富。

[误译] The west of China's minerals are rich.

[正译] The west of China is rich in minerals.

[评析] 原译文语法没有问题,但英语不这样表达,不能说矿产很富有。这样的译文使"矿产"拟人化。按照英语的习惯表达方法,应用 be rich in ... 句型。

【例186】中国电讯市场的竞争步伐加快了。

[误译] The pace of the competition in the telecommunication market in China has accelerated.

[正译] The competition in the telecommunication sector in China has accelerated.

[评析] 此例中的"加快竞争步伐"不一定要译成 accelerate the pace of the competition, 可省去 pace 不译, 否则英译文有拟人化的倾向。译成 accelerate the competition 意思更明确。

【例187】汉字在历史上有过不可磨灭的功绩。

[误译] Chinese characters have made indelible contribution in the past history.

[正译] The system of Chinese characters has played an invaluable role in our history.

[评析] Chinese characters 与 make contribution 一起使用, 有拟人化的倾向。英语没有这样的表达习惯。用 system 总括 Chinese characters 并改换说法, 使英译文地到自然。

【例188】宗教不能干涉政治。

[误译] Religion must not interfere with politics.

[正译] It is impermissible to interfere with politics in the name of religion.

[评析] 本句原文的非人物性主语"宗教"与动作性动词"干涉"可以搭配使用, 但是英译时要注意避免产生拟人化的现象, 改变主语便可以解决这个问题。

【例189】西方舆论纷纷预测。

[误译] The public opinion in the West predicts one after another.

[正译] The Western press has much to say in prediction.

[评析] 非人物性主语 public opinion 不能与动作性动词 predicts 搭配, 因为这使得句子有拟人化倾向, 不是英语的惯常表达方式, 要改换说法。

第七节 过强的语气

英译文语气过强也是中国式英语的一个标志。汉语语气较强，常含有夸张性的词语，汉语中也有不少绝对化的表达方式；而英语则讲究含蓄、委婉，不愿把话说足。译者应熟悉这种差异，英译时有意识地适当减弱英译文的语气。在一般情况下过分强调，反而减弱词语的意义。

【例190】到中国来访问的贵宾，我去年都跟他们讲过。

[误译] I have discussed that with all of the distinguished guests last year.

[正译] I have discussed that with many foreign visitors last year.

[评析] 本句汉语的言辞有些夸张，英译时需要减弱语气。因此，"所有到这里的贵宾"译为 many foreign visitors。

【例191】关于广东信托投资公司事件，我想这个问题也是大家所关心的。

[误译] On the question of Guangdong International Trust and Investment Company, I think this is also a question of interest to everyone.

[正译] On the question of Guangdong International Trust and Investment Company, I think this is also a question of interest to many of you.

[评析] "大家"不要译成语气很强烈的 everyone 或者等词 all，可弱化为 many。

【例192】中央的财政，银行，都拿不出钱来支持转基因技术。把钱浪费了。

[误译] The central government and including various state banks do not have money to support transgene technology because a lot of money has been squandered.

[正译] The central government and including various state banks do not have enough money to support transgene technology because a lot of money has been squandered.

[评析] 原汉语中所说的中央财政"拿不出钱来"支持转基因技术,只是一种较为夸张的说法,如果将英译文改成 do not have enough money,语气恰到好处。

【例193】WTO 的这些国家已经认识到没有中国参加的 WTO 是没有代表性的,是忽视了中国这个潜在的最大市场。

[误译] The WTO member states have come to realize that a WTO without China would not be representative, or the WTO would have neglected China, the largest potential market in the world.

[正译] The WTO member states have come to realize that a WTO without China would not be representative enough, or the WTO would have neglected China, the largest potential market in the world.

[评析] 本句汉语的表达方式有些绝对化,汉语原文中的"没有代表性的"这个短语语气过强,英译时应适当减轻语气。在英译文中可弱化为 would not be representative enough 等。

【例194】我们也准备做出最大的让步。

[误译] We are also prepared to make the biggest concession.

[正译] We are prepared to make the biggest concession within its ability.

[评析] "最大的让步"语气过强,将其弱化为 the biggest concession within its ability, 也可译为 the biggest possible concession。

【例195】我认为在这个问题上美国方面的人士犯了两个过低估计的错误。

[误译] I think on this question people in the United States have made two mistakes due to the underestimation.

[正译] I think on this question some people in the United States have made two mistakes due to the underestimation.

[评析] 英语语气往往不如汉语强,所以英译时常需要降温。"美国方面的人士"往往被译成 people in the United States,这样批评的对象太多,不如减弱语气,译成 some people in the United States 更

好。

第八节 词序差异

造成中国式英语的另一个原因是不注意汉英词序的差异,汉语中最重要的往往在前头,分量轻的殿后,而英语则反之,单词连用时是分量轻的在前,最重的一般在后头。

【例 196】他们是些无地及少地的农民。

[误译] They are peasants with no or little land.

[正译] They are peasants with little or no land.

[评析] 汉语从最严重的"无地"开始,然后到"少地",而英语则相反,单词的意义有弱变强,即 little or no land。

【例 197】某些企业要关、停、并、转,或者减少生产任务。

[误译] Some enterprises should either close down, suspend operation, be amalgamated with others, switch to other products, or cut production.

[正译] Some enterprises should either cut production, switch to other products, be amalgamated with others, suspend operation, or simply close down.

[评析] 汉语原文从最严重的情况开始罗列到最轻的情形:"关、停、并、转,或者减少",翻译成英语后要颠倒顺序,变为"减少、转、并、停或者关",以符合英语的表达方式。

【例 198】有五种爵位:公侯伯子男。

[误译] There are five ranks of nobility:duke, marquis, earl viscount and baron.

[正译] There are five ranks of nobility:baron, viscount, earl, marquis, and duke.

[评析] 汉语的"公侯伯子男",爵位由高到低,是汉语的思维方式;而英语的思维方式是由低到高,重点一般在后头,因此应按"男子伯侯公"的顺序来英译。

【例 199】海伦在 1991 年三月三日晚上十点出生。

[误译] Helen was born in 1991 March 3rd, at 10 pm.

[正译] Helen was born at 10 pm on 3rd March, 1991.

[评析] 按照英语前轻后重的表达习惯,英文日期的排列是从小单位到大单位。

【例 200】他从马来西亚柔佛州一个小镇来到这里。

[误译] He came from a small town in Malaysia Johore.

[正译] He came from a small town in Johore Malaysia.

[评析] 英文地点的排列是从也是小单位到大单位,把最重要的信息放在最后。

【例 201】中国饮茶的风尚,到了第七世纪的唐代,已经相当盛行了。

[误译] In the seventh century of the Tang Dynasty, the Chinese prevailing custom of drinking tea was in vogue.

[正译] By the Tang Dynasty in the seventh century, tea-drinking had become very popular in China.

[评析] 原译文有词序错误,英语时间的排列是从也是小单位到大单位,把最重要的信息放在后面。因此 the seventh century of the Tang Dynasty 应改为 the Tang Dynasty in the seventh century。另外,原译文用词累赘,prevailing 和 in vogue 意思重复。汉语说某种"风尚……盛行"不太别扭,但说 prevailing custom was in vogue 就相当于说 prevailing custom was prevalent, 其语义重复极为明显。可以把"风尚"换说为"习惯"(custom),或者不说饮茶的习惯(the custom of drinking tea),而直接说"饮茶"(tea-drinking)。原译文还有时态错误,原文表明到了过去某一时间已经形成某种局面,所以译文宜用过去完成时。

第九节 汉语主题结构

汉语主题结构,即译文句子主语的选择。汉英语言转换技巧从本质上都可归结于英语表达的技巧。在理想情况下,译者应该首先确切理解汉语原文的含义,然后尽量摆脱原文的字句束缚,用英语进行思考,按照英语的语言习惯来表达原文的意思。所以,要想掌握汉英语言转换技巧,关键在于熟悉英语的语言规律和各种表达方式。
汉译英的一个关键步骤是考虑译文的整个句子怎么摆放,如何构建
译文句子的总体框架,主要是确定拿什么作为英语主语。传统语法
认为汉英句子总体框架相同,都属于"主—动—宾"类型。按照这一
理论,当我们进行汉译英时,译文与原文在句子结构上,尤其是在主
语、谓语、宾语等重要成分的位置处理上,应当能做到大致相同。在
某些情况下,确实如此,我们能够直接把汉语原文的主语作为英译文
的主语。例如:

不要碰它。Don't touch it.

他是只纸老虎。He is a paper tiger.

他说他很忙。He says he is very busy.

这事使他丢脸。This matter makes him lose face.

请填表格。Please fill the form.

他的行动惊人地迅速。His movements were astonishingly rapid.

哭是没有用的。It's no use crying.

别流鳄鱼泪。Don't shed crocodile tears.

应该弥补代沟。We must bridge the generation gap.

欢迎到中国来! Welcome to China!

如何提高生产力? How to increase productivity?

在翻译方法上,这些基本上是词对词的翻译,而且是可以成立
的。译者应很清楚要警惕词对词翻译的不良后果,因为只有在某些
情况下而且是少数的情况下,源语(汉语)和目标语(英语)两种语言
中才有完全相等或几乎完全相等的表达方法。即使如此,其中仍有
须增加谓语动词、定冠词以及必须更换词序的问题,以求合乎英语的
语法和习惯表达方式。词对词翻译仅在一定程度上有其可能性。

国内一些学者的研究分析,汉语是注重主题的语言,其句子结构
是语义;而英语是注重主语的语言,英语句子结构是语法的。汉语
句子在结构上可分为话题和说明两部分,而英语句子只要满足主谓
(宾)这一结构,语法上就是合格的句子了。有些译者由于不了解英
汉语言在结构上存在的这一差别,汉译英时,不顾汉语句子主题突出
及英语句子主语为主的特点,逐词死译,造成译文结构不顺、意义含

糊。现在,越来越多的人接受了一种新的语言类型分类,把英语看成注重主语的语言,汉语则为注重主题的语言。具体地说,汉语经常采用"主题—述题"的句式,主语的句法功能弱,有时还不容易识别,但这并不影响我们对句子意思的理解;英语主语的句法功能强,几乎都采用"主语—谓语"的句式,主语是整个句子最关键的成分。就英语而言,主语一旦选定,句子的总体框架大致就确立了。

【例 202】这件事你不用操心。

[误译] This you don't need to worry about.

[正译] You don't need to worry about this.

[评析] 原文是很通顺很常见的汉语句子,"这件事"是主题,"你不用操心"是述题。这种汉语特有的句型,是千万不能逐字照搬到英译文。

【例 203】这件事你不用操心。

[误译] This you don't need to worry about.

[正译] This is not something you need to worry about.

[评析] 如果我们要在译文中突出汉语的主题"这件事",就需要把英译文在句式上做出相应调整,翻译为 This is not something....之类的句型。

【例 204】这件事你不用操心。

[误译] This you don't need to worry about.

[正译] It is unnecessary for you to worry about this.

[评析] 还可以把同样的一句汉语换个说法:把"不用"换个说法,就是"没有必要",可以使用英语常用而汉语没有对应结构的 it 或 there 打头的句式,把原句译为 It is unnecessary ... 或者 There is no need for you to worry about this.

【例 205】在他分管范围的每件大事,总是亲自筹划,积极组织。

[误译] Within his range of responsibility in each major task, he would plan personally and actively organize.

[正译] He would plan personally and organize each major task within his range of responsibility.

[评析] 根据汉语句子的结构特点,"在他分管范围的每件大事"是主

题,其余部分应当是说明部分,即述题。在翻译成英文时,应考虑到英语主谓宾的句式特点,将"每件大事"译作宾语,全句为 SVO 结构。使得译文能忠实地反映原文作者的意图。而有些译者缺乏有关英语和汉语语言对比知识,翻译时过于拘泥于原文结构,不敢根据译语特点进行必要的增删或重组。

【例 206】你们从电视里看到,总统跟我会见的时候,他把我的手拉着放在他的胸上面。

[误译] From TV you might see that the President, before our meeting, he shook hands with me, and he put my hand to his heart, to his chest.

[正译] From TV you might see that the President, before our meeting, he shook hands with me, and put my hand to his heart, to his chest.

[评析] 汉语喜欢用代词重复前面的名词主语,在这句中用"他"来指代"总统"。但在英语中,后面重复使用代词是不必要的。译者应尽量摆脱这种汉语主题—评论式的结构,把后面的 he 省去不译。在汉译英过程中应十分注意汉语和英语句子成分的差异与汉语主题结构句的翻译。

　　一般地说,无论汉语原句是典型的"主题—述题"结构还是与英语类似的"主—动—宾"结构,假如直接把原文的主题或主语译为译文的主语后,译文显得生硬,句子结构不平衡,或者与上下文在语气上不连贯,那么就要设法把原文的其他成分,也许是名词、形容词、副词或动词,译为英译文的主语。在此过程中,我们必须考虑到汉语和英语的各种差异,如在英语里面以事物作主语的句子比汉语里面更常见,用名词结构表示动作也比汉语要普遍等。依此规律来选择英译文的主语,就能使英译文更地道,更符合英语的表达方式。

第十节　措　　词

　　中译英最常见的错误不仅有语法错误,也有措词方面的错误。

造成错误的直接原因是常使用抽象名词或动名词,而不用动词。如果要想使我们的译文简洁,我们必须多使用动词,避免大量使用名词结构。

【例207】我们应促使音乐、语言和数学相结合。

[误译] We should promote the combination of music, language and mathmetics.

[正译] We should integrate music, language and mathmetics.

[评析] integrate 的解释是 to make into a whole by bringing all parts together, to unify, 意思与 promote the combination 一样, 但是用 integrate, 英译文更简洁有力、更地道。

【例208】各种产业正经历分化和整合,新旧矛盾相互交织。

[误译] Various industries are undergoing disintegration and realignment and the new and old contradictions are interwoven.

[正译] Industries are disintegrating, their elements are being realigned, and new contradictions are being interwoven with the old.

[评析] disintegration(分化)和 realignment(整合)有动词形式,而不译 undergo(经历),不影响本句的意义。industry 的复数形式就表示"各种",因此 various 不必译出。

【例209】应主要通过技术进步来发展加工业。

[误译] The development of the processing industry should be achieved mainly through technological upgrading.

[正译] The manufacturing industry should develop chiefly through technological upgrading.

[评析] 由于用了名词 development(发展),还要用动词 be achieved,不如直接用动词 develope,让英译文更简练一些。

【例210】全国植树造林,有利于当代和子孙,应坚持不懈地做下去。

[误译] The nationwide drive for afforestation, which benefits our contemporary, and future generations, should be carried on with perseverance.

[正译] We must persevere in the national drive for afforestation, which benefits both present and future generations.

[评析]"坚持不懈"有相应的动词 persevere,为什么要舍弃它而用效果不好的 carry on with perseverance 呢?

【例 211】这在理顺价格方面起积极作用。

[误译] All this played an active role in rationalizing prices.

[正译] All this helped to rationalize prices.

[评析] play an active role 是汉化很强的一个短语,它的意思完全可以用 help 代替。用 help,英译文意思更加明晰。

【例 212】我们应发挥专利制度在发展科学和经济方面的作用。

[误译] We should give play to the role of the patent system in expanding scientific undertakings and economic development.

[正译] We should use the patent system to encourage scientific research and economic development.

[评析] 这一句的原译与上一句原译的译文有着类似的问题。如果一个动词就能清楚地表达意义,就不要用动词+名词短语,这样反而弱化了词义。

【例 213】继续发展农村商品经济的关键在于深化价格体系改革和农产品流通方面的改革。

[误译] The key to a further expansion of the rural commodity economy lies in deepening the reform of the structure of pricing and distribution of farm produce.

[正译] The key to expanding the rural market economy is to deepen the reform of the pricing and distribution of farm produce.

[评析] expansion 中含有 further(继续)的意思,可略去 further 不译; expansion 和 deepening 在本句中没有 expanding 和 deepen 的直接表达力强。

【例 214】现在我们应集中精力加强全面整治淮河和太湖。

[误译] Right now we should focus our attention on stepping up the comprehensive harnessing of the Haihe River and Lake Taihu.

[正译] Right now we should concentrate on projects to harness the Huaihe River and Lake Taihu.

[评析] focus our attention 从意思上到用法上都逊色于 concentrate。

由于用了 concentrate,冗长的词组 stepping up the comprehensive harnessing 用一个动词 harness 便很好地表达了原文的意思。

译文要简洁,就要去掉可有可无的词,汉语的某些词语不必译出来,减去虚夸的修饰语。

第十一节 同 义 词

选择合适得体的词语,准确传达讲话人的意图。汉语和英语有较大的区别。汉语词义较笼统,表意较模糊,注重的是意念;而英语在词义上较具体,表意较准确,注重的是形式,句式结构严紧。这使得汉语和英语语境的构成的特点也随之不同。因此,在选词时要做到词义准确。

【例 215】国际公约

[误译] public international treaty

[正译] general multilateral convention

[评析] "国际公约"不能译成 public international treaty,因为这里的"国际公约"是指许多国家为解决某一重大问题而举行国际会议最后缔结的多边条约,所以选用 convention(国际公约国家、派别或军事力量之间的契约,尤指关于某一特定问题的国际公约,如战俘待遇),全文应译成:general multilateral convention。

【例 216】互不侵犯条约

[误译] pact of mutual non-aggression

[正译] treaty of mutual non-aggressions

[评析] 应译成 treaty of mutual non-aggressions,而不能译成 pact of mutual non-aggression, 因为 pact 常被认为比 treaty 较不重要或约束力较弱的协定。

【例 217】"明寓"从设计到装潢都体现了中国明朝时期的建筑风格,我相信您一定会喜欢这套古典式公寓。

[误译] "Ming House" is a classic Chinese residence emboding the architectural style of China's Ming Dynasty. I am sure you will like this classic appartment.

[正译]"Ming House" is a classic Chinese residence designed and decorated in the architectural style of China's Ming Dynasty. I am sure you will like it.

[评析]"体现"的英语对应词是 embody 和 demonstrate。但是, embody 主要用于表述想法和感情, 与这句的意义不符, 不能使用。demonstrate 虽有"(某事物)的实例, 表明"之意, 但原文的意思是:"明寓"就是以明朝风格设计和装潢的。通过直接使用 design 和 decorate 的被动语态, 准确地表达了原意, 在语体上也符合英语具体明了的表达习惯。

【例 218】我感谢陆登庭校长的邀请, 使我有机会在这美好的金秋时节, 来到美国你们这座古老而又现代化的学府。

[误译]I wish to thank President Rudenstine, for inviting me to this ancient yet modernized institution of the United States in this golden fall.

[正译]I wish to thank President Rudenstine for inviting me to this old yet modern institution of the United States in this golden fall.

[评析]看到"古老"一词, 往往首先想到 ancient, 但是虽然哈佛大学是一个有悠久历史的大学, 此处用 old 也比用 ancient 作定语更为恰当。用 ancient 显然是不合适的。

【例 219】近几年, 城市出现了大龄未婚女青年群。

[误译]In recent years, groups of old unmarried girls have made their appearance in cities.

[正译]In recent years, groups of elder unmarried girls have made their appearance in cities.

[评析]old 的意思是"年老的"或"老龄的"; elder 的意思是"年长的"或"大龄的"。

【例 220】这个研究所附属于科学院。

[误译]This institute is belonged to the Academy of Science.

[正译]This institute is attached to the Academy of Science.

[评析]belong to 虽有"属于"的涵义, 但它是不及物动词, 不用被动态。作"附属"解释的动词还有 affiliated。例如:It is a hospital af-

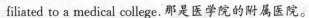

filiated to a medical college. 那是医学院的附属医院。

【例221】中国对于进入 WTO 的态度是积极的,我们为此已经进行了十一年的谈判。

[误译] China's attitude towards the accession to WTO is a active one, and we have been working for that objective for 11 years.

[正译] China's attitude towards the accession to WTO is a positive one, and we have been working for that objective for 11 years.

[评析] 态度上的积极应译为 positive,行动上的积极可译为 active。

【例222】我们现在正在积极地做准备工作。

[误译] We are making positive preparations for that visit.

[正译] We are making busy preparations for that visit.

[评析] 翻译"积极"不容易。"积极的影响"应译为 a positive influence;"积极地参加"也可为 take an active part in。但这里的"积极地做准备"无论是译为 positive preparations 还是 active preparations,都不是英语的惯常搭配,busy preparations 较准确。

【例223】他谢绝赴宴的邀请。

[误译] He refused an invitation to dinner.

[正译] He declined an invitation to dinner.

[评析] refuse 与 decline 是同义词,意为"拒绝",但 decline 意为"婉拒"、"婉言谢绝",refuse 意为"拒绝"。

【例224】你已经读完那本书吗?

[误译] Have you completed that book yet?

[正译] Have you finished that book yet?

[评析] 动词 finish 与 complete 都有"结束"、"完成"的意思。但是 finish 着重于结束;而 complete 着重于完成。如果没有上下文,误句有两种涵义:(1) 你已经写完那本书吗? (2) 你已经读完那本书吗? 而正句只能译成:你已经读完那本书吗? 例如:1 finished dinner at 12. 我 12 点钟吃完午饭。(着重结束)/He completed his homework early in the evening. 他晚上很早就把作业完成了。(着重完成)

【例225】他们救起一名溺水的队员。

[误译] They assisted the team member who was drowning.

[正译] They helped the team member who was drowning.

[评析] 动词 help 除作"帮助"解之外,尚有"救援"之意,而 assist 是指受助者有部分活动能力,有"辅助"、"协助"之意。

【例 226】我正在过街时,差点被汽车撞着。

[误译] I was crossing the street and was almost knocked by a car.

[正译] I was crossing the street and was almost hit by a car.

[评析] 动词 hit 意为"碰撞",常用于"车撞"。knock 意为"撞倒",

【例 227】产品质量有待提高。

[误译] The quality of the products should be raised.

[正译] The quality of the products should be improved.

[评析] 汉语"提高质量"英语应说 improve the quality of,不能说 raise the quality of;但可以说 raise the price 提高价格,raise efficiency 提高效率;raise the rent 提高租金,raise one's voice 提高声音等。

【例 228】月球影响潮汐。

[误译] The moon affects the tides.

[正译] The moon influences the tides.

[评析] 动词 affect 可作"影响"解,但主要指不良的影响,动词 influence 可以表示不良的影响, 也可表示好的影响。

【例 229】那位工程师在一次事故中受了重伤。

[误译] The engineer got seriously wounded in an accident.

[正译] The engineer got seriously injured in an accident.

[评析] wound 指在战、争或战斗中受了枪弹伤、刀创伤。injure 指在事故中受伤。上述二词都比 hurt (受伤)严重得多

【例 230】如果发生创伤,最重要的是预防感染。

[误译] If an injury should happen, it is then very important to prevent infection.

[正译] If an injury should occur, it is then very important to prevent infection.

[评析] injury (伤),pain(痛),disease(病)等的发生常常用 occur, develop 或者 result,不用 happen。happen 多指发生事故。

【例231】休息以后又开始上课了。

[误译] After a break class began.

[正译] After a break class was resumed.

[评析] 动词 resume 意为停顿之后重新开始。例如：They resumed their journey after short rest. 他们在短暂休息之后重新开始他的旅行。begin 只能表示某个动作的第一次开始。

【例232】雅典被举为下一届奥运会的会址。

[误译] Athens was chosen as the site for the coming Olympic Games.

[正译] Athens was selected as the site of the coming Olympic Games

[评析] 动词 select 有"精选"之意。例如：The peasants are selecting seeds. 农民正在选种。choose 也作"选择"解,但不强调经过周密考虑之后的选择。

【例233】本杰明·富兰克林的发现之一是：闪电是电。

[误译] One of Benjamin Franklin's findings was that lightning is electricity.

[正译] One of Benjamin Franklin's discoveries was that lightning is electricity.

[评析] discovery 常指科学上新的、重大发现, 例如：Balboa's discovery of the Pacific Ocean occurred in 1513. 巴尔伯于 1513 年发现了太平洋。finding(s)作"发现"、"发现物"解时,并不意味着是新的、重大发现。例如：He wanted to publish his archaeological findings. 他想发表他在考古学上若干发现。

【例234】如果病人无力支付,医生会免收诊费。

[误译] Doctors will not receive fares for services if patients are not able to pay.

[正译] Doctors will not receive fees for services if patients are not able to pay.

[评析] fee 多指学费、会费、诊费、服务费、入场费、税等,例如：The admission fee is 2 dollar. 门票为两美元。fare 主要指车费、船费等。如：Bus and taxi fares will be raised next year. 明年公共汽车费和出租车费要涨价。/What is the fare to New York and back?

往返纽约车费是多少？

【例 235】大气污染日益变为公害。

[误译] Air pollution is becoming one of the pubic dangers.

[正译] Air pollution is becoming one of the pubic hazards.

[评析] 名词 danger 与 hazard 作"危险"解时是同义词。例如：Mountain climbing is full of hazards. 登山充满危险。/In war a soldier's life is full of danger. 战时士兵的生命充满危险。但作"公共危险（公害）"解时须用 hazards。

【例 236】不久将来肯定会发生月食。

[误译] It is sure that there will be lunar eclipse in the near future.

[正译] It is certain that there will be lunar eclipse in the near future.

[评析] 英语中 sure 与 certain 都有"肯定的"、"无疑的"之意，可作表语，引出宾语从句，例如：She was sure(certain) she would succeed. 她确信自己会成功。但不能说：It is sure that...。此时可以使用 It is certain that... 的结构。例如：It is certain that she will pass the examination. 她肯定会考及格。

【例 237】体育文化已被全世界人民所接受。

[误译] Physical culture has been received by the people of the whole world.

[正译] Physical culture has been accepted by the people of the whole world.

[评析] to receive 是"接收"，to accept 才是接受。

【例 238】你能介绍我一本好书吗？

[误译] Could you introduce me a good book?

[正译] Could you recommend me a good book?

[评析] introduce 和"介绍"在这句话中是假对应词。如用 introduce，就等于说把一个人介绍给一本书认识认识，显然逻辑不通。这里的汉语意思实际上是"推荐"。同理，翻译"他向我们介绍了一些他的教学经验"时，更不能使用 introduce 这个词。而应译为：He told us something about his experience in teaching.

【例 239】他拒绝对这件事发表意见。

［误译］He refused to express his opinion on this matter.

［正译］He refused to comment on the matter.

［评析］to express one's opinion 与"发表意见"在这里是假对应词,不足以表达原文的意思。

【例240】尽管是一个大学生,我兄弟连一封英文信都写不好。

［误译］In spite of a college student, my brother cannot write an English letter properly.

［正译］Though he is a college student, my brother cannot write an English letter properly.

［评析］in spite of 有时译为"尽管",但其深层含义是"不为困难或障碍所阻",亦即"全然不顾"。所以,用在这句的译文中是不合适的,应改用"Though (he is)..."

【例241】在晚会上,邀请一位外国老师为我们唱几首民歌。

［误译］At the party a foreign teacher was required to sing some folk songs for us.

［正译］At the party a foreign teacher was requested to sing some folk songs for us.

［评析］require 是"要求"、"命令",指提出要求的人有权要司对方做某事。例如:The students are required to write a composition twice a week. 要求学生两星期写一篇作文。"request"是"请求"的意思,比"ask"稍正式一些。例如:Professor Zhang was requested to give a lecture on English usage. 张教授被请求作一次关于英语惯用法的讲演。

【例242】最近人口统计显示中国人口已超过十三亿。

［误译］The latest census shows that China's population has surpassed 1,3 billion.

［正译］The latest census shows that China's population exceeds 1,3 billion.

［评析］surpass 一般用于超过别人的成绩,速度等。exceed 则单纯指在数字、程度等方面超过。例如:The number of students in this school exceeds 5000. 该校的学生人数超过五千人。

第十二节 近 形 词

英语中还有一些单词拼写相似,两个单词之间只有一两个或两三个字母不同,他们有时意思也十分接近。遇到这些词拿不准的时候,就要查字典以避免误译。

【例243】电影也有国际评奖。

[误译] There are also some international rewards for movies.

[正译] There are also some international awards for movies.

[评析] reward 是报酬、酬劳的意思。例如:He got a reward of $900 for catching the criminal. 他因抓获罪犯而得 900 美元酬金。award 表示奖金、奖品,例如:Educational Development Awards 教育发展奖金。

【例 244】旅游业是很有希望的财源。

[误译] Tourism is a promising financial resource.

[正译] Tourism is a promising financial source.

[评析] financial resource 的意思是财力;financial source 的意思才是财源。

【例 245】那些家庭经济模式反映了庭院经济对每个家庭带来的影响。

[误译] Those household economical patterns reflect the influences upon each household made by the courtyard economy.

[正译] Those household economic patterns reflect the influences upon each household made by the courtyard economy.

[评析] economical 的意思是 not wasteful (节省);economic 的意思是"与经济活动有关的"。

【例 246】那所自然博物馆的门票为五美元。

[误译] The admittance to the Museum of Natural History is five dollars.

[正译] The admission to the Museum of Natural History is five dollars.

[评析] 名词 admittance 和 admission (= permission to go in) 都有"准许进入"的意思, admittance 比 admission 更为正式, admission 则更为常用。作为"入场费"、"门票"、"票价"解时只能用 admission (entrance price)。

【例247】第二次世界大战时中国与美国结成联盟。

[误译] China entered into ally with the United States in the Second World War.

[正译] China entered into alliance with the United States in the Second World War.

[评析] 名词 alliance 意为联盟；名词 ally 意为盟国。例如：China was one of the allies in the Second World War. 第二次世界大战时中国是盟国之一。ally 用作动词有"结盟"的意思, 例如：Great Britain was allied with France in the Second World War. 第二次世界大战时英国与法国结盟。

【例248】龙和凤是想像中的动物。

[误译] The dragon and phoenix are imaginative animals.

[正译] The dragon and phoenix are imaginary animals.

[评析] imaginary 是"想像的"意思, 用来修饰人们想像出来而事实上不存在的事物。例如：The equator is an imaginary line. 赤道是一条想像中的线。imaginative 意为富有想像力的。例如：A writer should be imaginative. 作家应富有想像力。

【例249】她对化学感兴趣, 但对物理不感兴趣。

[误译] She was interested in chemistry, but disinterested in physics.

[正译] She was interested in chemistry, but uninterested in physics.

[评析] 形容词 interested 意为对……感兴趣, 其反义词是 uninterested。disinterested 意为不偏不倚的。例如：His remarks were not disinterested. 他的话并非不偏不倚。

第十三节 单 复 数

英语普通名词有可数与不可数之分, 其中有些普通名词既可用作可数名词,又可用作不可数名词,但意义不尽相同。例如,paper 用作不可数名词时作"纸"解,而用作可数名词时则作"报纸"解,如:an evening paper(一张晚报)。另外,汉语词汇比较灵活,很多词汇可以是可数名词,也可以是不可数名词,但是英语中有些名词只能当抽象名词使用,必须与其他其体名词连用才能变得可数。这在汉译英时要尤为小心。

【例 250】在他的干预下,进行了不少盲目的重复建设。

[误译] Under his intervention there have been a lot of indiscriminate and duplicated constructions.

[正译] Under his intervention there have been a lot of indiscriminate and duplicated construction projects.

[评析] 英语中有些名词只能当抽象名词使用,必须与其他名词连用才能变得可数。所以, duplicated constructions 应改为 duplicated construction projects。

【例 251】我想今后不会有太多的金融机构破产,也许就没有了。

[误译] I don't expect to see too many bankruptcies of financial firms in the future, and maybe there will be none.

[正译] I don't expect to see too many bankruptcy cases of financial firms in the future, and maybe there will be none.

[评析] 汉语词汇比较灵活,"破产"可以是可数名词,也可以是不可数名词。但 bankruptcy 是不可数名词,为表示复数概念可以增词翻译为 bankruptcy cases。

【例 252】对失败一方来说,讲和条件通常是苛刻的。

[误译] The term of the peace was usually hard for the defeated side.

[正译] The terms of the peace were usually hard for the defeated side.

[评析] term 表示条件(conditions)或人际关系(personal relations) 的意思时,要用复数形式。例如:One should be on good terms with one's neighbors. 人们应与邻居和睦相处。

【例 253】多年的教学经验,帮助我改变了主意。

[误译] Years of teaching experiences has helped me to change my mind.

[正译] Years of teaching experience has helped me to change my mind.

[评析] experience 作单数是经验的意思，用作复数就是经历、阅历的意思。不少译者容易混淆 experience 单复数的意思。

第十四节　虚义实译

汉语中有些词意义比较虚泛、含糊，英译时要将其具体化，不经过这么处理的话，英译文可能会让人看不太懂。

【例 254】几十亿、几百亿的一个项目投产以后没有市场，相反，把原有的一些企业也挤垮了。

[误译] Some projects which have absorbed billions or tens of Millions of RMB yuan in investment, as soon as they are put into operation, they actually can't find any market for their projects. And some existing enterprises have collapsed because of these newly set up projects.

[正译] Some projects which have absorbed billions or tens of Millions of RMB yuan in investment, as soon as they are put into operation, they actually can't find any market for their projects. And some existing enterprises have to be closed or to be suspended because of these newly set up projects.

[评析] 汉语中有些词意义比较虚泛，英译时最好将其具体化。把企业"搞垮"如直译成 collapse，意思仍不太明确。应将其具体化为 to be closed or to be suspended，更清楚易懂。

【例 255】中央已经决定成立国家科技教育领导小组。

[误译] The Centre has decided to establish a leading group for the state science and education development.

[正译] The Central Committee of the CPC has decided to establish a leading group for the state science and education development.

[评析] "中央"也是一个泛义词，译者可根据具体情况分别译为 the Party Central Committee 或 the Central (National) Government。

【例 256】也就是中国的中央银行的监管能力能够达到的时候, 我们就会实行。

[误译] That is to say, we will achieve that objective, when the supervision and regulation capabilities of the Central Bank of China achieved.

[正译] That is to say, we will achieve that objective, when the supervision and regulation capabilities of the Central Bank of China are up to standard.

[评析] 汉语口语中有一些语义比较虚泛的词。在这句中,"能够达到"的语义不太具体,应将其其体化为 up to standard。

【例 257】有一点我不喜欢他,那就是他过于自信了。

[误译] The one thing about him that I dislike is his overconfidence.

[正译] The one characteristic about him that I dislike is his overconfidence.

[评析] one thing about him 这种译文意义表达得不太清楚,只用于非正式的口语,最好译为 one characteristic about him。

【例 258】这对加强国防十分重要。

[误译] This is fundamental to the strengthening of China's national defense.

[正译] This is fundamental to the building up of China's national defense.

[评析] 在这一句里,因为"加强"这个词没有具体含义,较虚泛。翻译"加强"用 build up, 比用 strengthen 好。build up 是增大、逐步建立的意思, build up 使英译文的意思清晰起来。

【例 259】今年我省在引进工作方面又取得了重大成就。

[误译] Major achievements has been made in our province this year in importing work.

[正译] Much more fruitful work has been done in our province this year in importing advanced technology and equipment.

[评析] "重大成就"不要译成 major achievements, 要做弱化语气处理。因为"引进工作"是一个很虚的词,最好不要空泛地译为其对

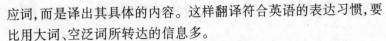

应词,而是译出其具体的内容。这样翻译符合英语的表达习惯,要比用大词、空泛词所转达的信息多。

【例 260】中国人口的 80％在农村,如果不解决这 80％的人的生活问题,社会就不会是安定的。

[误译] 80％ of China's population live in the rural areas. There will be no social stability unless their problem of livelihood are solved.

[正译] 80％ of China's population live in the rural areas. There will be no social stability unless their daily needs are met.

[评析] "生活问题"不能直译成 problem of livelihood,这样太抽象,意思太虚泛。如果译成 living conditions 又可能被误解为"生活条件"。这里"解决生活问题"就是指"满足生活的需要"。daily needs 包含了衣食住行等各方面,甚至精神文明方面的需要,是个含义面可宽也可以窄的词。

第十五节 解读原文

英译文能不能译好,理解是关键。有时若机械地按照字面的意思译,会违背原文的意思,甚至造成误解。这时译者就要开动脑筋,根据上下文来判断原文的真正含义是什么,然后加以很好地处理。词义的特性和联系实际的关系以上把词义的种种特性讲完了,这些特性是互相联系、互相渗透的,有一方面未讲清楚,便谈不上活用。词义的特性虽多,但用到具体句子时除词义的本质外,只能显出一种主要的特性,不会各种特性同时显现。一个词在具体句子内占有一定位置,起着一定作用,使句子成为有机联系的整体。这种有机联系性就是客观实际有机联系的反映。一个词放在一个句子内是否能和其他词构成有机的联系,是检验这个词用得是否恰当的句内标准。然后拿整句意思和客观实际去合一合,看看那一词用得是否恰当,才能做出最后决定,是翻译对了还是错了。翻译错的词义必然歪曲实际的真正面貌。

【例 261】我曾经请人转告他,中国如果不稳定就是个国际问题,后果难以想像。

[误译] I asked others to tell him that if the political situation in China became unstable, the trouble would become an international issue, with consequences that would be hard to imagine.

[正译] I asked others to tell him that if the political situation in China became unstable, the trouble would spread to the rest of the world, with consequences that would be hard to imagine.

[评析] "国际问题"不能机械地译作 international issue，如果这样译，各国就都可以采取行动，而这肯定不是说话人的本意。应当仔细解读"中国如果不稳定就是个国际问题"的真正含义，这句的意思应是中国如果不稳定会对周边有影响。

【例262】经济是一个大问题。

[误译] Economy is a big problem.

[正译] Economy is an important (a major) question.

[评析] 这句话的本意是说经济是一个很重要、范围很广的问题，如果翻译不假思索，每个字都以对应的英文单词翻译出来，就成了 Economy is a big problem. 其意思是经济出了大问题。

【例263】要注意解决好少数高级知识分子的待遇问题。我们不论怎么困难，也要提高教师的待遇。这个事情，在国际上都有影响。我们的留学生有几万人。

[误译] We must try to increase the material benefits for the few top intellectuals. No matter how many difficulties we have, we must try to improve the treatment of teachers, for it will have international influence. We have tens of thousands of students studying abroad.

[正译] We must try to increase the material benefits for the few top intellectuals. No matter how many difficulties we have, we must try to improve the treatment of teachers, for it will affect our intellectuals in other countries too. We have tens of thousands of students studying abroad.

[评析] "在国际上有影响"如果译为 have international influence，意思不是很清晰，这里应根据上下文判断，理解为会对我们在国外的留学人员产生影响，这就使较为含混的说法清楚易懂。

【例 264】 该国内部对该政策究竟怎么样,我们还要观察。

[误译] What the policies are to be pursued after all within the country, we still have to wait and see.

[正译] The country authorities have to decide among themselves what the policy to pursue, and so we still have to wait and see.

[评析] "该国内部"并非指"该国国内",而是指该国的领导层必须决定采取什么样的政策。因此现在译文加字是完全必要的。

【例 265】 对于他们批准的议定书,我们决定不予承认。

[误译] We have decided not to recognize the protocol by them as binding.

[正译] We have decided not to acknowledge the protocol by them as binding.

[评析] 议定书是客观存在的,只是不承认它有效力。因此不能译为 not to recognize the protocol。

【例 266】 这也使民族精神获得了新的解放。

[误译] This has also further liberated the national spirit.

[正译] This has also further liberated the nation ideologically.

[评析] 如果机械地把"民族精神"译成 national spirit,这样就曲解了原文的意思。national spirit 是代表民族的精神,譬如:勤劳、勇敢是一个民族的精神。这句话的原意是使得我们的民族在精神上和思想上获得新的解放。这句话还可以译为:Reform and the open policy have also emancipated the minds of the people.

第十六节 文体的误译

语言是人类交流思想的工具。表达思想的人,各有不同,其教育程度不同,阅历不同,身分不同,年岁、性别不同,心情,谈话的内容不同,人们所用的语言也不同。因此,语言的种类多种多样,有各种口头语言,有各种笔头用语,有正式的语言,等等。毫无疑问,各种语言,特别是口语与书面语,非正式语言和正式语言之间,存在着这样或那样的差别。在翻译时,要尽力把原文的这些特点体现出来。注意文体的不同,例如翻译"马"时:a knight's steed 用于文学体;但 a policeman's horse,用于一般体。death 用于一般场合,decease 用于正式场合或文件中,pass away 偏文偏古。例如:

【例 267】今年春季召开的全国科学大会,动员全国民为祖国的科学、技术现代化而努力。

[误译] The national Science Conference convened this spring sparked off the entire nation dig in towards the modernization of science and technology.

[正译] The national Science Conference convened this spring mobilized the entire nation work for the modernization of science and technology.

[评析] 用词不仅要准确、生动,而且还要注意语境的风格,比如文体的风格、人物的语言风格等。这一句汉语,明显是比较正式的政论文体或新闻文体,而 spark off 用词不准确,而且口语体,用在这里显然不合适。应改为书面体表达,可改为 mobilize。dig in 也属于口语,这是一篇具有重大意义的政论文章,所以应用书面语,不应用口语体去翻译这篇文章,可把 dig in 改为 work for。

【例 268】他们害怕竞争对手变得强大起来。

[误译] They are afraid of the emergence of their rivals.

[正译] They fear the emergence of their rivals.

[评析] afraid 一般用于日常口语,不像政治用语。这是一篇社论,该用 they fear 这类正式的词。

【例 269】中东的形势将仍是紧张而复杂,充满新的战争冲突。

[误译] The situation in the Middle East will remain tense and complicated, full of the danger of new military conflicts.

[正译] The situation in the Middle East will remain tense and complicated, fraud with the danger of new military conflicts.

[评析] full of 用在这样一篇严肃的社论里不当,可改为 fraud with。

【例 270】事实雄辩地证明了有志者事竟成。

[误译] The facts eloquently show that there is a will, there is a way.

[正译] The facts eloquently demonstrate that there is a will, there is a way.

[评析] show 与 eloquently 不能搭配,可把 show 换为更为庄严的字眼,如 demonstrate 等。

【例 271】他们在很大程度上必须依靠产品质量和营销。

[误译] They cannot but rely to a great extent on the quality of their product and marketing.

[正译] They have to rely to a great extent on the quality of their product and marketing.

[评析] cannot but 太口语化,用在这里与这篇社论的文风不相符,用 have to 要好一些。

【例 272】他们经济上畸形发展。

[误译] Their economy development is lopsided.

[正译] Their economy is distorted.

[评析] lopsided 太口语化,可改为 distorted。

【例 273】他们也许能推迟病毒的爆发。

[误译] They may be able to put off the spread of virus.

[正译] They may be able to delay the spread of virus.

[评析] put off 太口语化,一般指不十分重要的事情,所以在这里应以 delay 来代替 put off。

【例 274】早在 1805 年,他们就解决了这个问题。

[误译] Back in 1805, they solved the problem.

[正译] As early as in 1805, they solved the problem.

[评析] Back in 1805 太口语化,可改为:As early as 1805。

【例 275】几千年的历史经验已经证明:物极必反。

[误译] As the past experience of thousands of years has proved, things will develop in the opposite direction when they become extreme.

[正译] As the historical experience of thousands of years has proved, things will develop in the opposite direction when they become extreme.

[评析] past 与 thousands of years 不相配,可改为 historical。

第十七节 词义的褒贬强弱

人在表达自己的思想时,常常带有感情色彩,喜怒哀乐以及好恶等等。在汉译英时,注意词义的褒贬也是常常要注意的问题之一。

【例276】学生应该从这里得出一条经验,就是不要被假象所迷惑。

[误译] Students should draw experience here:Don't be misled by false appearances.

[正译] Students should draw a lesson here:Don't be misled by false appearances.

[评析] 这里的"经验"不是成功的经验,而是从错误或失败中得出的经验,所以用 experience 不太合适,而 lesson 表示教训、训诫、惩戒等义。所以用 a lesson 恰如其分。例如:a historical lesson written in blood 历史上血的教训。

【例 277】 你不要太急了,我比你还急。

[误译] Please don't be too impatient. Actually, I'm more impatient than you are.

[正译] Please don't be too anxious. Actually, I'm more anxious than you are.

[评析] "急"在这里如果用 impatient,贬义就太重,impatient 有"不耐烦的"意思。最好改译成 anxious。

【例278】打得赢就打,打不赢就走。

[误译] Fight when we can win and run away when we cannot.

[正译] Fight when you can win, move away when you cannot.

[评析] 汉语原文的"走"没有贬义,因而 move away 比 run away 更好地体现了原文的感情色彩。

【例 279】恐怖分子的暴行激起了人民极大的愤怒。

[误译] The violence of the terrorists roused the people to great anger.

[正译] The atrocities of the terrorists roused the people to great indignation.

[评析] 汉语原文的"暴行"和"愤怒"意义强烈,所以在英译文中选用

了 atrocities 和 indignation, 而不用 violence 和 anger。

【例 280】孙中山先生是个好人。

[误译] Dr Sun Yet-sen was a good man.

[正译] Dr Sun Yet-sen was a man of integrity.

[评析] 如果译作 a good man, 词义显得太轻, 与这位伟大的革命先
行者的身分不相称, 而 a man of integrity 用在这儿, 词义轻重合
适。

【例 281】爱因斯坦是一个聪明人。

[误译] Einstain was a clever man.

[正译] Einstain was a wise man.

[评析] wise 与 clever 都有"聪明的"意思。前者着重明智、智慧;后
者指一般的伶俐、灵巧。如果描写一位著名的科学家, 用 wise 较
妥;描写一般人的聪明、灵巧, 最好用 clever, 否则就有大词小用或
小词大用之误。

【例 282】这个产品只有六个月的历史, 还有许多地方需要改进。

[误译] Product has only six-month's history, and leaves much to be
desired.

[正译] Product is only six-month old, and leaves much to be desired.

[评析] 译文里不能译出 history, 因为这里用 history 是大词小用了,
况且六个月还够不上 history。

第十八节　专业术语

概念是思维的基本形式, 它反映着事物最本质的特征。对于某
个专业的汉英翻译, 除了需要熟悉专业术语外, 还要对专业词语的内
容和结构进行分析, 找出它们的共同点和不同点, 再把经过分析而得
出的深层含义从汉语转译成英语。该用专业术语时要用术语, 这样
才能确切表达原文意思, 并使译文风格符合其内容。例如:

【例283】他们曾派遣雇佣军进行公然的军事入侵。

[误译] They sent mercenary troops for outright militate invasion.

[正译] They dispatched mercenaries for outright militate invasion.

［评析］sent 用在这里太口语化了，不像政治语言，可改为 dis-patched。另外，mercenary troops 用在这里不妥，可用 mercenaries 或 mercenary forces。

【例284】兹证明张三（男，1990年10月3日生）现在未婚。

［误译］This is to certify that Zhang San (male, born on October 3, 1990) is now unmarried.

［正译］Zhang San (male, born on October 3, 1990): present marital status is unmarried.

［评析］在这份公证书中，所证明的事项是张三目前的婚姻状况，改译后的英译文较好地体现了这一点。

【例285】签订经济合同的通常做法是由有关当事人中的一方提出签订合同的建议，并在合同中明确规定主要条款的具体内容。

［误译］The usual way of signing an economic contract is that one of interested parties puts forward his suggestion that a contract be signed and clearly set forth the specific contents of major provisions in the contract.

［正译］In the course of signing an economic contract, the usual practice is for one of the interested parties to propose his suggestion that a contract be signed and clearly set forth the specific contents of major provisions in the contract.

［评析］此句的主要内容是指：签订合同时，通常的做法是提出签订合同的建议，规定合同的内容。因此，先将"签订经济合同"译成状语 in the course of signing an economic contract，再译"通常的做法是"为 the usual practice is，这里的"做法"是指习惯、惯例，因此 way 应改为 practice。中间的"由有关当事人中的一方提出签订合同的建议"应改译成带逻辑主语的不定式结构 for one of the interested parties to，体现出原文的由合同当事人提出建议；另外这里的"建议"应改用 propose 加名词从句，比 put forward a suggestion 显得更严谨些。

【例286】李明在中国居住期间没有受过刑事制裁。

［误译］Li Ming has not been punished according to the criminal law during his living in China.

[正译] Li Ming has no record of committing offences against the criminal law during his residence in China.

[评析] 此句中的 not to be punished 与表示一段时间的 during 短语连用不恰当,况且,此句证明的是"没有受过刑罚的记载",而"触犯刑律"也应译成 commit an offence against the criminal law,所以改译后的意义更具体明确;另外,"在中国居住期间"应译为 during his residence in China,"居住"这个词选用 residence 而不用 living,更强调一个住所的永久性和合法性。

【例287】本保证书自即日起生效。有效期将于贵公司收到全部已经买方承兑和我行背书保证的远期汇票之日终止。

[误译] This letter of Guarantee will come into force from this day and will lose its effect when your company has received all the usance drafts accepted by the Buyer and endorsed by our Bank.

[正译] This letter of Guarantee shall come into force on its issuing draft and remain valid until you have received all the usance drafts accepted by the Buyer and endorsed by our Bank.

[评析] 法律文书中表示义务或规定时,第三人称后要用 shall 不用 will。from this day 不确切,宜改为 on its issuing draft。will lose its effect 也翻译得欠妥,effect 在这里的含义是效应、结果,况且此句的关键内容是指有效期到何时终止,故应选择:remain valid until 结构;另外 your company 宜改为 you。

【例288】本细则的解释权,属于中华人民共和国财政部。

[误译] The right of interpretation for the Detailed Rules and Regulations, belongs to the Ministry of Finance of the People's Republic of China.

[正译] The right of interpreting the Detailed Rules and Regulations, resides in the Ministry of Finance of the People's Republic of China.

[评析] the right of interpretation for the Detailed Rules and Regulations 不能准确地表达出"细则的解释力",应改用 interpreting;句中谓语动词 belong to 也用得欠妥,因为 belong to 的含义是"属于

…的财产"，这里的"属于"是指权力、权利等为…所有，故应选用 reside in，例如：The power of decision resides in the higher authorities. 决定权属于上级机构。

第十九节　增　　词

为了使译文忠实于原文的内容，无论是英译汉，还是汉译英，有时必须改变原文的形式。有时为了行文的需要，都可以在译文里增加几个词。如果机械地按照字面直译，不仅不能表达原文的思想、精神与形象，而且还会使译文前后矛盾，闹出笑话。有时是因为不同语言习惯说法不同，有时因为原文经不起推敲，有时是为了照顾那些不十分了解中国历史、现状、不了解中国的一些典故、谚语的外国读者。为了忠实表达原文，有时需要加字，有时需要减字，有时需要改变原文字面。增词可以使译文流畅，这是因为有些词在一种语言里可能是必要的，而在另一种语言里就会显得多余了。

【例 289】我卖掉了彩电。

[误译] 1 sold out my color TV.

[正译] I sold out my color TV set.

[评析] "彩电"有两层意思：一是指具体的实物——彩色电视机(color TV set)；二是指电视机屏幕上映出的影像，即彩色电视(color television)。在这里，卖掉的只能是具体的实物——彩色电视机.

【例 290】他的科学著作在英语国家中得到广泛阅读。

[误译] His scientific works were widely read in English countries.

[正译] His scientific works were widely read in English-speaking countries.

[评析] "英语国家"的含义实际上是"讲英语的国家"。例如：Canada is one of the English-speaking countries. 加拿大是英语国家之一。

【例 291】作为一个世界贸易组织，缺乏中国，它也很难发挥作为一个世界贸易组织的应有作用。

[误译] As a world trade organization, WTO without China will be hard to play its due role.

[正译] As a world trade organization, WTO without the participation of China will find it hard to play its due role.

[评析] "缺乏中国"可以就译为 without China, 但是如果添加一些词,翻译成 without the participation of China, 使英译文的表述更加明确,也更容易理解。

【例 292】分清职责

[误译] define the duties

[正译] define the duties incumbent on each person or post

[评析] "分清职责"的意思在中文里十分清楚,即指每个人的职责或岗位责任。但英译文如果只译 define the duties 含义模糊。

【例 293】我们总要相信,全世界也好,中国也好,多数人是好人。

[误译] We must believe that in China and in the whole world, the majority of the people are good.

[正译] We must believe that in China, as everywhere else in the world, the majority of the people are good.

[评析] 原译文里的 in China and in the whole world 的含义是中国不属于世界,这不符合逻辑,因为中国是世界的一部分,所以加上了 everywhere else。

【例 294】1998 年是联合国确定的国际海洋年,中国政府愿借此机会介绍中国海洋事业的发展情况。

[误译] The year 1998 has been designated by the United Nations as International Ocean Year, and on this occasion I would like to introduce the progress of China's work in this particular field.

[正译] The year 1998 has been designated by the United Nations as International Ocean Year, and on this occasion I would like to introduce the progress of China's work in this particular field to the world.

[评析] 原文"介绍……的发展情况"句子是完整的。但在译文里却需要说明向谁介绍,因此加了 to the world。

【例 295】领导人对两国关系非常关心。

[误译] Our leaders have been much concerned about our bilateral relations.

[正译] Our leaders have taken interest in the development of our bilateral relations.

[评析] 对两国关系非常关心的实质意义是关心两国关系的进展。改正译文准确地理解了这一点,增词 development,使英译文十分贴切原文的意思。

【例 296】建国以来

[误译] since the founding of the People's Republic of China

[正译] since the founding of the People's Republic of China in 1949

[评析] 有些人,尤其是外国人并不知道"建国以来"具体指的是什么时间,需要加以说明,增译 in 1949。

【例 297】抗战期间

[误译] during the War of Resistance

[正译] during the War of Resistance against Japan

[评析] 同上例一样,有些人,尤其是外国人不太清楚"抗战期间"的战争双方是谁,也要加以说明,这里要增译 against Japan。

【例 298】结婚大办酒席,实在可以免去了。

[误译] Giving lavish feasts at weddings can well be dispensed with.

[正译] The practice of giving lavish feasts at weddings can well be dispensed with.

[评析] 汉语里有时不用表明事物范畴的概括性词语,译成英语时却往往需要增译一些概括性词语。原文并没有 practice 这个对应词,但增译它可以符合英语突出信息重点的要求。

【例 299】要提倡顾全大局

[误译] We should advocate taking the whole situation into consideration.

[正译] We should advocate the spirit of taking the whole situation into consideration.

[评析] 本句没有表明事物范畴的概括性词语,但是英译文有时需要增译一些概括性词语。汉语中"顾全大局"是一种精神,要提倡的是这种精神,在译成英语时,要对"顾全大局"的意思加以概括,否

则英语读者就理解不清了。

从以上这些例子可以看出为了准确表达原作意思,有时可以增词翻译。译者可以发挥创造性,就是摆脱原文的束缚,在译文里使用最好的表达方式。

第二十节　简　　洁

在中译英过程中,我们常常发现有些词没有实际意义,因此我们可以把他们减词省译。在写作上,我们讲究简洁明快的文风,英美人称之为 clean English,在翻译时,我们也应保持这种文风,要用简练的英文去表达原文丰富的思想。同时,"简洁"也是用以加强语气一种修辞手段。这就需要去掉一些可有可无的词、短语、成分或句子。在译完一篇文章或一部作品之后,要多读读,多看看,去掉译文中那些可有可无的词。

一、省译形容词

【例 300】他们做了艰苦的努力。

[误译] They made painstaking efforts.

[正译] They made efforts.

[评析] efforts(exertion of physical or mental energy to do something 努力)与 painstaking (taking great care or trouble 艰苦的)的意思相互包含,翻译关键词"努力"即可。

【例 301】我们对过去的历史应有所了解。

[误译] We should know a little of our past history.

[正译] We should know a little of our history.

[评析] "过去"与"历史"意思部分重合,在汉语中可以接受。而如英译成 past history,就是很不好的译文,在英语里它们不能一起使用。

【例 302】又处在信息革命的伟大历史时期。

[误译] What's more, it finds itself in a great historic period of information technology.

[正译] What's more, it finds itself in a historic period of information technology.

[评析] great 不必译出,翻译出来反而英文不通了,因为 historic 已含有 great 的意思,翻译出来是多此一举,而且译文不简洁。

【例303】我们取得了伟大的历史性胜利。

[误译] We have won a great historic victory.

[正译] We have won a great victory.

[评析] 胜利取得了以后,它便成为历史,因此,在英译文里 historic 不能与 victory 搭配,historic 不能像汉语的"历史"一样出现在这样的语境中。

【例304】这个地区遭受了严重的自然灾害。

[误译] The people in the region suffered a serious natural disaster.

[正译] The people in the region suffered a natural disaster.

[评析] disaster 的英语释义是 an occurrence causing widespread destruction and distress; a catastrophe,即 disaster 本身就含有"严重的"意思,因此,serious 不能与 disaster 搭配。

【例305】教育发展速度比较快。

[误译] The speed of the development in education has been comparatively fast.

[正译] Education has developed at a comparatively great speed.

[评析] speed(速度)与 fast(快)两个词的意思是重复的。因此,形容词 fast 可以省去不译。

【例306】我们对此进行了积极的尝试。

[误译] We have actively carried out the experiment.

[正译] We have carried out the experiment.

[评析] experiment(尝试)本身就是一个积极的行为和态度,所以,没有必要翻译"积极的"一词。

【例307】我们积极支持生态农业。

[误译] We actively support ecological agriculture.

[正译] We support ecological agriculture.

[评析] "支持"的英语对应词 support 已经含有积极的意思,加 actively 就多此一举了。

【例 308】 成功地完成

[误译] successful accomplishment

[正译] accomplishment

[评析] 不能误译成 successful accomplishment, 因为 accomplishment (something completed successfully; an achievement)含有 successful 的意思,因而应删除 successful 一词。

【例 309】 他们采取了有效的措施。

[误译] They have adopted effective measures.

[正译] They have adopted measures.

[评析] measures 的英语解释是 action taken to achieve a purpose; an action taken as a means to an end(作为到最后的手段而采取的行动), effective 重复了 measures 的含义。

【例 310】 生物系有效地落实了生物工程研究。

[误译] Bioengineering research is effectively implementation implemented in the biology department.

[正译] Bioengineering research is implemented in the biology department.

[评析] implementation 已经含有 effective(有效)的意思。

　　类似的例子还有:"有效保护"不能译为 effectively protect;"认真解决问题"不能译为 earnestly solve the problem;"积极发展"不能译为 energetically develop;"积极探索"不能译为 enthusiastically explore;"我们必须坚决制止"不能译为 we must firmly put a stop to;"他们自觉守法"不能译为 they conscientiously obey the law, 等等。

【例311】 他抓住了有利时机。

[误译] He grabbed the favorable opportunity.

[正译] He grabbed the opportunity.

[评析] 根据朗文当代高级英语辞典, opportunity 的英语解释是 a favorable moment or occasion, 所以 opportunity 这个单词涵盖了 favorable 的意思。"有利"和"时机"在汉语里意思也有重合。但是汉语可以说"有利时机", 英语不能说 favorable opportunity。

【例 312】他反对完全禁止这种习俗。

[误译] He is against complete prohibition of the habitude.

[正译] He is against prohibition of the habitude.

[评析] prohibition 就包含有 complete 的意思,在翻译出 complete 是多此一举。"彻底毁灭"不能译为 thorough destruction 也是同样的道理。

【例 313】我们要加快住宅建设。

[误译] We will accelerate the construction of residential housing.

[正译] We will accelerate the construction of housing.

[评析] residential 和 housing 都有住宅的含义,只须译出 housing。

【例 314】本届政府要减少财政赤字。

[误译] This government will reduce the financial deficit.

[正译] This government will reduce the deficit.

[评析] 在英语里,可以说 trade deficit(贸易赤字),budget deficit(预算赤字),但是不能说 financial deficit,因为 deficit 本身含有 financial 的意思。同理,"财政税收"不能译为 financial revenue。

　　无可否认,复杂的思想不是片言只字可以描绘出来,但是在可能情况下,要力求用词既简洁又准确,并使内容丰富,而不是词藻华而不实,内容却贫乏。

【例315】外贸有了新的发展。

[误译] Foreign trade has made fresh progress.

[正译] Foreign trade has made progress.

[评析] progress 本身就有 fresh 的意思。

【例 316】世界各国

[误译] various countries throughout the world

[正译] countries throughout the world

[评析] throughout the world 含有 various 的意思,没有必要用 various。

【例 317】我们和该国已经签订了导弹互不瞄准的协议。

[误译] We have signed with the country the agreement on mutual non-targeting of missiles at each other.

[正译] We have signed with the country the agreement on non-targeting of missiles at each other.

[评析] 有些译者在使用和汉英翻译英语时很容易出现语义重叠的现象,应注意避免。在上面一句英语中 mutual 与 each other 语义重叠,因而最好把 mutual 删去。

【例 318】我们应制止和取缔一切败坏社会风气的丑恶现象。

[误译] We should ban any ugly practice that corrupts social morals.

[正译] We should ban any practice that corrupts social morals.

[评析] practice 前不用加 ugly、evil 等单词;因为要制止和取缔的东西应是不好的东西。

二、省译副词

汉语里似乎修饰词用得较多,例如:顺利进行,胜利完成,热烈拥护,积极支持,努力做到,认真贯彻,彻底粉碎,深入批判,广泛开展,严肃处理。甚至有些人的文章里还出现"不切实际的幻想"、"毫无根据的诽谤"等等。一般说来,英语里的修饰词不像汉语里那么多,不少指导写作的书都告诫不要乱用修饰词。因此,汉语里的修饰词不一定非统统照译不可,而应加以推敲,决定如何处理。英译文里修饰词过多会显得装腔作势,效果适得其反,原来想加以强调的反而削弱了。例如:

【例 319】进一步简化手续,及时地积极地从国外引进,并且认真组织科学技术人员和广大职工做好消化和推广工作。

[误译] We should further simplify procedures and take prompt and vigorous action to import urgently needed technology, earnestly organize scientists, technicians and the mass of workers to assimilate and popularize imported technology.

[正译] We should simplify procedures and take prompt action to import urgently needed technology, organize scientists, technicians and workers to assimilate and popularize imported technology.

[评析] 如果照原文字面在 simplify 前加上 further,在 prompt 后加上 and vigorous,在 organize 前加上 earnestly 或 actively,在 workers 前

加上 the mass of,文字会显得重复和累赘,反而没有很好传达原文的意思。

此外,有的修饰词要不要译,需要根据情况,仔细斟酌,有时译了反而有损原意,例如"胜利召开"如译为 successfully convene, 会使人感到召开前遇到不少困难和阻碍,最后才得以开成,而原文可能根本没有这种含义。

【例 320】我们一定能够达到目标。

[误译] Our goal will certainly be attained.

[正译] Our goal will be attained.

[评析] 这里如使用副词 certainly,看似加强语气,实际上减弱了动词的力量。

【例 321】双方一致同意签订中日长期贸易协定。

[误译] Both sides unanimously agreed to the signing of a Sino-Japanese long-term trade agreement.

[正译] Both sides agreed to the signing of a Sino-Japanese long-term trade agreement.

[评析] 由于本句的动词是 agreed(同意),它本身就含有 unanimously(一致)的意思,因而没有必要加上 unanimously 一词。

【例 322】大一学生壁球一定能赢。

[误译] The freshmen will surely win in the squash game.

[正译] The freshmen will win in the squash game.

[评析] will win 的分量已够,再加上 surely 反而削弱了力量,使人觉得说话人自己还有一点怀疑。所以不加 surely 更为忠实原文。

【例 323】这对真正理解这本书十分重要。

[误译] This is very fundamental to a true understanding of the book.

[正译] This is fundamental to a true understanding of the book.

[评析] fundamental 是"基本的"、"根本的"、"十分重要的"之意,不需要再加副词修饰,或者使用比较级和最高级,也不必再用程度词修饰。类似的还有 basic, principal, major, initiative, original 等等。

【例 324】只要我们紧紧地依靠上帝

[误译] as long as we rely totally on God

[正译] as long as we rely on God

[评析] "紧紧地依靠"可译成 depend totally（或者 heavily）on, 但 rely on 本身语气已经很强, 不必再添加副词。

【例 325】价格要适当调整。

[误译] Prices should be appropriately adjusted.

[正译] Prices should be adjusted.

[评析] adjust 的概念是 to change so as to match or fit, cause to correspond, 调整的目的就是要调整得适当, 因而不要把"适当"（appropriately）译出来。

【例 326】坚持不懈地推进生物多样性。

[误译] We should constantly promote biodiversity.

[正译] We should promote biodiversity.

[评析] promote（推进）的意思是 to contribute to the progress or growth of, to further; constantly 的定义是 persistent, 两者含义重合, 所以删去副词 constantly。

【例 327】如果你想要取得他们的支持, 它必须进一步改善自己的形象。

[误译] You will have to further improve your image if you want to win their support.

[正译] You will have to improve your image if you want to win their support.

[评析] improve 定义是 make better, 而 further 的含义是 to a greater degree or extent, 两者意思有重合, 只须译出动词。

【例 328】有力地促进由粗放型模式向集约型模式转变

[误译] vigorously promote the shift from the mode of being extensive to that of being intensive

[正译] promote the shift from the mode of being extensive to that of being intensive

[评析] 误译为 vigorously promote, 是由于受到汉语影响, 逐字翻译造成的。promote 已经含有 vigorously 之义。

三、省译介词短语

【例 329】 我们愿意在和平共处五项原则的基础上同世界上所有国家发展友好合作关系。

[误译] China stands ready to develop friendly relations and cooperation with all countries in the world, on the basis of the Five Principles of Peaceful Coexistence.

[正译] China stands ready to develop friendly relations and cooperation with all countries, on the basis of the Five Principles of Peaceful Coexistence.

[评析] 汉语中有些话即使不说出来也可通过简单的逻辑推理判断出来,英译时可省去。在这句中,如把 in the world 省去,人们仍然知道这些国家在这个世界上,不是在别的星球上。英语讲究简洁,有些可以从逻辑推理中推断出来的话就不一定要明确地表述出来。

【例 330】 我们已经从其他国家有计划有选择地进口了一些成套设备。

[误译] We have imported in a planned and selective way from other countries some complete plants.

[正译] We have imported in a planned and selective way some complete plants.

[评析] import 一字已含有从外国进口的意思,所以, from other countries 或 from foreign countries 已成了多余的表达了汉语原文中有此表达,也是语言修饰需要,实际上不符合逻辑。但如说从某个具体国家进口,则必须译出。

【例 331】 要广泛动员中小学生学习科普知识。

[误译] Primary school and high school students should be mobilized on an extensive scale to learn popular science knowledge.

[正译] Primary school and high school students should be mobilized to learn popular science knowledge.

[评析] 不用加 on an extensive scale。因为 popular(普及的,通行的)

的含义是"人民"、"通俗的"、"大众化的",其意思与 on an extensive scale 重复。

【例 332】 他们把三个部门合成了一个部门。

[误译] They have combined the three departments into one department.

[正译] They have combined the three departments.

[评析] combine 的意思是把二个以上的东西合成一个,所以在这里 into one department 就成了画蛇添足之举。

【例 333】 这些困难都是暂时性的。

[误译] These hardships are temporary in nature.

[正译] These hardships are temporary.

[评析] in nature 是"性质上"的意思,在本句里,in nature 是个很虚泛的词组,不影响 temporary 意义的完整性,不应画蛇添足翻译出来。

【例 334】 我们就把这个学习方法建立在更加自觉的基础之上了。

[误译] We set up this studing method on the base of much more consciousness.

[正译] We employed this studing method much more consciously.

[评析] "基础"是虚指,没有实质意义,可以不用译出,否则,英译文反而不易理解。

【例 335】 在他们自愿基础上,好心地帮他们学习。

[误译] On the base of their willingness, it is our duty sincerely to help them study.

[正译] Given their willingness, it is our duty sincerely to help them study.

[评析] 根据原文句意,"基础"不必从按照字面的意义译出,在英文中没有 on the base of their willingness 这样的表达方式。

【例 336】 在不断增加粮食生产的基础上,他们正在进一步发展多种经济。

[误译] While steadily developing grain production, on this basis they are further expanding the diversified economy.

［正译］While steadily developing grain production, they are further di-
versifying the economy.

［评析］"在(不断增加粮食生产)的基础上"的意思已在 While steadily developing grain production 中得到了体现,可以省去不译,使英
译文意思明朗。

【例337】我国国民生产总值达到一万亿美元,日子就会比较好过。
更重要的是,在这样一个基础上,再发展三十年到五十年,我们就
可以接近发达国家的水平。

［误译］$ 1 trillion will mean a higher standard of living for Chinese.
More important, on such basis we will approach the standard of the
developed countries in another 30 to 50 years' time.

［正译］$ 1 trillion will mean a higher standard of living for Chinese.
More important, it will allow us to approach the standard of the developed countries in another 30 to 50 years' time.

［评析］根据汉语原文的语境,直译 on such basis 没有用 it will allow
意译的效果好,it will allow 用灵活的译法更好地衔接了上下文的
意思。

【例338】由于实行了加强宏观调控的十六条措施,使中国大约在两
年多一点的时间解决了经济过热的问题。

［误译］Thanks to these 16 measures adopted in strengthening macro-
regulation and control, within a period of about a little more than
two years, China successfully resolved the problem of economic
overheating and resumed the momentum of economic growth.

［正译］Thanks to these 16 measures adopted in strengthening macro-
regulation and control, within a period of a little more than two
years, China successfully resolved the problem of economic overheating and resumed the momentum of economic growth.

［评析］中文允许双重模糊。"大约"是一个模糊概念,"多一点"又是
一个不准确的概念。英译时一般只能译出其中之一,如 a little
more than two years,而不必将 about 再译出。汉语讲究总体效果,
不刻意追求细节上的准确性。但英语则比较刻板,表述要准确。

四、替换或省译名词

汉英两种语言有一个重大的差别,那就是英语不喜欢重复,如果在一句话里或相连的几句话里需要重复某个词语,则用代词来代替,或以其他手段来避免重复。所以汉译英时要千方百计避免重复,多用代称;英译汉时则要少用代称,多用实词。汉语不怕重复,连续使用某个词语是常见的事。汉语也用代词,但不如英语用得多。

【例 339】中国作为一个发展中的沿海大国,国民经济要持续发展,必须把海洋的开发和保护作为一项长期的战略任务。

[误译] As a major developing country with a long coastline, China, therefore, must take exploitation and protection of the ocean as a long-term strategic task before China can achieve the sustainable development of its national economy.

[正译] As a major developing country with a long coastline, China, therefore, must take exploitation and protection of the ocean as a long-term strategic task before it can achieve the sustainable development of its national economy.

[评析] 指国家,可以用代词 it 和 its,也可以用 she 或 her。在英语里,用代词来指国家和船只时,是可以用 it 和 its 和 she 或 her 的。

【例 340】政府帮助国有企业的领导整顿国有企业。

[误译] The government helps the leaders of state-owned enterprises to consolidate state-owned enterprises.

[正译] The government helps the leaders of state-owned enterprises to consolidate them.

[评析] 在原文中"国有企业"在不长的句子里出现了两次,如果逐字译成英语,则英译文罗嗦拗口,应用英语常用的方式,即代词来代替 state-owned enterprises。

【例 341】——这些票和那些票是一样的吗?

——不,这些是今天的,那些是明天的。

[误译] ——Are these tickets the same as those ones?

——No, these ones are for today and those ones are for tomorrow.

[正译] ——Are these tickets the same as those?

——No, these are for today and those are for tomorrow.

[评析] 学生已学过并使用过 this one, the blue one, the green one 等。如用复数,英语习惯只说 the blue ones, the green ones 等,却不太说 these ones, those ones。所以,可以说 Is this ticket the same as that one? No, this one is for today and that one for tomorrow. 该把 ones 删去。

【例 342】哈佛是最早接受中国留学生的美国大学之一。中国教育界、科学界、文化界一直同哈佛大学保持着学术交流。

[误译] Harvard is among the first American universities to accept Chinese students. The Chinese educational, scientific and cultural communities have all along maintained academic exchanges with Harvard.

[正译] Harvard is among the first American universities to accept Chinese students. The Chinese educational, scientific and cultural communities have all along maintained academic exchanges with this university.

[评析] 汉语原文"哈佛"出现两次,而正译文中 Harvard 只出现一次,第二次使用了代称 this university。这样译,既避免了重复,又体现了两句之间的联系,译文也就显得流畅。而如果译者忽视了英语的这一特点,注意力过分集中在单个句子上,照样重复,译文便成了两个孤立的句子了。

【例 343】非洲正在努力维护非洲文化的独特性。

[误译] The people of Africa are making great efforts to protect the unique culture of Africa.

[正译] The people of Africa are making great efforts to protect the unique culture of the continent.

[评析] 改正译文在第二次提到 Africa 时,为避免重复,用了 the continent 来变换一下指称。以符合英语的表达习惯。

【例 344】他们的方法是一个很好的方法。

[误译] Their method is a very good method.

[正译] Theirs is a very good method.

[评析] 本句还可以译为 Their method is a very good one. 但是如果译成 Their method is a very good method. 则是犯了英语用词力戒重复的大忌。

【例345】另外一种方法是生物化学方法。

[误译] Another method is the biochemical method.

[正译] Another method is the biochemical process.

[评析] 原文还可以译为：Another approach is the chemical method. 总之,尽量避免在一个句子中重复使用一个单词。

【例346】在中美两国元首实现互访以后,中美之间开始致力于建设一种建设性的战略伙伴关系,发展势头本来是很好的。

[误译] Since the exchange of visits between the heads of China and of the United States, China and the United States have started to work to build towards a constructive and strategic partnership. The momentum of growth of China-US relations has been quite good.

[正译] Since the exchange of visits between the heads of China and of the United States, the two sides have started to work to build towards a constructive and strategic partnership. The momentum of growth of China-US relations has been quite good.

[评析] 通常汉语喜欢原字重复,所以"中美"可以重复使用。英语中一般不喜欢过多重复,在译完 China and the United States 之后一般可改用 the two sides (countries)等。英语常用代词,常变换词汇,不喜重复;汉语少用代词而喜欢使用实称词,因而往往出现重复。在汉译英时,应借助英文的代词优势,务必避免重复。

【例347】互相尊重的精神是我们今天文化合作的基础。

[误译] The spirit of mutual respect is the basis of our cultural cooperation today.

[正译] The frame work of mutual respect sustains our own cultural cooperation today.

[评析] 误译的译法看起来是中国式英语。sustain 有"支撑"的意思,

它代替了 the basis of, 但比 basis 更有表现力。改译后, 不仅英文十分地道, 而且还较好地表达了原文的意思。

【例 348】这是我从几十年的野外研究中得出的经验。

[误译] That is the experience that we have learned from decades of my field research.

[正译] That is what we have learned from decades of my field research.

[评析] "经验"这个词在汉语里用得比较多。有些译者一看见这个词, 往往首先就想到 experience。如果每次都这样译, 就重复太多。

【例 349】从我们自己这些年的经验来看, 经济发展隔几年上一个台阶, 是能够办得到的。

[误译] Judging from the experience that we have had in recent years, it should be possible for our economy to reach a new stage every few years.

[正译] Judging from what we have accomplished in recent years, it should be possible for our economy to reach a new stage every few years.

[评析] 本句的改正译文根据语境用 what we have accomplished 来代替 experience, 使得英译文读起来比较顺。

【例 350】最近她来我家的时候, 我就告诉她一句话。

[误译] During her recent visit to my house. I told her one sentence.

[正译] During her recent visit to my house. I said to her.

[评析] 原句的词组"一句话", 不可直译成 one sentence。这样的译法符合英语的表达方式。可以译成语义比较虚泛的 I said to her, 能适用的范围很广, 不管是说几个字, 一句话, 还是一大段语, 都可以这么译。

【例 351】克隆动物是一个新事物, 没有现成的经验可以照搬。实践证明谨慎些有利。

[误译] Cloning animals is a new undertaking, so we have no precedent to go by. Our practice indicates that it should be beneficial to be more cautious.

[正译] Cloning animals is a new undertaking, so we have no precedent to go by. Our experience indicates that it should be beneficial to be more cautious.

[评析]"经验"和"实践"这两个词在汉语里都是常用的词。本句改正后的英译文用 experience(经验)来代替 practice(实践),看似意义不同,实际上 experience 用在这儿要比 practice 意思更贴切。

【例352】外国有的科学家说,这里的生态系统非常脆弱,是不可逆转的。我认为这个看法是正确的。

[误译] Some scientists abroad say that the ecosystem here is fragile and irreversible. I think the opinion is right.

[正译] Some scientists abroad say that the ecosystem here is fragile and irreversible. I think they are right.

[评析]原文第二句的从句明明是以"这个看法"为主语,如果译文以 they 为主语就是地道的英语,既合乎英语的说法,又符合原文的含义。

【例353】中国民主革命的先行者孙中山首先提出"振兴中华"的口号,他领导的辛亥革命,推翻了在中国延续几千年的君主专制制度。

[误译] Dr Sun Yat-sen, China's forerunner in the democratic revolution, was the first to put forward the slogan of "rejuvenation of China". He led the Revolution of 1911 to overthrow the autocratic monarchy system lasting several millennia in China.

[正译] Dr Sun Yat-sen, China's forerunner in the democratic revolution, was the first to put forward the slogan of "rejuvenation of China". He led the Revolution of 1911 to overthrow the autocratic monarchy lasting several millennia in China.

[评析]英译文里的 the autocratic monarchy 本身的意思就是一种制度,所以可以不翻译 system。

【例354】在地震前的 150 个出口生产项目中,有 120 个已经恢复生产,开始出口。

[误译] Of the 150 export items in production before the earthquake,

120 have resumed production and export.

[正译] Of the 150 export items before the earthquake, 120 have resumed production and export.

[评析]"出口"的东西一般都和"生产"有关,包含在"出口"词义中的"生产"意思不言自明。省去不必要的 in production。

【例 355】轻纺工业品

[误译] Industrial products from the light and textile industries

[正译] products from the light and textile industries

[评析] products 一般是指工业产品,所以 industrial 可省去不译,又如农产品 farm product。

【例 356】知识产权,不光要使领导者知道,干部知道,还要使广大人民群众知道。

[误译] Intellectual property right must be made known not only to the leaders and to the cadres but also to the broad masses of the people.

[正译] Intellectual property right must be made known not only to the leaders and to the cadres but also to the masses.

[评析] masses 就是广大人民群众,不必译成 the broad masses of the people,这样译文是画蛇添足。应省译"广大人民"。

【例 357】这些问题就是他提出的关于保护稀有动物的问题。

[误译] These questions are the questions (ones) he raised on the protection of rare animals.

[正译] These are his questions on the protection of rare animals.

[评析] 误译的译文用词显然是太罗嗦。而改正译文的译文将两个"问题"合而为一,用词非常简洁经济。而且,原文中的第二个"问题"是范畴词,无实质意义,完全没必要译出。

【例 358】中国经过全民族的努力,又以巨人的姿态重新站起来。

[误译] With the efforts of the entire nation, China has stood up again in a giant stance.

[正译] With the efforts of the entire nation, China has stood up again as a giant.

[评析]"以巨人的姿态"的实质含义就是作为一个巨人。因此 as a

giant 表达的意思就是以巨人的姿态,"姿态"不用译出。

【例 359】 中国是个文明古国,幅员辽阔,面积达 960 万多平方公里。

[误译] China is a country with ancient civilization. She has a vast territory and covers an area of 9.6 million square kilometers.

[正译] Covering an area of 9.6 million square kilometers and more, China is a country with ancient civilization.

[评析] 原译文是比较典型的中国式英语。问题主要是没有突出信息重心,不符合英语的表达习惯;而且语言罗嗦,第二句既然说了面积 960 万多平方公里,那么就自然表达了"幅员辽阔"这一概念,不需要再将其译出。

【例 360】 对于电讯行业来说,今后的五年是十分关键的五年。

[误译] The coming five years wil be very crucial five years to the telecommunication industry.

[正译] The coming five years wil be very crucial to the telecommunication industry.

[评析] 汉语可以重复说"今后的五年是十分关键的五年",即重复"五年",但是翻译成英语时,只要译成"今后的五年十分关键"的意思就够了,全部译出反而不是英语的表达方式。

【例 361】 我们要重视科研所、高等学校和重点企业的作用。

[误译] We must attach great importance to the role of scientific research institutes, institutions of higher learning and key enterprises.

[正译] We must recognize the great importance of scientific research institutes, institutions of higher learning and key enter-prises.

[评析] "作用"在本句的语境里是虚指,不译它不影响句义的完整,省译它后要调整句子,以使英译文地道。

【例 362】 当然,随着期货实践的发展,该完善的完善,该修补的修补,但总的要坚定不移。

[误译] Of course, as the practice of futures on, some of these policies should be improved or amended as necessary. But we should keep firmly to our general direction.

[正译] Of course, as the futures progress, some of these policies should be improved or amended as necessary. But we should keep firmly to our general direction.

[评析] 误译文中的 practice of 并非表示"……的实践",其实际意思是"有……习惯",把英译文读者引向了歧途。改正后的译文省译"实践",用"改革"作主语,抓住了问题的关键。减词后英译文的意思更明晰了。

【例 363】我们要积极吸收世界先进文明的成果和促进文化事业的发展。

[误译] We must actively absorb the achievements of advanced civilization in the world and promote the development of cultural undertakings.

[正译] We should assimilate the achievements of other cultures and promote our own cultural undertakings.

[评析] "发展"和前两例的"事业"与"建设"同样没有什么实质意义,可省译。还要留心"世界先进文明"的两种不同译法,原译文逐字死译,改正译文译得简洁传神;还有本句的"事业"具有实在含义,根据本句的意思,译为 undertakings,意思要比 cause 到位。

【例 364】我争取和保障人权运动的历史比你早得多。

[误译] I started my history of struggling for the pursuance and protection of human rights much earlier than you did.

[正译] I started my fight for the pursuance and protection of human rights much earlier than you did.

[评析] 个人的、时间较短的"历史"最好不要译成 history,此处的"历史"的真正含义是指时间。

【例 365】虽然识字是很好的一件事,但是,按鲁迅的说法,还有一个弊端。

[误译] Although literacy is something very desirable, it has, according to the words of Lu Xun, a drawback.

[正译] Although literacy is something very desirable, it has, according to Lu Xun, a drawback.

[评析] according to the words of sb 是逐词死译,不是英语的习惯表达方式。according to sb 指按某人的意见、说法、理论等,所以译文中的 the words 是多余的。

【例 366】这是一个伟大的成功,是科技史上未有的大成功。

[误译] This is a great success without parallel in the history of science and technology.

[正译] This is a great success, a great success without parallel in the history of science and technology.

[评析] 这句的英译文如果不重复 a great success,原文的强调意义则损失殆尽。翻译时,要看出原作者的写作意图,翻译时尽量保留作者的意图。

五、省译动词

省译动词也是翻译中常见的一种现象。英语名词、介词用得多,汉语则动词用得多。英译汉时,在英语没有出现动词的情况下,译文往往加上动词,可以使句子显得较为灵活。汉译英时,译文可以把原文使用的动词(不是谓语动词)删去,比较简洁。

【例 367】相互了解,是建立互信关系的前提。

[误译] Mutual understanding is the basis for establising mutual trust relations.

[正译] Mutual understanding is the basis for mutual trust relations.

[评析] 本句的"建立"不必译出,译出来反而不合乎英语的表达方式。

【例 368】中国始终是维护世界和平与地区稳定的坚定力量。

[误译] China is always a staunch force to maintain world peace and regional stability.

[正译] China is always a staunch force for world peace and regional stability.

[评析] 汉语原文的"维护",在英译文里可以不译。这是合乎英语的说法的。

【例 369】双方确定要探索两国在能源以及其他一些新领域开展长期

合作的现实可能性。

[误译] The two sides explored various possibilities of conducting long-term cooperation in such areas as energy.

[正译] The two sides explored various possibilities of long-term cooperation in such areas as energy.

[评析] 如果中文的"开展"不译成 conducting,后面的 cooperation 也可表示动作,也即译成 possibilities of long-term cooperation 便可。

【例370】你们的计划要进行调整。

[误译] Your plan will have to be made some adjustment.

[正译] Your plan will have to be adjusted.

[评析] 汉语词语为了音韵对仗,有时要添加一些词。如这句中的"进行",就没有多少实际意义。

【例371】我们要努力搞活国有大中型企业。

[误译] We should endeavour to invigorate the large and medium-sized state-owned enterprises

[正译] We should invigorate large and medium-sized state-owned enterprises.

[评析] 要"搞活"必定要"努力",invigorate 含有 endeavour 的意思。

【例372】所长当前的主要工作是做好科学技术研究成果的普及和应用。

[误译] The principal task at present for the director is to do a good job in disseminating and applying the scientific and technological research results.

[正译] The principal task at present for the director is to disseminate and apply the scientific and technological research results.

[评析] principal task 与 do a good job 是重复表达一个意思,根据本句的情况,删除 do a good job 使英译文流畅上口。

六、省译词组、句子

汉语的同一个句子、同一个词组可以连续使用。英语则不然,总是千方百计地换一个说法,以避免重复。有时一句话后半句表示的动作和前半句是一样的,只是把施事和受事颠倒一下。这在汉语里,后半句和前半句一般用同样的结构,略显重复。英语里则有一些简单的说法,如:vice versa, but not vice versa, otherwise, but not otherwise, but the opposite is not true 或者 but not the other way round 等等。

【例 373】为了推动中美关系的发展,中国需要进一步了解美国,美国也需要进一步了解中国。

[误译] To promote the development of China-US relations, China needs to know the United States better and the United States needs to know China better.

[正译] To promote the development of China-US relations, China needs to know the United States better and vice versa.

在汉语中,有时为了加强语气,有时为了求得句子的平衡、对称或其他修辞效果,往往使用重复词语或重复结构。这一例源自中国领导人在美国大学的演讲,为了强调中、美两国之间的深入了解对促进双方关系的发展的重要性,领导人在此用了重复句。译成英文时,按英语习惯,借用外来语 vice versa,从而使译文简洁有力,而且把原文的信息有力地传递了出来。

【例 374】责任制度,条件成熟的就可以实行,条件不成熟的不要实行。

[误译] The system of job responsibility can be adopted where the conditions are ripe and not be adopted otherwise.

[正译] The system of job responsibility can be adopted where the conditions are ripe and not otherwise.

[评析]“条件成熟了的就可以办”和“条件不成熟的不要办”除了一个是肯定句,一个是否定句以外,两句基本一样。读起来自然顺口,但是如果照汉语原样翻译,那么英译文会显得很笨拙,在这种情况下,用现成的词 not otherwise,英译文就简洁生动。

【例 375】现在的问题是,有一些少数的成员认为,好像中国很需要WTO,而 WTO 并不太需要中国。

[误译] Now, the problem is that a few member countries of WTO believe that China needs WTO badly, but WTO doesn't need China.

[正译] Now, the problem is that a few member countries of WTO believe that China needs WTO badly, but not the other way round.

[评析]"中国很需要 WTO"和"WTO 并不太需要中国",两句的主要差别就是主语和宾语颠倒了顺序,在这种情况下用 but not the other way round 是再贴切不过了,英译文显得很地道。

【例 376】不能把欧洲视为亚洲,也不能把亚洲视为欧洲。

[误译] It is therefore not advisable to identify Europe with Asia or to identify Asia with Europe.

[正译] It is therefore not advisable to identify Europe with Asia or vice versa.

[评析] 原文的这两句话的用词和意思都正好截然相反,vice versa 就是为这种语境而设的词,英译文简练清晰,符合英语的表达方式。

【例 377】革命是解放生产力,改革也是解放生产力。

[误译] Revolution means the emancipation of the productive forces, and reform, also means the emancipation of the productive forces.

[正译] Revolution means the emancipation of the productive forces, and so does reform.

[评析] 这两个汉语句子除了主语以外,用词完全一样。为了避免重复使用"解放生产力"这个动宾词组,可以用 and so does... 这一句型,表示第二个动作和第一个动作是一样的,and so does... 的使用,使英译文很地道。

【例 378】美国和欧盟国家已连续六次在日内瓦的联合国会议上提出这个议案,但是每一次都没有得到通过,都失败了。

[误译] The United States and EU countries have, for six years in a row, tabled the resolutions in the conferences in Geneva, but every time they have not been passed and have suffered defeat.

[正译] The United States and EU countries have, for six years in a row, tabled the resolutions in the conferences in Geneva, but every time they have suffered defeat.

[评析]"没有得到通过"与"都失败了"意思相同,只译出两者之一即

可。

【例 379】现阶段中国已经实现了粮食基本自给,在未来的发展过程中,中国依靠自己的力量实现粮食基本自给,客观上具备诸多有利因素。

[误译] China has basically achieved self-sufficiency in grain at the present stage, and there are many favorable objective factors for her to achieve self-sufficiency in grain by her own efforts in the course of future development.

[正译] China has basically achieved self-sufficiency in grain at the present stage, and there are many favorable objective factors for her to maintain such achievement by her own efforts in the course of future development.

[评析] 有一点值得注意。"实现粮食基本自给"在同一个句子里出现两次,但译文却不必要重复 achieve self-sufficiency in grain 当"实现粮食基本自给"第二次出现时, 可以译作 maintain such achievement。由此可以看汉语可以在一句话里重复某些词语,英语用简洁的说法来替代。

七、统管兼顾

汉语中常常有许多词组和短语作为修饰语。而这些词组中又以四字结构的形式为多,并常常成串出现。翻成英语时,要找出中心词与修饰词的关系,根据英语的词义和习惯加以组合、化简或者将重复词语或结构全部提出来,总译一次,加在全部有关词语或结构的前面,统管兼顾。有时也可以用代词或别的名词或相当于名词的词来代替重复使用的名词或名词词组。由于中,英文在语法结构,构词方法等特点的不同,翻译时可以进行语法意义、修辞意义以及避免重复等方面进行省略。

【例 380】这些新型汽车速度快,效率高,行动灵活。

[误译] These new cars have fast speed, high efficiency and agile action.

[正译] These new cars were fast, efficient and handy.

[评析] 在本句中,在主语"汽车"出现后,后面跟有主谓词组"速度"、"效率"、"行动",都是用来加强语气说明主语的特征,而英文的形容词、副词则有其包涵意义。因而,所修饰的主语无须赘述。翻译不好,还容易形成中国式英语。

【例 381】这部打字机真是价廉物美。

[误译] This typewriter's price is indeed low and quality is indeed fine.

[正译] This typewriter is indeed cheap and fine.

[评析] 原译文不仅是中国式英语,意思也不清晰。在本句里把形容词修饰的特征表达出来,显得有些画蛇添足。

【例 382】一个地方有一个地方的全局,一个国家有一个国家的全局,一个地球有一个地球的全局。

[误译] A locality has its own over-all interest, a nation has its own over-all interest and the earth its own over-all interest.

[正译] A locality has its own over-all interest, a nation has another and the earth yet another.

[评析] 原文的三个小句子都有"全局",可以用代词 another 来代替重复使用的名词"全局"。原文还可以这样翻译:A locality has its own over-all interest, and so do a nation and the earth.。

【例 383】他这个人历来都是勇于探索,勇于创造,勇于改正错误。

[误译] He has always been courageous enough to probe into things, courageous enough to make inventions and courageous enough to correct his mistakes.

[正译] He has always been courageous enough to probe into things, to make inventions and to correct his mistakes.

[评析] 这个句子出现三次同一个动词"勇于",如果都译出来就违背了英语忌重复的原则,而且英译文冗长。应该将重复词语"勇于"全部提出来,总译一次,统管兼顾。

【例 384】我们的政策,不光要使领导者知道,干部知道,还要使广大人民群众知道。

[误译] Our policy must be made known not only to the leaders, must be made known to the cadres but also must be made known to the masses.

[正译] Our policy must be made known not only to the leaders and to the cadres but also to the masses.

[评析]"知道"是原文"领导者"、"干部"和"广大人民群众"都有的动作,可以总括译一次,是英译文干净利索。

【例 385】发达国家有四大优势:先进的技术,先进的管理经验、资金雄厚、人才丰富。

[误译] Developed countries are strong in four areas: advanced technology, modem managerial expertise, abundant capital and experienced professionals.

[正译] Developed countries have an edge on four areas: technology, managerial expertise, capital and experienced professionals.

[评析] 在本句中结合整个句意,"四大优势"本身就含有了"先进"、"雄厚"、"丰富"的意思,所以不必把这几个形容词都一一翻译出来,这样英译文简练明晰。

【例 386】我饱尝了人间的苦辣酸甜。

[误译] I tasted to the full the bitterness, hotness, sourness and sweetness of life in the human world.

[正译] I tasted to the full the bitterness of life in the human world.

[评析]"苦辣酸甜"比喻痛苦、辛酸、幸福等各种人生经历。不必一一译出,"苦辣酸甜"在本句有"饱经沧桑"的意思,所以在这里主要指"苦",仅用 bitterness 即可。

第二十一节 范 畴 词

汉语中有不少范畴词,主要用于构成四字词组,而在语义上则不太重要。译者如熟悉这种现象,有些词可以省去不译。汉语频繁地使用范畴词,英语则较少使用,翻译时应删去部分的范畴词。汉语使用动词较多,英语使用动词较少,而英语的名词、介词也可表示动作,所以英译时可省去部分汉语动词。范畴词如"方面"、"方式"、"问题"、"情况"等等,在汉语里用得很多。这类词在句子里没有多少实际意义,但很有用,可以使句子流畅。汉译英时,往往不需要译出来。

【例 387】我们要促进文化教育事业。

[误译] We will promote the cause of culture and education.

[正译] We will promote culture and education.

[评析]"事业"在这里是范畴词,不具有实质意义,英译时,不用翻译"事业",英语中没有这样的表达方式。

【例 388】我国有十二亿多人口,陆地自然资源人均占有量低于世界平均水平。

[误译] China has a population of more than 1.2 billion, and its land natural resources per capita are lower than the world's average level.

[正译] China has a population of more than 1.2 billion, and its land natural resources per capita are lower than the world's average.

[评析] 原文里的 average 作为名词,在本句中属于"水平"的范畴,average 本身就包含着"水平"的意思。

【例 389】必须清除行政管理中的官僚现象。

[误译] We must clear away the phenomena of bureaucracy in the administrative management.

[正译] The administrative management must be cleansed of bureaucracy.

[评析]"phenomena"在这里只表示范畴,没有实质意义。如果译出,整个译文反而不地道。

【例 390】这件事情对我们的伙伴关系会带来负面影响。

[误译] It will have negative impact on our the relations of partnership.

[正译] It will have negative impact on our partnership.

[评析] 了解汉英差异的译者应该看到到原文的"关系"两字是范畴词,可省去不译,只翻译出 partnership,"关系"的意思就包含在其内了。

【例 391】第二就是看以后的考评工作是不是做得好。

[误译] Secondly, on how well the working of check and evaluation are carried out afterwards.

[正译] Secondly, on how well the check and evaluation are carried out afterwards.

[评析] 中文中的"工作"、"情况"、"问题"和"状况"等这类范畴词和抽象名词不必译出,如果本句的"工作"译成 the work of checking up 这是画蛇添足,加上后反而不通顺。

【例 392】他对现时的信息产业的发展状况感到乐观。

[误译] He is optimistic about the status of present development of information industry.

[正译] He is optimistic about the present development of information industry.

[评析] "状况"是范畴词,没有实质含义,可省去不译。

【例 393】他具有一心为工作,一心为他人的品质。

[误译] He has the quality of devotion both to his work and to the well-beings of others.

[正译] He is devoted both to his work and to the well-beings of others.

[评析] 可以省略原文中"品质"一词,因为"品质"在这儿用来表明范畴,已失去了具体含义,可以省略不译。the quality of devotion 是画蛇添足之举。

【例 394】他要讲经济问题和国际形势问题。

[正译] He is going to speak on the issues of economy and the international situation.

[正译] He is going to speak on the economy and the international situation.

[评析] "问题"在本句中是表示范畴的抽象名词,不必译出,以使译文符合英语的表达习惯。类似的情况还有"宣传教育工作"、"工业发展状况"、"出口计划的执行情况"等等,其中的"工作"、"状况"、"情况"都不必译出。汉语的某些抽象名词喜用范围词和定性词,以成英语时多数要省略或做变通处理。

【例 395】 我们要解决就业问题。

[误译] We should solve employment problem.

[正译] We should reduce unemployment.

[评析] 英译为 employment problem 显得生搬硬套，employment 不能与 problem 放在一起，因为 employment 怎么能成为 problem？地道的英语是 unemployment。原文的"问题"也是没有实质意义的范畴词，本来就不必翻译。译出后，反而容易引起误解。

【例 396】 我想土地荒漠化的问题总不能够再被忽视了！

[误译] The soil desertification , in my view, is an issue that cannot be ignored.

[正译] The soil desertification, in my view, should (must) not be ignored.

[评析] "土地荒漠化的问题"这个词组中的"问题"是虚指，没有实质意义，表示范畴。可以省译，如果像原译文那样译出，反而使句子意思不够明晰。

【例 397】 由于失业率增高，美元币值下降，股票市场处于困境之中，经济问题将是总统所面临的最严峻的考验。

[误译] With unemployment rate high, the dollar value low and the stock market in distress, the economy problem will be the President's sternest trial.

[正译] With high unemployment, the low dollar and the stock market in distress, the economy will be the President's sternest trial.

[评析] 英语较少使用范畴词，所以译文中的"率"(rate)、"币值"(value)和"问题"(problem)都应该省去不译，这样英译文才是比较地道的英文。

【例 398】 应加强国防建设。

[误译] The building of national defense should be strengthened.

[正译] The national defense should be strengthened.

[评析] "建设"在本句原文中是需要的，否则就感到句子意思不完整，但它在这句里是范畴词。在是英译文中如果有 building，不仅译文罗嗦，而且意思模糊，不好理解，也不是地道的英语。

【例 399】 我们信息高速路的建设和其成就喜人。

[误译] Our information highway construction and the achievement are satisfactory.

[正译] Our information highway and the achievement are satisfactory.

[评析] 原文"建设"是范畴词,不必译出。

【例 400】 我想这样文章的出现也反映着现在的一股潮流。

[误译] I think the emergence of such kind of article has reflected the wave at present.

[正译] I think the emergence of such an article has reflected the wave at present.

[评析] 英语中 kind, sort 等词的使用频率明显低于汉语中的"样"、"种",因此"样"、"种"等词不一定要译成 kind,有时可省去不译。"这样的文章"不一定要译成 such a kind of articles,可简单译成 such an article 或 such articles。

【例 401】 这所附属中学的学生们热衷科学研究活动。

[误译] The students in the affiliated high school are addicted to the scientific research activities.

[正译] The students in the affiliated high school are addicted to the scientific researches.

[评析] "活动"设定"科学研究"的概念,是虚指,在本句表示范畴,不必翻译。

【例 402】 市政府应扶持中小型地方企业。

[误译] The municipality should support medium and small sized local enterprises.

[正译] The municipality should support medium and small local enterprises.

[评析] "型"在本句是范畴词,没有实质意义,可省去不译。

【例 403】 我国的经济建设,需要一个和平的国际环境,需要一个国内安定团结、天下大治的局面。

[误译] China's economic construction needs an international environment of peace and a domestic situation of stability, unity and great order.

[正译] For its economic development, China needs an international environment of peace and a domestic stability, unity and great order.

[评析] 原文的"局面"是范畴词,省去不译反而使英译文的意思更为清晰明了;另外,英译文要改换主语,否则会出现拟人化及主谓搭配的问题。

【例 404】各行各业都应服从并服务于经济发展的进程。

[误译] Work in all fields should be subordinated to and serve the progress of the economic development.

[正译] Work in all fields should be subordinated to and serve the economic development.

[评析] "progress"在本句中没有实在意义,它隶属于"economic development",可以省译。

第二十二节 对偶词组

汉语的对偶词组,即由四个字构成的习语,在修辞上很匀称;英语一般没有这种形式。这类词语分两种,第一种是由四个字一起构成而缺一不可的,否则就会影响意思的完整性。英译时要将四个字的意思整体表达出来。例如:

相形见绌 pale by comparison

相得益彰 bring out the best in each other

枯木逢春 get a new lease of life

饱经风霜 weather-beaten

前功尽弃 all one's previous efforts wasted

功败垂成 suffer defeat on the verge of victory

见利忘义 be actuated by mercenary views 或者 forsake good for the sake of gold

这些四字词组大都可以意译。

第二种,四个字的前两个和后两个词的意义明显是重复的,传达的信息也是重复的。按语言学中的信息论来说,重复信息的价值等于零,因此只译其中两个字即可,全部译出在英语中反显得累赘、多余。例如:

深情厚谊 profound feeling

精疲力竭 exhaustion

赤手空拳 bare-handed 或者 bare-fisted

铺天盖地 overwhelmingly

如胶似漆 dote on each other

破釜沉舟 burn one's bridges (boats)

土崩瓦解 fall apart

街谈巷议 street gossip

高谈阔论 spout 或者 speak with fervour and assurance

深仇大恨 deep hatred

贪官污吏 corrupt officials。

类似的例子还有:

【例 405】在现代化建设发展的关键时期,我们召开这样一个承前启后、继往开来的大会,具有极为重要的意义。

[误译] With the modernization construction at the critical stage, it is of extremely great significance for us to have convened such a congress that inherits the past and ushers in the future, and builds on the past and prepares for the future.

[正译] With the modernization drive at the critical stage, it is of extremely great significance for us to have convened such a congress that builds on the past and prepares for the future.

[评析] 汉语讲究重复、对仗,追求韵律美;英语则讲究简洁,避免词汇重复、语义重叠。"承前启后"与"继往开来"在语义上差别不大,可以只译出其中之一。如将两者都译出,成为 inherits the past and ushers in the future, (and) builds on the past and prepares for the future,会显得十分罗嗦,而且不严谨。

【例 406】全体公司员工进行了几十年艰苦卓绝、奋发图强的斗争。

[误译] All the company stuff waged arduous struggles and went all out for the prosperity of the company for several decades.

[正译] All the company stuff waged arduous struggles for several decades.

[评析] 汉语有时连用几个四字成语作定语,以加强语气。译文需考虑句子的整体结构,避免累赘,可以适当压缩。本句中的"艰苦卓绝、奋发图强的斗争"就只需译作 arduous struggles。

【例 407】我们应贯彻、落实这个战略决策。

[误译] We should carry out and put into practice the strategic policy decision.

[正译] We should implement the strategic policy decision.

[评析] "贯彻"和"落实"是一个意思的两种说法,在汉语里,这样重复表达是为了音韵对仗,有时要添加一些词。但是译成英语时,只须译出其一。因此应将 carry out and put into practice 改译为 implement。汉语里还常常有两个意思相近或相同的两字词组并列使用,英译时,也只需译出其一即可。

【例 408】应探索各种途径和手段促进儿童的语言发展。

[误译] Various channels and ways should be explored to promote the language development of children.

[正译] Various channels should be explored to promote the language development of children.

[评析] 在本句 channels 和 ways 都是一个意思的两种不同表达方法,应取其一。

【例 409】他们要到海外看望家人和亲属。

[误译] They are going to visit their family members and relatives overseas.

[正译] They are going to visit their relatives overseas.

[评析] family members(家庭成员)意思是包含在 relatives(亲戚、亲属、亲缘)的概念之中的,应省译 family members。

【例 410】我们要建立充满活力与生机的经济结构。

[误译] We will establish a economic structure imbued with vigor and vitality.

[正译] We will establish a vigorous economic structure.

[评析] 我们从 vigor (physical or mental strength, energy, or force) 和 vitality(physical or intellectual vigor; energy)的定义中可以看出它们的意思基本一致,这里只需其中一个。

【例 411】我们应努力开拓国际和国内市场,打开新的国际市场以及进一步开发农村市场。

[误译] We should enthusiastically explore both the international and domestic markets, opening up new international markets and further exploring the rural market.

[正译] We should try to open up new international and domestic market, especially exploring the rural market.

[评析] "开拓"和"打开新的"是一个意思用另一种说法重复了一遍,这在英语中是要避免的,应将其合并一处。

【例 412】为了确保这两种产品顺利转换和成功交接,科研人员将继续与企业合作。

[误译] To make sure that there will be a smooth transition and a successful transfer of the two products, the scientific researchers will continue to cooperate with the enterprise.

[正译] The scientific researchers will continue to cooperate with the enterprise to ensure that the transfer of the two products proceeds smoothly.

[评析] 除了要将"转换"和"交接"这两个意义相近的动词合并以外,还要注意本句的语序,汉语一般是先表达目的,再表达行为;英语则相反,先说行为,再表达目的。要注意汉英的这一差别,使英译文的到自然。

【例 413】这家航空公司需要加强改进和完善运行机制。

[误译] The airline company should make intensive efforts to change and improve their operation.

[正译] The airline company should make intensive efforts to change their way of operation.

[评析] change 在从这一句的语境的来看,是往好变的意思,与 improve 意思一样,应只译其一。

第二十三节 句 型

一、"是"字结构句

"是"在汉语语法中称为"判断词",它的意义通常相当于英语的系动词 be,但它不像英语的系动词 be 那样有形态、时态、人称和数的变化。尽管我们通常将"是"称为"判断词",由"是"字构成的句子却并非总是判断句。事实上,"是"字句是一个含义极其丰富、表达力极强的句式,是汉语中的特殊句型。在大多数情况下,汉语的"是"句型,其前后的内容仅仅是相关,其前后的意思往往并不等值,这时如果翻译成 be,就不符合英语的表达习惯,所以要根据语境翻译成其他词语。

【例 414】他的工作作风是以大刀阔斧、严厉著称。

[误译] His style of work is a kind of taking bold and drastic actions and also of being quite stem.

[正译] His style of work is characterized by bold and drastic actions as well as sternness.

[评析] 本句汉语的"是"前后的内容相关,而不等值,"是"在这里表示事物的特征。这时最好改用表示相关的词语 is characterized。

【例 415】过快地要求一个国家开放它的资本市场,过分的资本流动性,往往是欲速则不达。

[误译] To urge a country to liberalize or open its capital market too quickly or to ask or to request an overflow of capital in a country would only be what we say "more haste, less speed".

[正译] To urge a country to liberalize or open its capital market too quickly or to ask or to request an overflow of capital in a country would only result in what we say "more haste, less speed".

[评析] 本句原文"是"的前后不等值,这里汉语的"是"字用在动词之前表示有所否定,以加强句子的语意,英译文要根据"是"字所处的

位置和上下文,增添不同的词以表示"是"字所加强的意义。改正译文根据上下文改用 result in 来替代 be。

二、"有"字结构句

【例 416】现在有很多的产品领域出现了供过于求的情况。

[误译] In certain areas of products, there is the phenomenon of over-supply than demand.

[正译] In certain areas of products, the supply is greater than demand.

[评析] 中国学生往往把"有"、"存在"、"出现"等词译成英语的 there be 句型。这有时会使句子结构复杂化。其实,不用 there be 句型,结构反而更简单。

【例 417】心脏病有许多分类方法。

[误译] Heart disease has many classifications.

[正译] There are many ways of classifying heart disease.

[评析] 动词 have 表示"所有"。例如:我有三本词典。I have three dictionaries. 有些拟人化的事物也可以用 have,例如:这座城镇有许多高楼大厦。The town has many great buildings. 但 have 这个词不宜滥用,否则会导致拟人化的问题。一般要用"there is (are)",这个词组来表示存在的"有",例如:那条街上有三幢新房子。There are three new houses on the street.

【例 418】另外,有些人比较担心核电站的安全问题。

[误译] And another question is there are some people who are worried about the safety of nuclear power plants.

[正译] And another question is some people who are worried about the safety of nuclear power plants.

[评析] 原译文很拖踏,there are 的使用使英译文句子结构无必要得复杂,本句完全可以简单明快地译为 some people are worried about。

【例 419】但是这两年来国内的市场出现了相对的饱和。

[误译] However, over the past two years there have been relative saturations on the domestic market.

[正译] However, over the past two years the domestic market relatively saturated.

[评析] 原译文用 there have been 句型后接一个抽象名词,它的英译文意思不好理解,省去不译,可简化译为 the domestic market has been relatively saturated 这样一个句型简单、语义清晰的英语句子。

第二十四节 句 子

汉语句子结构比较松散,连词用得不多,但意思是连贯的。英语句子结构比较紧凑,句子内部连接之处,一般都要用具体的词语来体现。这句子中间的连接往往就是需要译者发挥创造性的地方。

【例 420】七年前,也是三月份,开过一次会,我讲过话。主要讲了两个意思,两句话。

[误译] Seven years ago, also in the month of March, we held another conference at which I spoke. I talked mainly about two points, two sentences.

[正译] Seven years ago, also in the month of March, we held another conference at which I spoke. I talked mainly about two points that can be summarized in two sentences.

[评析]"两个意思"后面用一个定语从句衔接"两句话",清晰表明"两个意思"和"两句话"之间的关系。

【例 421】说过去说过来,就是一句话,坚持这个办事原则不变。

[误译] After all that's been said, There is just one sentence: we shall keep to these principles of handling affairs.

[正译] After all that's been said, I can sum up our position in one sentence: we shall keep to these principles of handling affairs.

[评析] 原文的前两句不好在意思上衔接,用"就是"二字可以引出"一句话"。

【例 422】在新世纪即将到来的时候,在我国改革开放和现代化建设

发展的关键时期,我们召开这样一个承前启后、继往开来的大会,
具有极为重要的意义。

[误译] With the advent of a new century and with China's reform,
opening up and modernization drive at the critical stage, it is of extremely great significance for us to have convened such a congress
that builds on the past and prepares for the future

[正译] With the advent of a new century and with China's reform,
opening up and modernization drive at the critical stage, we held
such a conference that builds on the past and prepares for the future.
And this is of great significance.

[评析] 汉语原文较长,对于"我们召开这样一个承前启后、继往开来
的大会具有极为重要的意义"这一句,可使用"拆句法",按原文顺
序翻译,可使译文意思明晰。

【例 423】他为人处世的原则是一贯的,有三句话,第一句……。

[误译] His tenet of bearing himself is consistent and there are three
sentences. First ...

[正译] His tenet of bearing himself is consistent and can be summed
up in three sentences. First ...

[评析] 本句改正译文用一个"有"字引出"三句话"。这些说法,在英
语里都不能照办,因此译文用 to be summed up 来解决两句的衔接
问题。

【例 424】他们自己总结经验,由内向型转为外向型,就是说能够变成
工业基地,并能够打进国际市场。

[误译] They summerized their experience and shifted the zone's economy from a domestic orientation to an external orientation, which
meant that it would become an industrial base and offer its products
on the world market.

[正译] They reviewed their experience and decided to shift the zone's
economy from a domestic orientation to an external orientation,
which meant that it would become an industrial base and offer its
products on the world market.

[评析] 汉语原文里的"总结经验"和"经济转型"之间的关系不许明言,但是翻译成英语时,必须要表达清楚其间的关系,decided 在句中起到了过渡意思的作用。

【例 425】我一两年前去过一次上海,那里确实是一派兴旺气象。

[误译] I visited Shanghai a couple of years ago and the economy there is really flourishing.

[正译] I visited Shanghai a couple of years ago and found the economy flourishing.

[评析] 原文没有说"去过上海"和"兴旺气象"是什么关系,也不需要说,因为意思是清楚的。译文则需要有适当的词来过渡一下,因此要用 found 这个动词。

【例 426】要提倡科学,靠科学才有希望。

[误译] We must promote science, and rely on science, then we have hopes.

[正译] We must promote science, for that is where our hopes lies.

[评析] 这句原文看似简单,但是如果不理清思路,英译文就会没有逻辑。

【例 427】抓住机会,拓展自己,关键是要自强。

[误译] I am to seize opportunities and promote myself, it is crucial to strive to become stronger.

[正译] If I am to seize opportunities to promote myself, it is crucial to strive to become stronger.

[评析] 这个例子很典型,说明汉语可以不用连词,而英语要用连词。译者必须揣摩原文的内在关系,在译文中选用适当的连词。

第二部分　英译汉

第四章 英译汉概说

第一节 英译汉的翻译过程

英译汉一般要经过两个程序。第一步,理解原文。英译汉的成败,开始于对原文的分析阶段。分析原文,并不只是弄清原文词语的表面意义,寻找译文中的对等词语以进行逐字逐句的转换,而是包括分析表层、挖掘深层、揣摩风格等几个方面。既要理解内容,又要研究形式,既要琢磨原文的词法、句法和修辞特点,又要考虑作者的观点、态度、手法以及某些词语的特殊含义 第二步,译成汉语。透彻理解原文是翻译的前提和基础。如果对原文的理解失误,译文表达得无论多么好都会失去意义,因为译者是在以讹传讹。中国人在阅读理解英文过程中,往往会遇到多方面的难点。认真分析这些难点,逐步把握它们的规律并钻研译成汉语的对策,对英译汉的表达是至关重要的。这当然只是大致的划分,在实际工作中,这个程序并不是单向的。一个句子,往往要从英文到中文、中文到英文仔细推敲,反复研究多次,直到这句话的译文与原文意思完全符合了,才算告一段落。待到一段文字、一篇文章译好以后,还要通读一遍,看看这一句话那一句话是否有不妥不顺之处。在这个阶段,有时还要回过头来细细琢磨原文,英文词义不辨明就无从表达;但是辨明了英文的意思,词义没有确切地表达出来,也不叫翻译。

翻译时的思维具有双重性的特点,一方面是进行概括的思维,一方面是进行具体的思维。从概括思维中理出各词词义的内在联系,从具体思维中确定词的最后译法。心理学家倾向于认为,任何一个学会了语言和阅读的人,都拥有一个心理词典。所谓认知一个词,就是在心理词典中查到了与这个词相对应的词条。我们知道,一个词通常都具有多种意义。在阅读、理解原语篇章的过程中,译者是如何迅速地在自己的心理词典中搜索出目标词的具体意义呢? 有些翻译经验的人都知道,我们在阅读理解过程中一看到词的书写形式,就可以在心理词典中直接达到它的意义表征。但这个意义表征正确与否,必须有目标词所处的语境来检验。换言之,目标词在译者心理词典中的意义表征须与语境一致才算完成了对一个词的正确认知。一些心理学家认为,语境对词的认知产生直接影响且控制心理词典。由此可以说,语境对词的认知作用越大,就越不容易发生误译。相反,语境效果的作用非常弱时,译者对篇章中词的认知错误频率就高。例如:

【例428】The man, wearing such dark glasses, obviously could not see clearly.

[误译] 这人因戴着这种黑眼镜,显然看不清。

[正译] 这个戴着这种黑眼镜的人显然看不清。

[评析] 如果把这个分词短语看做定语,就可以译为:"这个戴着这种黑眼镜的人显然看不清";而如果把它看做状语,就可以译为:"这人因戴着这种黑眼镜,显然看不清"。因此需要仔细分析,根据分词短语 wearing such dark glasses 所处的位置,它应是定语。

【例429】He wants a girl to finish the cleaning.

[误译] 他需要一个会把清洁工作做完的姑娘。

[正译] 他需要有一个姑娘来做完清洁工作。

[评析] 如果没有上下文的话,原文可以译为:"他需要一个会把清洁工作做完的姑娘",即 to finish the cleaning 作定语修饰 a girl;原文也可译成:"他需要有一个姑娘来做完清洁工作",即 to finish the cleaning 作目的状语,修饰 wants。但是根据动词句型 want sb to do,"他需要有一个姑娘来做完清洁工作"应是正确译文。

理解英文要求准确无误,这是翻译工作的基础。翻译时,如果对英文句子还没有很好理解,便径自动笔,是译不好的。怎样准确地理解英文? 这是一个范围十分广泛的题目,它涉及英文学习的各个方面。准确地理解英文,就是掌握所译英文的词语及整句的意思。要做到这一点,首先必须看上下文。看上下文就是看英文的词(或词组)与词、词与句子、句子与句子、文章的这一部分意思与其他部分意思之间的有机联系,了解它们之间的语法关系及逻辑关系,从而准确地理解作者所表达的思想。准确,是指译文与原文实质内容上的一致,而不是它们形式上的一致。但是译者往往由于对外文理解不深,不能透过原文的形式掌握其精神实质,仅见其形,未见其神,加之对于"准确"的要求有片面的理解,于是翻译时便过多地受原文形式的约束,迁就原文的字面和结构,不敢或不愿有所突破。这样译出的文字,形式上与原文似乎一致了,但与原文的意思相去甚远。

【例430】It is possible that they never imagined that any considerable amount of public opinion would be rallied in their favor.

[误译] 这是可能的:他们从未想像过有任何相当数量的公众意见会聚集到对他们有利方面来。

[正译] 他们可能决没有想到,竟会有相当多的舆论支持他们。

[评析] 改正译文的译法做到了准确而流畅。原译文的译法,中文英文形式上是一致的,但未将原文的意思表达出来,不准确,也不流畅。这就是死译。改正译文将 it is possible that 译为"竟"既准确又流畅。

【例431】To appease their thirst its readers drank deeper than before, until they were seized with a kind of delirium.

[误译] 为了解渴,读者比以前越饮越深,直到陷入了昏迷状态。

[正译] 读者为了满足自己的渴望,越读越想读,直到进入了如痴如醉的状态。

[评析] 改正译文没有按照原文的形式排列,也没有按照原文的字面意思翻译,但抓住了原文的精神实质,既准确又流畅。原译文逐词死译,照搬字典释义,似乎是准确,但是反而使人不能明白作者要说什么。

　　理解原文的过程是一个十分复杂的过程,是一个语义辨认、语法分析、逻辑分析三者相互作用的过程,总起来说是一个根据上下文关系进行推理演绎的过程。原文的词与词之间、词组与词组之间、句子与句子之间、段落与段落之间,都存在着内在的联系。各个语言单位,各个段落的句子以及说明每个中心议题的各个段落都不是孤立的,它们彼此之间的组合都必然受到逻辑思维的支配。所以,通过上下文的逻辑联系来推断多义词在一定语境中的确切含义,往往是理解原文的关键之一。英文常用词,绝大部分为多义词。极为复杂。不仅有表面的、直接的、一般的涵义,还有引申的、内涵的、特定的意义。词典给出了众多的释义,是我们选择的依据。但需结合上下文的文意仔细推敲选择,不能照搬,也不能任意选出一个,应付了事。而且,不论任何详尽的词典,也不能将单词的全部涵义尽数收录。所以往往需要根据文意,仔细揣摩,以词典释义为依据,适当变通。有时,一个词还会由作者根据需要赋予某种新义,译者便只有根据上下文的意境,细加体味,推测作者的思路、意图,予以确定。总之,词义的确定既应根据词典,又不能死搬。语言的灵活多变便在于此。一个语言学家说过:"在新的上下文里使用的每一个词都是新词",确实一点不错。在实际翻译活动中,可能遇到各种各样情况。但只要记住一点:一个单词,不论词典释义有多少,一旦进入句子,受上下文制约,只能有一个意思,这个意思只能根据上下文确定。只要符合上下文意,即使不符合词典释义,也算正确。反之,尽管符合词典释义,但不符合上下文意者,仍然可能是错误的。翻译质量的好坏主要决定于英汉两种语言的水平。

一般说来,大多数中国译者对英语的熟练程度不可能赶上或者超过对自己母语的熟练程度。因此,在英译汉时应特别注意首先吃透英语原文,切忌望文生义或浅尝辄译。英语、汉语之间的差异错综复杂,既有语言表达方式方面的不同,又有思维逻辑以及文化、习俗等方面的不同,这就造成理解和表达上的重重困难。掌握一些翻译技巧,有助于扩大思路,提高熟练程度,可以起到锦上添花的作用。但不打好英、汉两种语言的扎实基础,即使对翻译窍门很熟悉,也不可能搞出好的翻译来。所以,要提高英译汉的能力,除了对汉语应予重视外,当务之急还是要通过大量的精读和泛读打好牢固的英语基础。此外,英译汉练习也可以作为一种手段检验并加强对英语语法的掌握程度。

第二节 英译汉的必要条件

除了要有较高的英语和汉语水平,英译汉还要有一定的专业知识。

英语的许多词一放到特定的语境中就有了明确的意指。此外各个学科都趋向于利用常用英语词汇来表达各自的专业概念或事物。例如 phase 在常用英语中的词义是"阶段"。但它在物理学中的词义是"相",在土壤学中是"分段",在数学中是"位相",在动物学中是"型",在天文学中是"周相",在军事学中则变成了"战斗阶段"。所以翻译时必须符合各专业的术语。各学科和专业共用一个词表达不同的专业概念,是英语词义的一个相当突出的共性特征。翻译中可根据材料类别选用汉语的不同表达法。由于缺乏相关的专业知识而导致的专业术语的乱译、误译或干脆不译等等屡见不鲜。比如将 projecting power([军事]投送力量)误译为"发电";将 regime([国际军控]机制)误译为国际军控"政权";将 pacifism(和平主义)误译为"消极主义";将 hyper-nationalism(极端民族主义)误译为"超民族主义";将 Secretary of Defense(美国的国防部长)误译为"国防部秘书";将 Diet Resolution(日本的"国会决议")误译为"食品决议",这些专业术语的误译都是由于缺乏相关的专业知识而造成的。

译者的背景知识匮乏时,容易产生误译。

英、汉两种语言之间存在着多种差异,许多情况之下成了英、汉互译的极大障碍。翻译之难,主要难在处理语言的差异上,难在寻觅译文的近似值表达上。有的语言表达法,涉及一些微妙的含义以及特殊的文化含义、民族习俗等。

背景知识也是一种上下文。这种背景知识也许能在上文或下文中找到,有时也许作者并没有写出来,但常常是不言自明的。

【例432】The European Empires in Africa have disappeared.

[误译] 在非洲的欧洲帝国已经消失了。

[正译] 欧洲人在非洲建立的一些帝国已经消失了。

[评析] the European Empires in Africa 指的是欧洲帝国主义国家在

非洲的殖民统治。若直译为"在非洲的欧洲帝国",读者是不能确切了解其含义的。

【例 433】There was nothing mass produced about the school, but if it was individualistic, it also had discipline.

[误译] 这所学校并不是大量出人才的。但如果说这所学校强调个性,可是它也注意纪律。

[正译] 这所学校并不是批量生产的。但如果说这所学校强调个性,可是它也注意纪律。

[评析] mass produced 指"批量生产",在注重个性的西方文化里含有某种贬义,误译文错把它译成褒义的"大量出人才",这说明没有强调集体主义和数量的中国文化价值观在起作用,对西方文化的背景知识不甚了了。

【例 434】But the Second Front exists, and is a main preoccupation already of the enemy.

[误译] 但是,第二战场是存在的,它已是集中力量进行的主要任务。

[正译] 但是,第二战场是存在的,它已成为敌人的心头大事。

[评析] preoccupation 指急务,使人全神贯注的事物。文中的敌人指的是德国法西斯,第二战场根本不是他们要集中力量进行的主要任务,只是他们的心头大事。这一点,看上下文或具有一定的背景知识,便能理解。

【例 435】In May 1935, the lobbies of the House of Commons and the newspapers were full of rumors of the impending, reconstruction of the Government.

[误译] 1935 年 5 月,院外集团里和报纸上都在盛传政府即将改组的谣言。

[正译] 1935 年 5 月,下院休息室里和报纸上都在盛传政府即将改组的谣言。

[评析] lobbies 在英国是议会的休息室,在美国则指垄断组织为收买或胁迫议员使立法为其服务而设立的机构或派出的人员。这里谈的是英国 1935 年的情况,当然不能理解为美国的院外集团。

第三节　英译汉错误分析概说

一篇好的英译汉译文,既要求对英语原文的理解正确无误,又要求汉语译文的语言通顺流畅。但两者之中,正确理解原文是关键。而要做到正确理解原文,就需要有扎实的语言基础。误译现象的发生往往是由于译者根本不知道自己是否理解了英语原文的真实意义,不能根据上下文推断多义词的含义,翻译时往往造成误译。

英语中有两句名言:

You know a word by the company it keeps. 理解一个词,要看它的结伴关系。

No context, no text. 脱离上下文,就不能正确理解词义。

这里的 company 和 context 既指结伴关系和上下文,又包含具体情境或语境的涵义。

英汉两种语言,除一些专用名词、科技术语以外,绝对等值的词为数很少,原因主要是英汉词汇都有一词多类、一词多义的现象。例如英语的 like 同时兼类动词、名词、介词和形容词。汉语的"轻松",同时兼类动词、名词、形容词。汉语的"影响"在不同的语境中有多种意思:他的思想影响了几代人。意为激励;这种坏书对青少年有很大影响。意为腐蚀,产生负效应;你别站在那里影响我看电视。意为妨碍、挡住视线等等。

由于许多英语词汇都具有三个词义范畴——即结构词义,涉指词义和情景词义,所以不少情况下这些词的确定的、充分的词义不在其本身,而必须到上下文中去寻找。例如形容词 light 处在孤立位置时,它的词义是游移不定的,可能是"轻的"、"轻率的"、"轻挑的"、"轻松的"、"轻柔的"、"轻巧的",等等。名词 story 一词则具有"事件"、"事情"、"情况"、"情形"、"报道"、"消息"、"电讯"、"内容"、"内情"、"真相"、"传说"、"说法"、"热门"、"有意的渲染"、"谎言"、"身世"、"遭遇"、"情节"、"案情"等释义。有时同一个英语词,英国人和美国人用法不同,亦即英国英语和美国英语存在差异,这种现象亦应当心。翻译一个词,必须先从它在上下文中所处的地位以及与其他词的搭配关系去理解,去选择适当的翻译表达。其基本原理是:译词看句子;译句子看段落;译段落看全文。孤立地译词是下策。实际上,一个词在上下文中的实际词义往往在词典中找不到字面的对应词。原文难度越大,越需要学会既遵守词义理据,又能融会贯通,灵活变动的思考,以把握一个词的种种含义,做到求义于词典又不拘泥于词典。

第五章 与语法有关的误译

美国翻译理论家尤金·奈达指出"语法分析是翻译过程中极其重要的一环。"要翻译好一句话,词义准确之后紧接着就是分析整个句子的语法结构,而且两者往往是必须同时进行,因为两者是相互影响的。即便是一个词,本身也有语法问题。英语原文的句子,即便是在懂得了词义的基础上,如果有时句子的语法结构不严密,或比较复杂容易引起误解,或者语法分析不对,句子结构弄错,也会造成误译,甚至与原句的意思大相径庭。这时就需要结合上下文所构成的语法环境确定词义才能弄懂句子的完整意思。即先确定词的语法功能,再确定词义。在语法结构方面,主要表现为对原文中修饰关系、逻辑关系、主谓关系、动宾关系、时态、语态等缺乏正确的理解。

第一节 冠词的误译

在英译汉中,在冠词问题上最值得注意的是要弄清有无定冠词和不定冠词在一些固定词组中的差异、定冠词和不定冠词在一些固定词组中的含义,以及它们在不同上下文中的含义,否则一字之差而意义却不同,甚至恰恰相反。例如:

in trade 开铺子

in the trade 内行,行家

at a crossroads 在十字路口

at the crossroads 抉择的重要关头

in front of the car 在车的前面

in the front of the car 在车的前座

in office 执政

in the office 在办公室里

in word 口头上,表面上

in a word 总而言之

a red and a white flower 一朵红花和一朵白花

a red and white flower 一朵红白花

【例 436】A fluent speaker never lacks a word but an accurate speaker never lacks the word.

[误译] 一个讲话流利的人从不缺少一个词,但一个讲话精确的人从不缺少那个词。

[正译] 一个讲话流利的人从不缺少词汇,但一个讲话精确的人从不缺少恰当的词汇。

[评析] 这里的 a word 与 the word 不作"一个词"、"那个词"解,前者泛指词汇,后者特指某些恰当的词汇。

【例 437】This is a most interesting book.

[误译] 这是一本最有趣的书。

[正译] 这是一本非常有趣的书。

[评析] 在一般情况下,在形容词和副词前的 most 是最高级的标志,但在 most 前加不定冠词 a 并不表示最高级,意思是"十分"、"非常",例如:a most important matter 一件十分重要的事

【例 438】He took the chair at the board of directors.

[误译] 他在公司的董事会上坐过那张椅子。

[正译] 在公司的董事会上他担任主席。

[评析] take the chair 是一个固定词组,是"担任主席"的意思,如果表示"入坐"要用 take a chair,两者意思完全不同。

【例 439】In his first year in office, he has given all men and creeds, no matter how preposterous, a respectful hearing.

[误译] 在办公室的第一年,他对所有的人,所有主张,不管这些人多么荒唐,这些主张多么荒谬,他都洗耳恭听。

[正译] 在他任职的第一年,他对所有的人,所有主张,不管这些人多么荒唐,这些主张多么荒谬,他都洗耳恭听。

[评析] in the office 表示"在办公室"。但这里是 in office,是一个固定词组,意思是执政、任职。同样情况的还有:go to church 和 go to the church,前者是"去做礼拜",后者是"到教堂去"。如果对这些

固定词组不加分析,望文生义,就会产生误译。

第二节 名词的误译

英语名词汉译涉及的问题范围很广。从翻译方法上看,英语名词汉译主要是采用词的增加(包括词的重复)和词性转化这两种基本的翻译技巧:词的增加,如抽象名词汉译时补充"情绪"、"现象"以及"是否"等,普通名词复数汉译时增加"几"、"一些"以及"之间"等;词性转化,主要是动作名词汉译时一般可转化为动词。然而,翻译的灵活性毕竟很大,英语名词的汉译,也应根据原文的各种不同情况灵活处理。例如,名词的数对于正确理解名词的含义关系就很大。有些译者由于没有掌握名词的一些语法特征,容易产生对原文的理解错误或在译文中表达不当等问题。

一、可数名词与不可数名词

名词的意义是很活跃的,有时一个名词用作单数或复数,用作可数或不可数,前面有没有定冠词,意义大不相同。因此借助名词的语法特征往往能帮助我们理解其意。英语普通名词有可数与不可数之分,其中有些普通名词既可用作可数名词,又可用作不可数名词,但意义不尽相同。例如,paper 用作不可数名词时作"纸"解,而用作可数名词时则作"报纸"解;an evening paper,一张晚报;experience 用作不可数名词时作"经验"解(a translator with experience 一位有经验的译者),用作可数名词时则作"经历"解(an unusual experience 或 unusual experiences 不平凡的经历);value 价值,values 标准;等等。

还有一种情况,如 people 和 peoples 都是可数名词,但加了 s 与不加 s 意义上有所不同:people 人们, 人民;peoples 各国人民, 各民族;a crossroad 交叉路;a crossroads 十字路口。由于英语可数名词单数与不可数名词在形式上相同,翻译时稍不注意,就容易产生误译。

【例 440】 The Unite Nations Organization was born at the end of the Second World War out of the reaction of peoples determined to save succeeding generations from the scourge of war.

[误译] 联合国组织是在第二次世界大战末期根据人民决心要拯救后代免于战争灾祸的反应而诞生的。

[正译] 联合国组织是在第二次世界大战末期根据各国人民决心要拯救后代免于战争灾祸的反应而诞生的。

[评析] people 作为总称, 作人民、人们解。前面加上定冠词 the people, 也可作"人民"解, 即 people 不加 s 或者不加 a 作"人民"、"人们"解。例如: People say that the Chinese people are a great people. 人们说中国人民是一个伟大的民族。但是如果 people 前面有不定冠词 a, 或者后面加上 s, 成为 a people 或 peoples, 意思就变了, 就作民族、国家解, 这里的 peoples 还需增词译为"各国人民", 宜在汉语中体现其复数的含义。

【例 441】Anthropologists wondered where the remote ancestors of the Polynesian peoples now living in the Pacific Islands came from.

[误译] 人类学家曾想弄清楚现今居住在太平洋群岛上的波利尼西亚人的远祖是从哪里来的。

[正译] 人类学家曾想弄清楚现今居住在太平洋群岛上的波利尼西亚各民族的远祖是从哪里来的。

[评析] 这句中的 peoples 不能译为"人民", 应译为"各国人民"、"各民族"解。例如: the Chinese people, 译为"中国人民", 但 the unity among the peoples of our country 里的 peoples 作"各民族"解, 应译为"我国各民族间的团结", 根据上下文将 Polynesian peoples 译为"波利尼西亚各民族"。

【例 442】The question became whether man could control the disease he had invented.

[误译] 因此, 问题就成了人们能否控制住他们自己造出来的这种疾病。

[正译] 因此, 问题就成了人类能否控制住他们自己造出来的这种疾病。

[评析] man 用作单数, 前面又不用冠词, 则作 mankind 解。例如: Slowly it dawns on man in general that science is something of interest and concern to all mankind. 人类渐渐懂得, 科学使全人类感兴

趣,并和全人类密切相关。因此,上文的 man 译成"人们"是错误的。

【例 443】The Einsteins, however, could not afford to pay for the advanced education that young Albert needed.

[误译] 然而,爱因斯坦无力负担年轻的阿尔伯特深造所需要的费用。

[正译] 然而,爱因斯坦的父母无力负担年轻的阿尔伯特深造所需要的费用。

[评析] 这句中 the Einsteins 是复数,不是指阿尔伯特·爱因斯坦本人,所以不能理解为"爱因斯坦无力负担……";the Einsteins 在这里是指爱因斯坦的父母。Einstein 是 Albert 的姓。英语中凡是在人名的姓后加 s,姓前面再用上定冠词 the,就是用来指父母、夫妇、兄弟姐妹等,有时也指全家。

【例 444】The search went on in Europe, in the Americas, in Java, in China, in Malta.

[误译] 研究工作继续在欧洲、美国、爪哇、中国、马耳他进行。

[正译] 研究工作继续在欧洲、南北美洲、爪哇、中国、马耳他进行。

[评析] 这句中有五个专有名词,除了 the Americas 以外,其余都不加 s。这里的 the Americas 不能译为"美国",单数 America 用来指美国或美洲,而复数 the Americas 则是指南北美洲。在确定一个名词的词义时,分清这个词是可数还是不可数很重要。在翻译时要注意名词变成复数后词义的变化。

【例 445】The United Nations has forged a framework guaranteeing the flourishing of man and respect for his values.

[误译] 联合国已经形成了一个保证人类繁荣和尊重他的价值的体制。

[正译] 联合国已经制定了一个保证人类繁荣、尊重人类各项道德准则的体制。

[评析] 这句的 values 是复数,意思不再是价值,而表示生活的理想、道德标准、社会准则;不仅复数的 values 意思发生变化,这里还需增词"各项"两字,以在汉译文中体现出复数的含义。

【例 446】 Agreement on control and reduction of cost within the executives of the joint venture is impossible, as it has been for so many years.

[误译] 如多年来所表明的那样,合资公司管理层要达成控制和削减成本的协议是不可能的。

[正译] 如多年来所表明的那样,合资公司管理层要在控制和削减成本问题上取得意见一致是不可能的。

[评析] agreement 既可用作不可数名词,又可用作可数名词,并且含义不同。用作不可数名词时意思是"一致意见",是抽象概念;用作可数名词意思是"协议",如 to come to an agreement(达成协议), to sign agreements(签订协议),是具体的东西。但本句的 agreement,前面既无 an, 词尾也不加 s, 很明显是用作不可数名词,应作"取得意见一致"解。混淆两者,会造成政治概念上的错误,因为许多问题很难取得一致意见,但仍然可以达成协议。

【例 447】 No war has ever started with such a victory for one side at the very beginning of the hostilities.

[误译] 从未有一场战争在刚开始时有敌对状态的一方就取得了如此重大的胜利。

[正译] 从未有一场战争在一开始一方就取得了如此巨大的胜利。

[评析] hostility 单数是作"敌意"、"敌对状态"解,但这句中的 hostilities 是复数,不能译为"敌对状态",而是作"战争"解。例如: to arouse somebody's hostility 引起某人的敌意/the outbreak of hostilities 战争的爆发/force 武力,暴力/forces 军队,兵力。

【例 448】 (There is a definite link between smoking and heart disease and lung cancer.) But this doesn't make you too uncomfortable because you are in good company.

[误译] 但这并不能使人们感到太不舒服,因为你是在一个好的公司里。

[正译] 但这并不能使人们感到太不舒服,因为和你一样抽烟的人很多。

[评析] company 用作可数名词和不可数名词意思不同。用作可数

名词作"公司"解,而用作不可数名词,却是"伙伴"、"伴侣"的意思。例如:

【例449】His high school and college days marked the time when his intellectual interests were broadening and when he sought the company of books.

[误译] 他读高中和大学的时候,正是他的知识趣味不断扩大,开始寻找图书公司的时候。

[正译] 他读高中和大学的时候,正是他的知识趣味不断扩大,开始寻求以书为友的时候。

[评析] 这里的 company 是个不可数名词,应作"伴侣"解,而如译成"寻求图书公司",就把 company 当作可数名词了。上面一句中的 good company,前面没有冠词,显然是一个不可数名词。

【例450】We attacked restrictive practices wherever they existed; we instituted measures for the more rational deployment of labor; and we greatly improved the relationship between management and workers.

[误译] 哪里存在限制性的实践,我们就在哪里加以反对。我们实施了许多旨在于更加合理地安排劳动的措施,我们极大地改善了管理与工人的关系。

[正译] 哪里存在限制性的做法,我们就在哪里加以反对。我们实施了许多旨在更加合理地安排劳动力的措施,并极大地改善了劳资双方的关系。

[评析] practice 作不可数名词时是"实践"、"练习"的意思,作可数名词时表示"做法"、"惯例";本句中的"labor"和"management",作不可数名词时分别作"劳动"和"管理"解。但这两个词有不可数名词的特征:前面没有冠词,又不是复数,却是作为总称,有可数名词的意思,分别作"劳动力"、"劳工"和"管理部门"、"资方"解。

　　英语普通名词中还有一种情况,动作名词一般不加 s,加了 s,含义就不相同。例如:the use of silicon chip 硅片的使用,使用硅片/the uses of silicon chip 硅片的用途/the trouble of translation 翻译的难处/translations of English literature 英国文学译作

【例 451】A successful scientist applies persistent and logical thought to the observations he makes.

[误译] 凡是有成就的科学家总是对观察进行持续不断的和合乎逻辑的思考。

[正译] 凡是有成就的科学家总是对观察到的结果进行持续不断的和合乎逻辑的思考。

[评析] observation 作"观察"解, observations 指观察到的情况、资料或结果以及观察后发表的意见。

【例 452】One recent use of radar was in the determination of the distance to the moon.

[误译] 雷达最近的一种使用是测定到月球的距离。

[正译] 雷达最近的一种用途是测定到月球的距离。

[评析] 原译文混淆了 use 的可数名词与不可数名词的意义。use 作不可数名词时, 意思是使用, 例如：The telephone number 999 is for use in emergencies. 作可数名词时, 意思是"用途", 例如：This little knife has plenty of uses. 本句里的 use 一词前面有数词 one 修饰, 是可数名词, 应作"用途"解。再如 Peacetime uses for radar are many. 雷达在和平时期的用途很多。

【例 453】The price which society pays for the law of competition, like the price it pays for cheap comforts and luxuries, is also great.

[误译] 社会的竞争法则付出的代价犹如它为便宜的舒适和奢侈付出的代价一样巨大。

[正译] 社会的竞争法则付出的代价, 犹如它为廉价的舒适家用商品和高档消费品付出的代价一样巨大。

[评析] comfort 和 luxury 都是抽象名词, 但是构成复数后, 词义就成为这种抽象名词所产生的具体东西或结果。例如：The hotel has all modern comforts. 这家旅馆配有所有现代化的舒适设备。/In some places white bread is a luxury. 有些地方连白面包也是奢侈品。

【例 454】As a result of those economies, many of our most important new projects in other fields became possible.

156

［误译］由于这些经济,我们在其他方面的许多最重要的新工程才得以实施。

［正译］由于采取了这些节约措施,我们在其他方面的许多最重要的新工程才得以实施。

［评析］这句中 economies 的单数形式是 economy, economy 可作"经济"(与"政治"相对而言)、"经济制度"解,也可作"节约"解。这里的 economy 作"节约"解,因为 economies 构成复数后,在这个上下文中就变成具体的"节约措施"的意思。

二、另类名词

英语中有像 singer, translator 等普通名词,是从动词 sing, translate 变成的,这类名词有时仍宜译成汉语动词。

【例455】You are a good singer.

［误译］你是一位很好的歌唱家。

［正译］你唱歌唱得很好。

［评析］原文的 singer 是由动词变成的名词,表示唱歌的人,如果译为"歌唱家"就太夸张了,原文也没有那个意思,最好将 singer 译成汉语动词。

【例 456】Lincoln was a good speaker and student of political philosophy.

［误译］林肯是一个杰出的演说家,又是一个政治哲学系的学生。

［正译］林肯擅长演说,又刻苦学习政治哲学。

［评析］林肯没有上过学,怎么会变成政治哲学系的学生的呢? 实际上这是英语的表达法。我们说一个人唱歌唱得好,既可以说 He sings beautifully. 也可以说 He is a beautiful singer。而后一种说法很广泛。所以这里的 speaker 和 student,实际上在汉语里是"说"和"学习"的意思。

【例 457】In the early 1600's, the Hollanders were great farmers.

［误译］十七世纪初,荷兰人是大农场主。

［正译］十七世纪初,荷兰人种田在行。

［评析］farm 的动词意义是耕种、种田、务农,因而 farmer 这个由动

词变成的名词译成汉语动词较为合适。这里 great farmers 的意思
是种田非常出色。

【例 458】Few students of the Far East doubted that Japan intended to
use the opportunity offered by the plight of Russia and Britain to
grab the oil she desperately needed.

[误译] 远东很少有学生怀疑日本打算利用俄国和英国的困境来攫
取它迫切需要的石油。

[正译] 研究远东问题的人几乎都认为日本打算利用俄国和英国的
困境来攫取它迫切需要的石油。

[评析] students of the Far East 和 students of geography 的表层结构
是一样的,但深层结构完全不同。后者是表身分,可译为"地理专
业的学生",而前者是表动作,应译为"研究远东问题的人"。这就
是说英语中有一种表达法:由于上下文的行文关系,或句子结构的
平行关系,有时用一个表示人的身分职业的名词,如 teacher, student, singer, translator 等来表示一个动作。如不注意这种表达
法,照样直译,就会出现误译。

第三节 代词的误译

一、人称代词

人称代词的汉译一般来说比较简单。we 我们;you 你, 你们;
they 他们,这些单词有时也许可以不看上下文就能确定其含义了,但
是有时必须要看上下文。在翻译 you、he(him)、she(her)、it 和 they
(them)时,就不能千篇一律地译为你(们)、他、她、它和它们(或他
们),应根据这些词在上下文和句中的不同含义,采取不同译法。有
时这个词甚至根本不作你或你们用。they 有时也不能译作"他们",
we 有时可以理解为"人人"。

【例 459】We have 365 days in a year.

[误译] 我们一年有三百六十五天。

[正译] 一年有三百六十五天。

[评析] 本句的 we 不能译为"我们",因为 we 在正式语体中还表示人

们、人类,例如:Do we have the right to destroy the world in which
we live？难道人类有权去破坏我们所生活的这个世界吗？根据本
句的语境,此处 we 表示人类。改正译文省译"我们",将原文的状
语 in a year 译为汉译文的主语,符合汉语的表达习惯。

【例 460】We have shortcomings as well as good points.

[误译] 我们都有优点也有缺点。

[正译] 人人都有优点也有缺点。

[评析] 本句的 we 也不能译为"我们",在这句里 we 泛指人们,根据
上下文,译成"人人"。例如:We all make mistakes. 每个人都会犯
错误。

【例 461】You can never tell.

[误译] 你无法预料。

[正译] 谁也无法预料。

[评析] you 在这里泛指一个人、任何人。在这种情况下,you 可以译
为"谁",或者省译。例如:You have to be careful with people you
don't know. 对陌生人要小心。

【例 462】They told us that the output of the steel plant was three
times as high as it was in 1960.

[误译] 他们告诉我们这个钢厂的产量等于 1960 年产量的三倍。

[正译] 据说这个钢厂的产量等于 1960 年产量的三倍。

[评析] 原文的 they 根据语境表示人们、大家。常常可以译为"听
说"、"据说"。例如:They say we are going to have a new school. 听
说我们将有一所新学校。

【例 463】There is always some water in the air around you. You cannot
see for it is in the form of water vapor.

[误译] 你周围的空气中常有水分。你看不见它,因为它是以水汽形
式存在的。

[正译] 人们周围的空气中常有水分。人们看不见它,因为它是以水
汽形式存在的。

[评析] you 在这里是泛指的用法,意思接近 one。例如:When you
live in England you soon get used to rainy weather. 住在英格兰的

人会很快适应多雨的天气。

【例 464】Gravity is what makes you weigh what you weigh.

[误译] 地心引力使你能称自己的重量。

[正译] 地心引力使我们(或"人们")能称自己的重量。

[评析] 这句中的两个 you 用来泛指一般人,相当于 people,因此,不一定译为汉语"你(们)"。这里的第一个 you 可译为"我们"或"人们",第二个 you 可译为"自己"。

【例 465】The United Nations has forged a framework guaranteeing the flourishing of man and respect for his values.

[误译] 联合国已经形成了一个保证人类繁荣和尊重他的价值的体制。

[正译] 联合国已经制定了一个保证人类繁荣、尊重人类各项道德准则的体制。

[评析] his 一词在这里是泛指,不能译成"他的",而应重复前面出现的人类。这也是英汉主要差异之一。

【例 466】One can only add that the global banking system is being transformed into a vast electronic web that transcends national borders.

[误译] 一个人只能进一步指出,全球金融系统正在转变成一个跨越国界的巨大电子网络。

[正译] 人们只能进一步指出,全球金融系统正在转变成一个跨越国界的巨大电子网络。

[评析] 这句中的 one 用来泛指人们,作 people 解,不作"一个人"解。

【例 467】In a self-service shop one serves oneself.

[误译] 在自助商店里,一个人自我服务。

[正译] 在自助商店里,人们自我服务。

[评析] 这句中的不定代词 one 用来泛指人们,因此不能译为"一个人"。

【例 468】That train of reasoning has all its various parts and terms——its major premise, its minor premise, and its conclusion.

[误译] 这一系列的推理具有其各个不同的部分和名称:其大前提,

其小前提和其结论。

[正译] 这一系列的推理具有各个不同的部分和名称:大前提,小前提和结论。

[评析] 英语频繁使用表所属的代词,而汉语的习惯则相反。这句中有四个 its,译成汉语都可省略不译。

还有一种情况也值得注意:英语人称代词在句中可出现在所指原词之后,也可出现在前,而汉语句子里的代词一般总在所指原词之后。因此,如果英语原文中代词在前,所指原词在后,那么译成汉语需将原词置前,代词移后。

【例 469】After she'd been married just over a year, Nora's first baby was born.

[误译] 她结婚刚一年,诺拉就生下了第一个孩子。

[正译] 诺拉结婚刚一年,就生下了第一个孩子。

[评析] 这句中的代词 she 出现在 she 所指的 Nora 之前,如果照原文逐词译为"她结婚刚一年,诺拉就生下了第一个孩子",似乎给人的印象是她和诺拉像是两个人,所以把这句译成汉语时需将"诺拉"提前,而 she 可省略不译。

【例 470】Several times on his trips to China, which he made as a guest of the Chinese Government, Bill's birthday occurred while he was in Beijing.

[误译] 作为中国政府的客人访问中国,比尔好几次都赶上在北京过生日。

[正译] 比尔作为中国政府的客人访问中国,好几次都赶上在北京过生日。

[评析] 英语有时在句子里先出代词,然后再出它所指的人或物。汉语一般总是先出实词,然后才用代词。知道了英汉两种语言使用代词的差异,本句应将原文的名词 Bill 提前译出。

【例 471】The crafty and insidious policy of the barrister, blinded him to his ambition.

[误译] 这个律师的狡黠、阴险的策略使他忽视了他的野心。

[正译] 这个律师的狡黠、阴险的策略使他忽视了其人的野心。

[评析] 从意思上分析,句中的 him 和 his 当然不会是指同一个人。中文若都用"他",便会产生误解。"其人"即这个律师。

【例 472】The whole area of national and local government was subjected to a most searching financial scrutiny, and wherever they occurred, inefficiency and waste were attacked and non-essential projects were brought swiftly to an end.

[误译] 我们对中央和地方主管的各个领域都进行了极其严格的财政检查。无论它们出现在哪里,我们就坚持反对效率不高和浪费的现象,同时一些非必需的项目也迅速让其下马。

[正译] 我们对中央和地方主管的各个领域都进行了极其严格的财政检查。不论在哪里出现效率不高和浪费的现象,都一概加以反对。同时一些非必需的项目也让其迅速下马。

[评析] 这句中的 they 指后面的 efficiency 和 waste。但是原译文的"它们"和"效率不高和浪费现象"并不是一回事。英汉两种语言代词的用法不同。英语中代词在句中的位置比较随便,它可以出现在所指代的名词前,而不影响意思。而汉语代词一般是用在所指代的名词后面。如放在前面,就可能会被理解为不是指后面的名词。所以当句中的代词在所代的名词之前时,应加以调整,把名词先译出,而后译其代词。

【例 473】He remembered his age. He was thirty-six.

[误译] 他记得他的年龄,他 36 岁了。

[正译] 他记得自己的年龄,他 36 岁了。

[评析] 代词 his 如果要译,也不一定译作"他的",可译作"自己的"。

【例 474】Although the traditionalist may have good intuitions about his language, his grammar only enables him to make invulnerable statements about language.

[误译] 虽然传统语法学家对自己的语言可能有着良好的直觉,但是他的语法只能使自己对语言提出一些无懈可击的论述。

[正译] 虽然传统语法学家对自己的语言可能有着良好的直觉,但是他们的语法只能使自己对语言提出一些无懈可击的论述。

[评析] 英语单数人称代词可以用来泛指属类,而汉语则需用复数。

这句中的名词单数 the traditionalist 用来泛指传统语法学家,它后面的人称代词 him 和两个 his 也是用来泛指,但译成汉语都不宜译为"他"和"他的",其中 his grammar 中的 his 应译为"他们的(语法)",而 him 和另一个 his 在这里可译为"自己(的)"。

二、不定复合代词

不定复合代词有时很不好翻译,千万不能逐词死译,需要将其意思译出。

【例 475】Theory is something but practice is everything.

[误译] 理论是重要的事物,实践是最重要的事物。

[正译] 理论固然重要,实践更重要。

[评析] 本句涉及两个不定代词,其实有比较、强调的含义。

【例 476】In learning English, grammar is not everything.

[误译] 学英语,语法不是一切。

[正译] 学英语,光学语法是不行的。

[评析] 原文句中的 grammar is not everything 的实质含义是语法不能解决所有的问题。

【例 477】A translator has to know everything of something and something of everything.

[误译] 翻译人员对一些事情要什么都懂,对什么事情都要懂得一些。

[正译] 翻译人员搞学问,既要精深,又要渊博。

[评析] 原文文虽然形似,但用词欠文采,缺神韵。改正译文虽脱乎原形,却凝练而神似,可谓雅俗共赏。

三、另类代词

he, they, one 是人称代词,只是为了划分归类方便而命名的。实际上 they, one 既可指代人,也可指代无生命的事物,而问题也就出在这里。当这些代词周围有两个或两个以上可能指代人、或人和事物的词时,由于分析不当,往往造成误译。即使弄清了指代,也可能由于表达不妥,而造成所指不清。在运用代词方面,英汉两种语言是有所不同的。汉语很少用代词来组织文章。在翻译人称代词时,除了上下文分析,认定指代外,还要注意英汉两种语言对人称代词的不同用法。

【例 478】 These were bitter memories. But workers felt it worthwhile recalling them because of the lesson they carry.

[误译] 回想往事是辛酸的,但他们觉得很值得回忆因为他们记住了教训。

[正译] 回想往事是辛酸的,但他们觉得很值得回忆因为这(指"回忆")里面包含着教训。

[评析] 这句的 they 前面有两个复数名词:一个是有生命名词 workers,另一个是无生命名词 memories,从形式看可以指 workers,也可以指 memories,但根据句中动词 carry 和其宾语 the lessons 的意义,这里的 they 只能 memories,不可能指 worker。

【例 479】 Our friends were obviously quite disturbed by the attitude of those in the country who is thought to misrepresent the arguments of the experts and reject them out of hand.

[误译] 我们的朋友对国内有些入企图歪曲专家们的论点和对他们轻易加以驳斥这种态度深感不安。

[正译] 我们的朋友对国内有些人企图歪曲专家们的论点和对这些论点轻易加以驳斥这种态度深感不安。

[评析] 这里的 them 根据全句的语境意义不是指 the Chinese,而是指 the arguments。

【例 480】 Where people once tried to influence natural events with magic and supernatural forces, they now had science to guide them.

[误译] 以前人们试图用巫术和超自然的力量来影响自然事件,而现在他们用科学来指导解释它们。

[正译] 以前人们试图用巫术和超自然的力量来影响自然事件,而现在人们用科学作为他们的指导。

[评析] 原译文误认为 they 是指 people,them 指 natural events,读起来也通顺。但是指代除了意思要通顺,语法也要正确。这个句子中有三个东西可被 they, them 指代 people、natural events、supernatural forces。根据过去与现在相比：Where people once . . . . they now, they 应该指 people。而 them 也应指 people, 因为根据 guide 这个动词的习惯搭配, 一般说 guide sb. 不说 guide sth. 。因此译成 "指导解释它们", 把 them 看成指代 natural events, 语法上不对。

【例 481】(Executives must be able to handle change in broad segments of industry, society, and government.) But perhaps the change that's most challenging of all is that within themselves.

[误译] 但是极富挑战意味的变革或许还是这些部门内部的改革。

[正译] 但是极富挑战意味的变化或许是发生在他们自己身上的变化。

[评析] 原译文把 themselves 当成是指代 broad segments of industry, society, and governments。但是这样译与原文意思不符。这句前的一句是说行政人员必须应付企业、社会、管理诸多方面的变化。紧接着, 用了一个 but 引出最富有挑战的变化：行政人员自身的变化, 因为这句后面紧跟的是：Many things cause executive metamorphosis—family or financial change, declining health . . . (造成行政管理人员自身变化的因素有许多, 如家庭或财政的变化, 身体健康状况的下降……)。所以上下文对于确定代词起关键作用。

四、替代词语

英语中替代词的使用频率远远超过汉语。也就是说, 只要可能, it, he, they, one, 甚至 as, so, do 等都可用来指代或替代前面提到过的某一事物或内容。而有些译者往往不注意这些代词所指代的确切东西, 结果造成误译。例如代词 it：My point is that the frequent complaint of one generation about the one immediately following it is inevitable. 我的看法是, 一代人对下一代人抱怨, 是难免的。句中 it 指代什么, the one 又指代什么。这个 it 看似 is inevitable 的主语。实际上是 following 的宾语, 指代 one generation。所以对代词的理解非常重要。as, so, do 在句中可以替代一个语法成分, 但是由于 as 作为连词, 可以引导一个从句, 作"正如"、"因为"等解；so 作为副词可以作"所以"解；do 作为实义动词, 可以作"干"、"做"解, 分析不当, 就会把

这两种不同功能混淆起来,造成误译。所以关键还是要对句子结构进行认真地分析。

【例 482】It is commonplace that a society reveals its reverence or contempt for history by the respect or disregard that it displays for older people.

[误译] 一个社会对历史是尊重还是轻视是通过历史对老人是敬重还是漠视来显示的,这一点是不足为奇的。

[正译] 一个社会对历史是尊重还是轻视往往是通过它(社会)对老人的态度是敬重还是漠视来反映的,这一点是不足为奇的。

[评析] 按照单复数指代原则,这一句中的 it 可指代前面的 society 和 history。原译选择了 history,但是从上下文意思来说显然不通。原文是讨论社会、历史、老人三者之间关系,作者认为只有对老人尊重的态度,才是对历史的尊重和负责。因此句中的 it 应指社会。可见对代词,首先用指代的一致性原则,如果不行就要分析上下文。

【例 483】Long afterwards the pilot recalled that when he got into trouble he was asked whether he was an American. "It seemed," he said, "pointless to deny it".

[误译] 很久以后,这个飞行员回忆起他被捕时有人问他是不是美国人这一事。他曾说"否认它看来毫无意义。"

[正译] 很久以后,这个飞行员回忆起他被捕时有人问他是不是美国人这一事。他曾说"否认我是美国人看来毫无意义。"

[评析] it 往往可以指代一个句子的意思。本句中的 it 是指 he was an American 这个句子。如果译为"……否认它看来毫无意义"就错了。

【例 484】Evening would come before you know it.

[误译] 到了黄昏,你才会知道它。

[正译] 黄昏不知不觉就要到来。

[评析] 根据上下文的意思,这里的 it 是指前面的整个主句 evening would come,所以可译为:"黄昏不知不觉就要到来"。

【例 485】After all, all living creatures live by feeding on something else, whether it be plant or animal, dead or alive.

[误译] 因为，毕竟活着的生物，不论是植物还是动物，死的还是活的都靠吃某种别的东西生存。

[正译] 所有活着的动物毕竟都是靠吃别的东西来生存的，而不管这些东西是植物还是动物，是死的还是活的。

[评析]“活着的生物”竟然还包括“死的”，而“死的”还要“靠吃某种别的东西生存”，这显然是不合逻辑的。我们从译文逻辑上的错误，可判定译者对原文理解有误。原译者把人称代词 it 误认为是替代 living creatures 的了，实际上，it 是替代 something else 的。逻辑是检查自己或其他译者对原文理解得是否正确的一个重要方法。虽然译文合乎逻辑不一定就正确，但译文不合逻辑却几乎可以肯定在理解方面有问题。自觉地运用逻辑思维形式和逻辑规律，对于透彻地理解原文，避免错误，提高翻译水平，具有非常重要的意义。

【例 486】 Having reviewed various technical possibilities, I would now like to comment on the dangers that might be presented by their fulfillment and to compare these with the consequences of efforts to prevent this development.

[误译] 分析了技术上的各种可能性后，我想现在要对他们的实现所带来的问题进行评论，并把这些与努力的后果相比较，以便阻止其发展。

[正译] 分析了技术上的各种可能性后，我现在想对这些可能性如果变为现实而可能带来的危险谈些看法，并把这些危险与竭力阻止这个技术发展所带来的后果作些比较。

[评析] 原译文有三个代词的误译 their, these, this。含糊地用“他们的”、“这些”、“其”来译，反映了译者并没有吃透或理解这三个代词指代什么。首先是 their。their fulfillment 相当于 the fulfillment of them。那么 them 指代什么呢？Dangers 或 possibilities？从复数指代原则来分析，似乎都可以，但是从意思搭配上来分析，应当是 possibilities。可以说实现可能性，不能说实现危险。从上下文来看，也是说可能性变成现实后可能会带来的种种危险，而不是危险

成为现实后可能带来的危险。these 同样可以指代 possibilities 和 dangers。原文把 these 与阻止 this 发展的做法带来的后果作比较。假设 this 是指遗传技术,一个是发展这种技术可能带来的种种危险(而不是种种可能),一个是阻止这种技术发展会带来的种种后果。原文把这两种做法产生的结果:危险与后果相比较。因此,these 是说 dangers。而 this 也清楚了,是说遗传技术。只要读懂上下文,就不会误译这三个代词。

【例 487】Few countries supported such aggressive acts and therefore the military burden had fallen on the aggressors alone. So would the agony of their new armed intervention in the affairs of other countries.

[误译] 几乎没有什么国家支持这种侵略行径,因此军事负担已落在侵略者自己身上。所以会有新的武装干涉别国事务的苦头。

[正译] 几乎没有什么国家支持这种侵略行径,因此军事负担已落在侵略者自己身上。如果他们再武装干涉别国事务,吃苦头的也只会是侵略者自己。

[评析] so 不是连词,不作"所以"解。其基本结构是 I can swim, so can I. 这句中的 so 就是代前一句的 had fallen on the aggressors alone;另外 So would the agony of their new armed intervention in the affairs of other countries. 相当于 The agony of their new armed intervention in affairs of other countries would also fall on the aggressors alone.

【例 488】We faced the question that year, as to some extent we still do today...

[误译] 我们在那年乃至今天在某种程度上面临的问题仍然是……

[正译] 我们在那年面临的问题,乃至今天在某种程度上面临的问题仍然是……

[评析] 应与不喜欢重复,所以用 do 来代替 faced the question,而汉语却常常重复用词,改正译文注意到了这一区别,重复了前文的 faced the question,符合汉语的表达习惯。

【例 489】And someone with a history of doing more rather than less

will go into old age more cognitively sound than someone who has
not had an active mind.

[误译] 历史上干得多而不是干得少的人比没有积极动脑筋的人更
易在认知上比较健全地进入老龄。

[正译] 习惯于多动脑筋的人,在进入老年之后要比起一个从来不积
极动脑筋的人的认知能力更为健全。

[评析] 这里的 doing 不是实义动词。从上下文意思来分析,这里没
有干得多,干得少的话题,而是在讨论对外界信息、事物是否多动
脑,保持大脑警觉的问题。从语法结构来分析,someone with a
history of doing ... will go into old age more cognitively sound than
someone who has not had an active mind 是一个平行的比较结构。
因此 doing 是一个代动词,代替 has not had an active mind。

【例 490】You can almost put it down as a general rule that he often in-
vite "honest criticism", but seldom gets it, and usually doesn't follow it when he does.

[误译] 你几乎可以把这一点看成一种惯例:他经常请人提出"直率
的批评"。可是他听不到什么批评,而且当他干的时候也通常不照
着去做。

[正译] 你几乎可以把这一点看成一种惯例:他经常请人提出"直率
的批评"。可是他听不到什么批评,而且即使听到了,通常也不照
着去做。

[评析] 原文中的第一个 it 是形式宾语,代后面的 that 从句;第二个
it 和第三个 it 都是指代 honest criticism。问题是对 when they do
这一从句的理解。句中的 they 不能译成"他们",因为可能指前面
的 presidents 或 aides。根据上下文,这里的 they 应当指"历届总
统",而不是"他们的助手"。但 when they do 译成"当历届总统干
的时候"也不对。因为这里的 do 不是一个实义动词,而是一个代
动词,代替前面出现的 get it。由于前面没有 as, than 标志,这种代
动词就较难识别。因此要更加细心区别。

【例 491】I would inevitably make mistakes at one time or another and
operate on someone who did not need surgery or sit on someone who

did.

[误译] 说不定什么时候我会出错,这是不可避免的。我会给不需要手术的病人开刀,也可能会把干事的病人忽略过去。

[正译] 说不定什么时候我会出错,这是不可避免的。我会给不需要手术的病人开刀,也可能会把需要动手术的病人忽略过去。

[评析] 这句的 did 就是代替 needed surgery,不可错看成实义动词。

五、指示代词

指示代词如 this, that, these, those, so, many, 等等,是指能够指代除人之外(baby 除外,英语中 baby 可用 it 来指代)的生命和事物的代词。需要根据上下文来判断它们到底指的是什么。this 和 these 一般可译成汉语"这"和"这些",而 that 和 those 则可译为"那"和"那些",但有时候则不能,而应重复所指名词或译为其他词语。这方面有两种常见的误译。一是当某个代词周围有两个可能指代的生命或事物时,译者不加分析,含糊地用"它"或"这"译出。二是有些代词,尤其是心不仅可指代名词,而且还可指代一个句子的意思或指代句子中某个语法成分,译者习惯用"这"和"它"译出,造成误译。要克服这两种错误,就要对代词所在的句子,甚至上下文进行认真的语义和语法分析。

【例492】 Health is above wealth, for this cannot give so much happiness as that.

[误译] 健康比财富更重要,因为这个不能像那个那样给人们带来幸福。

[正译] 健康比财富更重要,因为财富不能像健康那样给人们带来幸福。

[评析] 这句中的 this 和 that 显然不能译为"这"和"那",但是在意义上 this 还是指前面离它较近的名词,即句中的 wealth,而 that 指离它较远的 health。这种用法的 this 和 that 与 the latter 和 the former 相同,也可用"后者"和"前者"来译,但不如在译文中重复所指名词那样意义明确。

【例493】 There are two classes of people: the selfish and the selfless;

these are respected, while those are looked down upon.

[误译] 世上有两种人：自私者和忘我者；这些人受到尊敬,而那些人则遭鄙视。

[正译] 世上有两种人：自私者和忘我者；忘我的人受到尊敬,而自私的人则遭鄙视。

[评析] 这句中 these 与 those 不能译成汉语"这些"和"那些",应分别重复所指原词：these 指它前面靠近的 the selfless,译为"忘我的人"；those 指较远的 the selfish,译为"自私的人"。由于原文没有按照 the selfish and the selfless 的顺序评论这两类人,造成误译。最好将 these 和 those 译为所指代的名词,以使句子意思清晰。

【例 494】(In the best sense of that difficult word, science is a democratic method.) That has been its strength：that and its confidence that nothing can be more important than what is true.

[误译] 这就是科学的力量,科学的力量以及科学的信心：没有什么东西比真理更重要。

[正译] 这就是科学的力量,民主的方法以及相信没有什么比真理更重要的科学的信念。

[评析] that 是一个指示代词。本句中第一个 that 指代前面的 a democratic method 是对的。但第二个 that 并不是指代 its strength。从形式上来看, its strength and its confidence 这样理解很通顺,但是 that 如果是指 strength,它前面不应用冒号,而应用逗号。用冒号所表示的不是同位关系,而是说明关系,说明什么叫 its strength。因此这个 that 还是指前一句的"民主的方法"。

【例 495】In this way facts lead to ideas, ideas to more facts, these to revised or new ideas and so on. The process never ends.

[误译] 这样,事实产生思想,思想产生更多的事实,这些又产生修正了的或新的思想,等等。这个过程永不止息。

[正译] 这样,事实产生思想,思想产生更多的事实,更多的事实又产生修正了的或新的思想,等等。这个过程永不止息。

[评析] 这句中的 these 指它前面靠近的 more facts,不能译为"这些",应重复它所指的 more facts。

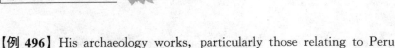

【例 496】His archaeology works, particularly those relating to Peru and Bolivia, are still of considerable value.

[误译] 他的考古学著作,特别是那些有关秘鲁和玻利维亚的至今依然具有重大价值。

[正译] 他的考古学著作,特别是有关秘鲁和玻利维亚的考古学著作至今依然具有重大价值。

[评析] 这句中的 those 指前面的 archaeology works,译成汉语也应重复"考古学著作"。

【例 497】This is what he said:"Man proposes; Heaven disposes."

[误译] 这是他说的话:"谋事在人,成事在天。"

[正译] 以下是他说的话:"谋事在人,成事在天。"

[评析] 这句中的 this 指下文 Man proposes...,this 可用来指下文将说及的事物,而 that 则用来指上文已提到的事物,与其译为"这是他说的话……",不如译为"以下是……"。

【例 498】"Do unto him as he does unto others." That is what he said.

[误译] "己所不欲,勿施于人。"那是他所说的。

[正译] "己所不欲,勿施于人。"以上是他所说的。

[评析] that 一般只用来指上文。这句中的 that 不宜译为"那",可译为"以上"。又如:That brings me to this question:What is a people? 这里的 that 指上文,this 指下面的问题,可译为:"这(或'以上')使我想起了这样(或'下面')一个问题:一个民族的含义是什么?"

【例 499】"High" and "tall" are synonyms:this may be used in speaking of what grows—a tree;that in speaking of what does not grow—a mountain.

[误译] "High"和"tall"是同义词,这个用来指生长的东西,如树,那个用来指不生长的东西,如山。

[正译] High 和 tall 是同义词,后者用以指生长的东西,如树,前者用以指不生长的东西,如山。

[评析] 原句中的 this 和 that 不作"这个","那个"解,this 是指上文提到的两个中较近的一个,即后面一个词 tall,因此可译为"后者",而 that 则指其中的前一个,即 high,可译为"前者"。

六、连接代词

【例 500】To try to give an idea of what my hometown is like now I shall start with what there isn't in my hometown before.

[误译] 要说一说我家乡现今是个什么模样,我还是从我家乡以前所没有的什么说起。

[正译] 要说一说我家乡现今是个什么模样,我还是从我家乡以前所没有的什么的事情说起。

[评析] 连接代词 what 分"疑问代词型"和"关系代词型"两种,前者用作疑问代词,可译为"什么",后者用作关系代词,相当于 the thing which,应译为"东西"。原句中有两个 what,what it is like 中的 what 和 what there isn't in China 中的 what 含义并不相同。第一个 what 是疑问代词,可译为"什么",第二个 what 是关系代词,就不能译为"什么",应译为"事情"或"东西",但在这里可省略。

七、所有格与语态

【例 501】We pledge ourselves to prove worthy of our trust.

[误译] 我们保证我们自己不辜负我们的信任。

[正译] 我们保证不辜负对我们的信任。

[评析] 这句的 our trust,结构上相当于 trust in us,our 在这里实质上是动作名词 trust 的宾语,带有被动意义,即"对我们的信任"或"我们受到信任"。如果译为"我们的信任",就带有"我们信任别人"的意思,那就把这里的 our 误解为主动意义。

【例 502】They will be kept in ignorance that a mighty figure has arisen in their defense.

[误译] 不让他们知道,一位坚强有力的人物已经在他们的保卫中站了起来。

[正译] 不让他们知道,一位坚强有力的人物已经站起来保卫他们。

[评析] 这句中的 in their defense 相当于 in defense of them,不是"他们保卫别人",而是"别人保卫他们"。原译是由于把 their 的被动意义误解为主动意义而造成的错误。

【例 503】 The paper said that the country's agents had infiltrated the then government and engineered Sadat's overthrow.

[误译] 报纸说该国特务渗透入当时的政府,策划了萨达特的推翻。

[正译] 报纸说该国特务渗透入当时的政府,策划了推翻萨达特的阴谋。

[评析] 这句中的 Sadat's overthrow 如果译为"萨达特的推翻",意思是"萨达特推翻别人"。这里专有名词 Sadat + 's 不是主动意义的用法,而是被动意义的用法,结构上相当于 overthrow of Sadat 或 agents engineered to overthrow Sadat,意义是"特务策划推翻萨达特的阴谋",不是"萨达特推翻别人"。"阴谋"两字是根据 engineered 的含义而增词补译的。

第四节　动词的误译

英语、汉语有一个很大的不同,英语很讲究动词,一个句子总少不了一个动词,即使是说明人物的状态、情况、性质的句子,也得用上一个动词,叫系动词,be 就是最主要的一种;汉语则没有这种讲究。汉语句子的谓语不一定非有动词不可,其谓语的主要成分可能是个动词,也可能是个名词或形容词。

一、及物动词与不及物动词的混淆

英语动词中的及物动词与不及物动词,动词过去时与过去分词,动名词与现在分词等在形式上有时相同,如不正确辨认,容易产生理解错误。

【例 504】 Within the first few hours, he issued the orders to murder over the radio and television.

[误译] 在最初几个小时,他下令毁坏无线电和电视。

[正译] 在最初几个小时,他通过无线电和电视下令进行屠杀。

[评析] murder 作动词时往往用作及物动词,但这句中的 murder 是用作不及物动词,to murder 在这里修饰 orders,意思是"下令进行屠杀"。over the radio and television 不是 to murder 的宾语,而是

介词短语用作状语,修饰 issued,作"通过无线电和电视"解。

【例 505】They were obviously quite impressed by the arguments that the students were advancing.

[误译] 他们对学生们正在前进这种论点显然颇为赞同。

[正译] 他们对学生提出的论点显然颇为赞同。

[评析] to advance 用作不及物动词时解释"前进"但这句的 were advancing 不是用作不及物动词,而是及物动词,作"提出"解,它的宾语是 arguments,所以应译为"提出论点",因此 that the Chinese were advancing 不是名词从句,不作 arguments 的同位语,而是定语从句,关系代词 that 的先行词是 arguments。这是及物动词被误解为不及物动词。

二、情态动词

英语的词汇有形态变化,例如动词有人称、时态、语态、情态和语气以及非谓语的变化(不定式,分词),名词有格和数的变化,形容词和副词有级的变化,许多词汇还有因为添加前后缀引起的词义的变化等等。英语通过词汇的形态变化,表示句子丰富多彩的语言关系和逻辑关系。汉语基本没有形态变化,它主要靠词语、词序及暗含逻辑关系来表达句子的语言意义。翻译英语的形态变化时,汉语一般用加词或变换说法的办法来表示。汉译英时,应把汉语的时态、语态、情态、语气等用英语的形态变化表达出来。

【例 506】I could have laughed to hear him talk like this.

[误译] 听到他这样讲话,我本可以笑出来。

[正译] 听到他这样讲话,我差点笑出来了。

[评析] could have done 表示过去有可能发生的动作没有发生,英语通过词形变化表达了这样的意思。译成汉语时采用增词手段,加译了"差点"。

【例 507】He was astounded but highly pleased that the man who presided over his destinies should come pleading to him.

[误译] 他又惊又喜,那位掌握着他的命运的人应该来向他央求。

[正译] 他又惊又喜,那位掌握着他的命运的人居然来向他央求。

[评析] should 作为情态动词有"应该"的意思,但是当句子中有 pity, surprise, shame, shock 等表达说话人感情色彩的词时,从句中的 should 就往往被译成"居然","竟然"等,把说话人的同情、吃惊、羞怯、不满、赞叹、怀疑等感情表达出来。原文中有 astounded 和 pleased 表示惊喜的词,所以 should 应译成"居然",如果译成"应该",就误译了。

三、否定

英语的否定形式、否定意义有时与汉语的表达方式差异很大,在英译汉时尤其要注意。

1.·否定转移

【例 508】He is not a majestic personal figure like my father, and he doesn't inspire fear like grandfather.

[误译] 和我父亲一样,他不是一个代表威严的人物;和我祖父一样他也不会让人望而生畏。

[正译] 他并不像我父亲那样是一个代表威严的人物,而且也不像我祖父那样叫人望而生畏。

[评析] 在 not...as / like...这个句子结构中,as 和 like 都应属于主句的否定范围,这种结构语法上称之为否定转移。其语法特征是否定词虽然和谓语在一起,而否定范围却不在谓语成分,而是转移到后面的状语上。如果不弄懂这种语法现象,就可能造成像原译文那样的误译。原译文和原句的意思正好相反。这种否定转移还表现在其他一些类似结构中,如:not...because...;not/hard1y/scarcely.../too/without...等。

【例 509】You should not despise him because he is backward.

[误译] 你们不该看不起他,因为他落后。

[正译] 不要因为某人落后,你们就看不起他。

[评析] not...because 的意思是"不要因…便",它是一个固定结构,表面否定前面的动词,但实际否定后面的原因状语从句。例如:
Just because I don't complain, you mustn't suppose that I am satis-

fied.你不可只因为我不发怨言就可以为我满足了。

【例510】I don't teach because teaching is easy for me.

[误译] 我是因为教书容易才不教书的。

[正译] 我并不是因为教书容易才教书的。

[评析] 原文的 not 虽然在 teach 前面,但否定的是宾语从句 because teaching is easy for me,原文在意义上相当于 I teach not because teaching is easy for me.。not 虽然放在谓语动词前面,但实际上否定的是宾语从句。

【例511】We don't read novels for amusement.

[误译] 我们为了消遣不读小说。

[正译] 我们读小说不是为了消遣。

[评析] 这句的 not 虽放在 read 前面,但否定介词短语 for amusement,原文在意义上相当于 We read novel not for amusement,应译为"我们读革命小说不是为了消遣"。not 虽然放在谓语动词前面,但实际上否定介词短语。

2. 部分否定

【例512】Just as all truck drivers and construction workers are no longer necessarily man, all secretaries and receptionists are no longer automatically women.

[误译] 正因为所有的卡车司机和建筑工人不再必须是男人,所有的秘书和接待员自然不再是女人。

[正译] 正如卡车司机和建筑工人不再都必须是男人一样,秘书和接待员也不再一定都是女人。

[评析] 理解本句的关键在部分否定这一语法现象上。稍不注意就会译成完全否定句,而且 as 也往往会引起误解。所以此误译。部分否定主要是由 all, every, both, everything, everybody 等含有全部意义的词与否定词构成。否定词虽然与谓语动词在一起,但实际是对前面由上述诸词构成的主语进行部分否定,通常译为"不全是"、"并非每一个"、"不总是"等。

【例513】We did not build institutes of technology to educate our boys for export, said one Indian scientist last week.

[误译] 上星期一位印度科学家说："我们过去没有办教育我们子女向国外输送的技术学院。"

[正译] 上周一位印度科学家说，"我们建立技术(理工)学院来培养年轻人，不是为了向国外输送。"

[评析] 原文虽然是用谓语否定的形式，但从实际含义来分析，是部分否定，具体的意思是虽已办了技术学院，但办技术学院的目的不是为了向国外输送人才。原译把形式上的谓语否定当作实际上的谓语否定，是因为没有结合上下文来分析逻辑关系。

【例 514】All the bacteria are not harmful.

[误译] 所有细菌对人体无害。

[正译] 并非所有细菌对人体有害。(即一些细菌对人体有害，一些对人体无害。)

[评析] all 用在否定结构中并非表示全部否定，而是表示部分否定。意思是"并非一切都是"，这样的代词还有 both, every 以及它的复合代词。下面几个常用的副词 everywhere, wholly, always 用在否定句中也表示部分否定。

3. 双重否定

【例 515】The greatness of a people is no more determined by their number than the greatness of a man is determined by his height.

[误译] 一个民族的伟大取决于其人口的多少不比一个人的伟大决定于他的身高多。

[正译] 一个民族的伟大不取决于其人口的多少，正如一个人的伟大不决定于他的身高。

[评析] 本句中 no more...than... 不能按表面意思理解为"不比……多……"。其中 no 不仅否定前半句，而且也否定后半句，是一种双重否定句。这种结构往往译为"……不……正如……不……(一样)"的格式。

【例 516】A home without love is no more a home than a body without a soul is a man.

[误译] 没有爱情的家庭不比没有灵魂的身体多。

[正译] 正像没有灵魂的身体不称其为人一样,没有爱情的家庭也不
　　　称其为家庭。

[评析] 在 no more...than 结构中 than 前后两部分都是否定含义,
　　　是一种双重否定句型,与 no more...than 相对应的还有一个 no
　　　less...than 结构,而在 no less...than...结构中 than 前后两部分
　　　则都是肯定含义。实际是以减少的否定词来加强肯定的意思。例
　　　如:Sunlight is no less necessary than fresh air to a healthy condition
　　　of body. 日光和新鲜空气对人体的健康状况同样是必要的。

四、动词形式的混淆

　　英语中有些动词的过去式和其他动词的现在式在拼写上是完全
一样的。例如 bore, 可能是两个意思完全不同的词。bore 作“钻”、
“挤”解;但是 bear 的过去式也是 bore, 作“忍受”解。不注意时态变
化的规则,不分析上下文,就会误译。

【例 517】 He founded the University of Chicago Laboratory School,
　　　the first of its kind, around the turn of the century.

[误译] 大约在本世纪初他发现了芝加哥大学实验学院,这是类似的
　　　这种学院的第一个。

[正译] 大约在本世纪初他创立了芝加哥大学实验学院,这是类似的
　　　这种学院的第一个。

[评析] 把 founded 译为“发现”,是把 founded 看成了 find 的过去时。
　　　实际上作“发现”解的 find 的过去时形式是 found, 而不是 founded。
　　　founded 是 found(建立, 创立)的过去时形式。类似的误译还有
　　　lay, 既可是 lie(躺下, 说谎)的过去时, 也可是 lay(放, 搁)的现在
　　　时。

【例 518】 His family ground its own grain in a windmill on the city
　　　wall.

[误译] 他家里人是把稻谷放在安装在城墙的风车地上。

[正译] 他家里人是把稻谷放在安装在城墙上的风车里碾磨的。

[评析] 原译是把 ground 看成作“放在地上”解的 ground, 语法上可

以讲得通;his family 作为集体名词,后面的 ground 可以用复数动词,但是意思不通,风车是圆的、转的,怎么会有"地上"。实际上这里的 ground 是 grind 的过去时形式。grind 是动词,作"碾磨"解,它的过去时形式恰好是 ground。类似容易造成误译的还有wound,它既可是 wound(伤害)的现在时形式,也可以是 wind(卷绕)的过去时形式,所以一定要仔细分析辨认。

【例 519】Drive carefully on that road in bad weather—it's very winding.

[误译] 气候恶劣的情况下,在那条路上开车要小心,因为风非常大。

[正译] 那条路弯弯曲曲,天气不好时开车要小心。

[评析] 毫无疑问,句中的 winding 是不及物动词 wind 的现在分词形式。问题是在于作"刮风、吹风"解的 wind,还是作"弯曲、迂回"解的 wind。译者认为 wind 作名词是"风",因此想当然地认为 wind 作动词是"刮风"的意思。实际上动词 wind 没有"刮风"之意,它有两个意思,一是"通风",二是"弯曲",(两者仅是同形词,读音也相异。)显然只有"弯曲"、"蜿蜒"的意思才符合上下文。

五、时态的混淆

英语的时间概念主要通过动词词形变化来表示,而汉语动词没有词形变化,其时间概念主要靠副词表示。因此,在把英语句子中的动词译成汉语时有时应增加有关副词,这在翻译同一句子中两个表示不同时间概念的动词时尤其如此。例如:

【例 520】In the gentle and serious voice with which he had welcomed me, he said ......

[误译] 他用欢迎我的又亲切又严肃的语气说……

[正译] 他像刚才招呼我那样又亲切又严肃地说……

[评析] 过去完成时 had welcomed 这一动作发生在 said 之前,将 had welcomed 单单译为"欢迎",并未把过去完成时的含义表达出来,应在"欢迎"(或"招呼")前面加上"刚才"或"原先"等。

【例 521】I haven't heard from him since he lived in Beijing.

[误译] 自从他住在北京以后,我就再没收到过他的信。

[正译] 自从他从北京搬走以后，我就再没收到过他的信。

[评析] 原译文没有准确表达原文的意思。这有一个语言陷阱，很容易错误理解。应当引起注意的是，在 since 引导的时间状语分句中，无论用的是非持续性动词的一般过去式还是持续性动词或状态的一般过去式，通常都表示动作或状态的完成结束。例如：It is already 10 years since he became a teacher. 他改行不当教师已经十年了。/Since he was at Fudan University, it has gone through a great change. 他离开复旦大学后，这里发生了巨大变化。/Since I used this kind of computer, it's design has completely changed. 自从我不再用这种电脑后，它的设计完全变了。

【例 522】It was the last service he was to render his fellow countrymen.

[误译] 这是他为他的乡亲作出的最后一次贡献。

[正译] 这是他要为他的乡亲作出的最后一次贡献。

[评析] was to render 表示过去将要发生而当时尚未发生的动作，如果译为"他为……作出的……"，意思是动作已经完成，那是把 was to render 误解为过去时 rendered。正确的译文应在"作出的"前面加上"要"或"即将"。

【例 523】The superpowers are beside themselves with rage at the Chinese bomb. They reckoned that the two "atomic giants" could between them rule the atomic roost.

[误译] 超级大国对于中国的原子弹暴跳如雷。他们以为两个"原子巨人"可以在原子弹方面称王称霸。

[正译] 超级大国对于中国的原子弹暴跳如雷。他们当时以为两个"原子巨人"可以在原子弹方面称王称霸。

[评析] 这里，前句的谓语动词是现在时 are，后句是过去时 reckoned，如译为"他们以为……"，并未将过去时的意义表达出来，特别是前一句的动词 are 是现在时，在这种情况下，应在"以为"前面加上"当时"或"曾经"，以表示原文中 reckoned 的过去时意义。误译混淆了动词的过去时与现在时，以致造成错误。这句说明应如何把英语谓语动词过去时的含义确切地表达出来。

【例 524】Upon his return to Islamabad in Pakistan, Yahya Khan told his chief foreign affairs officer to cable the message in code to their ambassador to the United States for transmission to Kissinger at the White House. Nixon had asked the Pakistanis to bypass the State Department for security reasons.

[误译] 叶海亚·汗回到巴基斯坦伊斯兰堡后,就叫外交部负责官员发密码电报给他们驻美国的大使转白宫的基辛格。尼克松为了保密起见要求巴基斯坦方面跳过国务院。

[正译] 叶海亚·汗回到巴基斯坦伊斯兰堡后,就叫外交部负责官员发密码电报给他们驻美国的大使转白宫的基辛格。尼克松为了保密起见曾经要求巴基斯坦方面跳过国务院。

[评析] 这句中的 had asked 是过去完成时,表明这一动作发生在…… told…to cable…之前,所以应在"要求"前面加"曾经"。原译没有能正确表达出这个时间关系,造成混乱。

【例 525】This country is one of the countries which struggled for independence and is in the vanguard in all matters concerning problems of the developing world.

[误译] 该国是一个曾为独立进行斗争的国家,现今在有关发展中国家问题的所有事务中都站在前列。

[正译] 该国是一个曾为独立进行过斗争的国家,现今在有关发展中国家问题的所有事务中都站在前列。

[评析] 这句中的 struggled 是一般过去时,两个 is 是一般现在时。如果把 struggled 译为"(一个为独立)进行斗争(的英雄国家)",那就没有把过去时的含义译出来,因为原文说该国"是在过去一段时间内为独立进行了斗争",所以应译为"……曾为独立进行过斗争……"。至于句中的两个 is,第一个可译为"是",第二个译成汉语时应补充"现今",以强调和过去时"曾为独立进行过斗争"的对比。

【例 526】Since the industrial revolution began, the physical science has in general been in the forefront of the scientific movement.

[误译] 自从工业革命开始以来,物理科学总的说来已经处于科学运动的前列。

[正译] 自从工业革命开始以来,物理科学总的说来一直处于科学运动的前列。

[评析] 英语中的现在完成进行时通常用来表示:开始于过去某点时间一直继续到现在的动作。但这句中的动词 be 由于本身表示一种延续的状态,就不用现在完成进行时而用现在完成时表示一种继续到现在的情况。初学者习惯于把英语现在完成时译为"已经",但这里的 has been 译为"已经处于……",就不妥当,应译为"一直处于……",这样才表达了 has been 所包含的"继续到现在"的原意。又如 Censorship has been in force since early in World War II. 也不能译为"审查制度从第二次大战初期就实行了",应译为"……一享实行到现在"。

【例 527】 It will also form the introduction to the compendium volume to be published by UNESCO.

[误译] 它也将作为联合国教科文组织中出版的摘要本的引言。

[正译] 它也将作为联合国教科文组织以后要出版的摘要本的引言。

[评析] 如果把这句译为"它也将作为联合国教科文组织中出版的摘要本的引言",这样译法好像是说这个摘要本"已经出版",那就不符合动词不定式 to be published 所表示的"将要发生的动作"的原意,所以应译为"……以后要出版的摘要本的引言"。又如 The most important factor, however, has been the magnitude of the problems. to be solved, 这里的 协 be solved 有"需要解决而尚未解决"的含义,因此 the magnitude of the problems to be solved 不能译为"解决的问题的规模大小",全句应译为"然而,最重要的因素还是有待解决的问题的规模大小。"

关于英语时态的翻译,还有一个问题也值得注意。英语叙述时间的顺序在句中比较灵活,它可以先叙述后发生的事情,后叙述先发生的动作;而汉语一般是先发生的事先说,后发生的事后说,否则就得用某些副词来表示时间的先后这一概念。请先看下面一个例子:

【例 528】 No one will deny that what we have been able to do in the past five years is especially striking in view of the crisis which we inherited from the previous government.

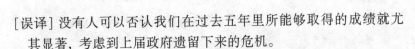

[误译] 没有人可以否认我们在过去五年里所能够取得的成绩就尤
其显著,考虑到上届政府遗留下来的危机。

[正译] 考虑到上届政府遗留下来的危机,我们在过去五年里所能够
取得的成绩就尤其显著,这一点是没有人可以否认的。

[评析] 这句英语原文中的四个谓语动词分别用了四种不同时态。
句中最先出现的是一般将来时 will deny,其次出现的是现在完成
时 have been able to do,再其次出现的是一般现在时 is,最后是一
般过去时 inherited。从这句英语的时间顺序来看,最后发生的动
作 will deny 在句子一开始倒先说了,而最先发生的动作 inherited
则放在句子末尾。汉语译文中叙述时间的顺序和英语原文适得其
反,完全根据动作发生的时间先后顺序重新安排,即把最先发生的
inherited 放在最前面,最后发生的 will deny 放在句末。因此,在
翻译这类英语句子时,英语动词时态是一个重要的线索,我们可以
根据动作发生的时间先后来重新安排汉语译文中动词的顺序。

六、被动语态与主动语态的混淆

【例 529】Tremendous research work is required to bring about such
fantastic speeds.

[误译] 巨大的研究工作需要产生这样神奇的速度。

[正译] 要达到这样神奇的速度,需要进行巨大的研究工作。

[评析] 这句的 is required 为被动语态,如果改为主动语态,require 的
宾语是 research work。在被动语态中,research work 移前用作主
语,to bring about such fantastic speeds 并不是 require 的宾语,而是
目的状语,所以不能译为"需要产生……",应译为"要达到……需
要进行巨大的研究工作"。

【例 530】They were imprisoned, refused anything to read.

[误译] 他们受到拘禁,拒绝阅读任何书刊。

[正译] 他们受到拘禁,不准阅读任何书刊。

[评析] 这句中的 refused 不是单独用作主动意义的谓语动词过去
式,不是主动语态,因此不是动词过去时,不能译为"拒绝阅读任何
书刊"。这里的 refused 是过去分词,它前面是省略了构成被动语

态谓语动词的一部分, 即系动词 were。因此译文中不能用"拒绝", 而应改用含有被动意义的"不准"。

【例531】Here then are the questions the author thought the average people would like answered.

[误译] 下面是作者认为一般人想要解答的问题。

[正译] 下面是作者认为一般人想要得到解答的问题。

[评析] 这句中的 answered 是过去分词, the average people would like answered 相当于 the average people would like (the questions) (to be) answered (by the author or someone else), 这里的 (to be) answered 是被动语态, answered 是过去分词, 作"被解答"解, 所以译为"想要得到解答"。如果译为"……一般人想要解答的问题", 意思是"一般人自己想要解答这些问题", 相当于英语的主动语态... the average people would like to answer the questions, 那就是把 answered 的被动语态含义误解为主动语态。

【例532】Since all the artware came from a third country, it could be said to have done so by the commission agents.

[误译] 鉴于所有的工艺品都来自第三国, 代理商可以说该国已经这样做了。

[正译] 鉴于所有的工艺品都来自第三国, 可以说该国是通过代理商这样做的。

[评析] 如果把这句的后半句译为"……代理人可以说该国已经这样做了", 就把被动语态中的动作 could be said 的发出者搞错了。原句没有提及动作的发出者, 但实际上相当于... it could be said that 或 people could say that it (a third country) did so by agents, 这里的 by agents 不是修饰 could be said, 而是修饰 to have done, 所以译为"……可以说该国是通过代理商这样做的"。

【例533】The strength thus developed, however, carried within it the seeds of its own decline.

[误译] 这股力量这样发展了, 然而在其内部就带有衰退的因素。

[正译] 然而, 这样发展起来的这股力量, 在其内部就具有衰退的因素。

[评析] 这句中的 developed 是过去分词，不是一般过去时，这里的过去分词可能会误解为一般过去时。

七、虚拟语气与陈述语气的混淆

【例 534】 Had this been an analysis on why there is scarcely any poetry here, it would have been useful.

[误译] 这篇文章要是对这里为什么几乎没有诗歌这一点进行一次分析的话，可以有所裨益。

[正译] 这篇文章要是对这里为什么几乎没有诗歌这一点进行一次分析的话，本来可以有所裨益。

[评析] 这句中的 Had this been... would have been useful 是虚拟语气，表示一种过去不存在的状况，译成汉语时从句中固然应该甩"要是"或"如果"等词语，但主句中也应表示出是与真实情况相反的意思，可以在"可以有所裨益"前面加上"本来"。原译忽略了这一点，译成了陈述语气。

【例 535】 Yet they could easily have learned that the success or failure of an enterprise is closely linked with the qualities of its labour force.

[误译] 他们不难知道企业的成败与劳动力的素质有着密切的关系。

[正译] 他们本来不难知道企业的成败与劳动力的素质有着密切的关系。

[评析] 这句的 could have learned 也是虚拟语气，如单单译为"知道"，就没有表达出与事实相反的含义，所以应在"知道"前面加上"本来"二字。

【例 536】 It is good these labourers leave the country. The job they would have secured can go to others.

[误译] 这些劳工离开本国是件好事。本来是他们做的工作可以让给别人。

[正译] 这些劳工离开本国是件好事。本来可能属于他们的工作可以给别人。

[评析] 原文中 these people 指的是外流的专门人才。这里原译者忽视了原文中所用的虚拟语气，把假设当成了事实，与原意不符。

第五节 形容词与副词的误译

一、形容词与副词的混淆

【例 537】But firemen succeeded in confining the outbreak to ware-houses containing less inflammable materials.

[误译] 然而,消防队员成功地把火势控制在存放少量燃烧物品的仓库范围内。

[正译] 然而,消防队员成功地把火势控制在存放不易燃烧物品的仓库范围内。

[评析] 原文的 less 不是形容词,并不修饰 materials,因此不能译为"少量",它在这里是用作副词,修饰形容词 inflammable,应译为"不易燃烧的"。

【例 538】In step with recent Chinese research into earthquake-related phenomena, some Japanese are turning to more exotic methods of prediction.

[误译] 与中国人最近研究地震有关现象采取一致的步调,有些日本人正在采用更加奇异的方法进行预测。

[正译] 与中国人最近研究地震有关现象采取一致的步调,有些日本人正在采用更多的奇异方法进行预测。

[评析] 这句的 more 同上句的 less 相反,不是副词,而是形容词,它不是修饰 exotic,而是修饰 methods,应译为"更多的……(方法)"。

二、形容词和副词转换

形容词和副词在英语里是两个非常活跃的词类。其词义往往岁前后搭配而变化,其用法也特别灵活。若与汉语相比较,则会发现有时与汉语是一致的,有时则有很大的差距,这两个词类有些共同的特点,而且翻译时往往可以互相转换。

【例 539】He was a quiet and thoughtful man.

[误译] 他很安静,很体贴。

[正译] 他举止优雅,待人体贴。

[评析] 原译文的译法不顺畅,生涩,这里的 quiet 和 thoughtful 译作"举止优雅"和"待人体贴",更符合汉语描述人物的说法。

【例 540】 We have acquired a keen sense that among them, the most important are income taxes, social security taxres, and gift taxes.

[误译] 我们得到敏锐的感觉,其中,最重要的是所得税、社会保险税和赠送品税。

[正译] 我们强烈地感受到其中最重要的是所得税、社会保险税和赠送品税。

[评析] 在本句中原文的形容词可以译成副词,原文里的副词可以译成形容词,或改变句式,用主谓结构。本句的 have acquired a keen sense of 译作"强烈地感受到"。

【例 541】 The thethod of cost-benefit analysis was popular in the enterprises long before 1980s.

[误译] 在二十世纪八十年代前,成本—效益分析的方法早就在这些企业采用了。

[正译] 成本—效益分析的方法在二十世纪八十年代前很久就在这些企业采用。

[评析] 这句中的副词 long 不是修饰它前面的谓语动词 was widespread,而是修饰它后面的介词短语 before the liberation。

【例 542】 As a private American citizen I recognize that many of the burdens and opportunities of our relationship have now passed to the non-governmental sectors of our two societies: to individuals, our corporations, universities, research institutes, foundations, and so on.

[误译] 作为个人美国公民,我知道我们关系中的许多机会现在已经转到了我们两个社会的非政府部门,即转到了公司、大学、研究机构、基金会等。

[正译] 作为一个普通的美国公民,我知道我们关系中的许多机会现在已经转到了我们两个社会的民间部门,即转到了公司、大学、研究机构、基金会等。

[评析] private 和 American citizen 连用,译作"普通的"。non-governmental 译作"民间","非政府的"这是常见的译法。汉译英时,"非政府的"、"民间的"也往往译作 non-governmental。

第六节　主语引起的误译

句子是表达一个完整思想的、具有一定语法特征的、最基本的语言单位,也是翻译人员理解、传达原文思想的基本单位。不能只看半句话就动笔。我们阅读英文,只有看完了整个一句话,才能明白作者说的是什么意思。英语句子成分按其作用分,有主语、谓语、表语、宾语、定语、状语。这些成分也有主要和次要之分。主要成分是一般句子结构所不可缺少的,这就是主语和谓语。主语是句子中被表述的对象,谓语对主语加以表述的成分,它说明、描写或叙述主语。如果谓语是个系动词,它后面则跟有表语,用来表示主语的身分和特征。如果谓语是个及物动词,它后面则跟有宾语来作为动作的对象。

一、无主语

在理解句子时要首先找主语、谓语这两个主要成分。不管句子如何不同,不管如何复杂难解,我们只要找到主语、谓语,整个句子的脉络就清楚了。反之,如果主语、谓语没有找到,或没有找准,其他句子成分即使弄明白了,全句的意思也还是不清楚。

【例 543】Let us, not leave this period without a further look at the role of compensation trade.

[误译] 请不要让我们离开这一时期而不去进一步看看补偿贸易的作用。

[正译] 我们在结束这一时期的论述时,不能不进一步研究一下补偿贸易的作用。

[评析] 这是一个祈使句,从语法上看,省略了主语 you,但对这个被省略了的主语不要看得过分认真,以为真是要求对方 (或读者)让我们做什么事似的。Let us go. 咱们走吧。这里的 us 包括了对方,全句的意思是劝他和自己一起走。当然,Let us go. 也可以理解为请求对方"允许"的意思,在这种场合,可以译为"你让我们走

吧。

【例 544】Just think the difficulty.

[误译] 正好考虑困难问题。

[正译] 考虑一下困难吧。

[评析] 这个祈使句的意思是要对方考虑一下困难。just 在这里起缓
和语气的作用,如 Just shut the door, will you? 关上门,好吗? 这里
的 just 不能理解为"正好"的意思。

二、误译主语

英语中常用 it, there 这两个引词来作形式主语。it 是个代词,当
引导词是它的一个发展。当主语是动词不定式、动名词或关系代词
所引导的从句时,这个主语常退到谓语动词之后,而用让放在句首来
代替它。

用副词 there 来作引词时,句子的主语就是动词 to be 后面的名
词。我们在遇到这样的句子时,要注意两点:it 和 there 就等于后面
的真正主语,而不是别的什么东西;it 和 there 只起语法作用,已失去
原来的意义,不再有"它"或"那里"的意思。

由让这个引词所代表的东西有时会很长,很复杂,在这种情况
下,让真正的主语回到 it 的位置上会费事一些

【例 545】It will strengthen you to know that your distinguished
achievement is so widely respected and appreciated.

[误译] 这会使你坚定地认识到你的杰出成就是如此广泛地受到尊
敬和赞赏。

[正译] 当你知道你的杰出成就是如此广泛地受到尊敬和赞赏时,你
就会力量倍增。

[评析] 原译把 it 看成是指代前文中说到的某件事,所以译成:"这"。
实际上这里的 it 并不是一般的代词,它是一个先行词,作为形式
主语,代替 to know 这个不定式短语。也就是说 to know 不定式短
语是句子的真正主语,因为太长,用 it 来作为它的形式主语。而
在翻译中,往往会把作先行词的 it 和作一般代词的 it 混淆起来,
从而造成误译。

【例 546】 It was agreed that personal expenses of the delegates should be defrayed by their respective constituencies。

[误译] 代表们的个人费用应由各该选区自行支付得到同意。

[正译] 大家一致同意,代表们的个人费用应由各该选区自行支付。

[评析] 这个 it 用于句首,是形式主语,后跟一个被动语态的动词,再跟一个从句。it 在这里代表了整个从句所说的意思。动作的执行者被省略了,翻译时可改为主动语态, It is agreed... 在这种语境下可以译为"大家同意"。类似的表达还有：It is reported... 据报道…/It is well-known... 大家知道…/It is believed... 据信…/It is asserted... 有人主张…/It is declared... 据称…/It is announced... 据宣布…/It is supposed... 有人推测…/It is learned... 据了解…

【例 547】 It was thought that fixed stars were suns, each with its own planets which were probably worlds themselves.

[误译] 这固定的星光被认为是恒星,每一个都有它自己的行星,每一个行星可能就是一个世界。

[正译] 大家认为,恒星都是太阳,每一个都有自己的行星,而每一个行星便有可能是一个世界。

[评析] 原文的 it 是形式主语,表明整个从句的意思。在这样的句子中,动作或行为的执行者被省略了,因此,翻译时可以改为主动语态,如 It is said that... 可以译为"大家说"、"有人说"等来代表动作或行为的执行者;或者也采取省略的办法,译为"据说"。It is thought that... 一般译为"大家认为",或者"有人认为"。

【例 548】 It will be remembered that the *Morning Advertiser* computed the numbers attending a former meeting at 300,000.

[误译] 将记得,《晨报》曾将以前一次集会参加的人数估计为三十万。

[正译] 人们应当记得,《晨报》曾将以前一次集会参加的人数估计为三十万。

[评析] it 用于句首,后跟一个被动语态的动词,再跟一个从句,这时 it 是形式主语。由于动作的执行者被省略了,因此, It will be remembered...翻译时可改为主动态,译为"人们应当记得"或者"大家应当记得"。

【例549】To do this aircraft will fly at 2,000to 4,000 mph.

[误译] 要制造这种飞机,每小时将飞行2,000至4,000英里。

[正译] 要做到这一点,飞机每小时要飞行2,000至4,000英里。

[评析] 名词 aircraft 的单复数为同一形式,句中的 aircraft 紧接在 this 之后,容易误解为单数。把此句译为"要制造这种飞机……",是由于原文 aircraft 与 this 之间没有逗号,误把 this 与 aircraft 连在一起,作 to do 的宾语,从而一错再错,又把 to do this aircraft 作为句子的主语。实际上,这里的 aircraft 是集合复数,作句子的主语,to do this 是目的状语。to do this 之后可以用逗号,也可以不用。

【例550】Are these (pure science and applied science) two totally different activities, having little or no interconnection as is often implied?

[误译] 这两种(理论科学与应用科学)完全不同的活动是否像通常所说的那样,几乎没有什么或者根本没有相互联系呢?

[正译] 这两者(理论科学与应用科学)像通常所说的那样,是两种几乎没有什么或者根本没有相互联系的完全不同的活动吗?

[评析] 这句中的 these 不是用作定语修饰 activities,不能译为"这两种完全不同的活动是否……没有……相互联系呢",因为 having 前面用了逗号,说明 having little or no interconnection 是修饰 activities 的定语,这里的 having 不可能和 are 一起用作谓语动词,因此这句的主语不是 activities,而是 these,所以译为"这两者……"。

【例551】There was greater economy of labour and some use of the system of alternative parts, spares.

[误译] 人的使用经济得多,而在循环使用制度下,零件的使用也经济得多。

[正译] 人力更为节约,并且采用了互换性配件系统,即备用件互换系统。

[评析] 在这个句子中,there 引起两个主语:economy 和 use。spares

则是 alternative parts 的同位语。显然,原译文没有搞清句子的结构和主语,所以发生了误译。

三、汉语主题

汉语是注重主题的语言,其句子结构是语义的;而英语是注重主语的语言,英语句子结构是语法的。

【例552】His skills qualify him for the job.

[误译] 他的技艺使他有资格担任这一工作。

[正译] 他有技术,能担任这一工作。

[评析] 英语句子只要满足主、谓和宾、补等结构,语法上就是合格的句子了。而汉语句子在结构上可分为话题和说明两部分,"他有技术,能担任这一工作"。原译文逐词死译,造成译文结构不顺。

【例553】Her efforts gained her a reputation.

[误译] 她的努力为她赢得了声誉。

[正译] 她很努力,名声很好。

[评析] 原译文有典型的翻译腔,不符合汉语的表达习惯。有些译者由于不了解英汉语言在结构上存在的差别,不注意英语句子主语为主及汉语句子主题突出的特点,使得汉译文不地道,意义含糊。

第七节 定语与状语的误译

由于一些定语或状语所处的位置,有时定语与状语容易混淆。

【例554】Some of our most skilled people don't get the salaries of maids in the US.

[误译] 连我国一些最有能力的人在美国还比不上女佣人的工资高。

[正译] 我们有些技术最好的人才薪金还不如美国女佣人高。

[评析] 这句里的介词短语 in the US 显然是修饰 maids 的定语,而不是地点状语。

【例555】The composer began his musical career as a violinist.

[误译] 作曲家开始了小提琴手的音乐生涯。

[正译] 作曲家以拉小提琴开始他的音乐生涯。

[评析] 这句的介词短语 as a violinist 不能作定语,并修饰 career,如果译为"开始了小提琴手的音乐生涯"不合逻辑,既然是位"作曲家",怎么能"开始小提琴手的音乐生涯"? 从形式上看 as a violinist 可作定语,也可作状语,修饰 began,但语法分析应服从内容,这里的 as a violinist 作状语,应译为"……以拉小提琴开始……",或"作曲家的音乐生涯是以拉小提琴开始的"。

【例 556】We teach this song in English over the radio.

[误译] 我们在电台里用英语教唱这首歌曲。

[正译] 我们在电台里教唱这首英语歌曲。

[评析] 这句中的介词短语 in English 从形式上看既可用作定语,修饰名词 this song,译为"这首英语歌曲",又可用作状语,修饰动词 teach,译为"用英语教唱这首歌曲"。然而,根据实际情况,电台英语学习节目中一般教唱的是英语歌曲,而不是用英语教唱歌曲。

【例 557】The Committee recommended the adoption of that draft resolution without objection.

[误译] 该委员会建议通过那项无异议的决议草案。

[正译] 该委员会在无异议的情况下建议通过那项决议草案。

[评析] 这句中的介词短语 without objection 用作状语,修饰动词 recommended,不是用作定语,既不是修饰 that draft resolution,也不是修饰 the adoption,不能译为"……建议通过那项无异议的决议草案",也不能译为"……建议无异议地通过……"。

【例 558】His first act as an engineer was to investigate in the workshop.

[误译] 他的第一个行动是以工程师身分下车间调研。

[正译] 他当了工程师以后的第一个行动是去车间调研。

[评析] 这句中的 as an engineer 不是修饰 was to investigate 的状语,而是用作定语,修饰 act。原译把定语误解为状语了。as an engineer 不可能修饰它后面的动词 was to investigate,否则意思变成"他的第一个行动是以工程师身分下车间调研",那就和原意大相径庭。

【例 559】Having reviewed various technical possibilities, I would now

like to comment on the dangers that might be represented by their
fulfillment and to compare these with the consequences of efforts to
prevent this development.

[误译] 分析了技术上的各种可能性后,我现在想对如果这些可能性
成为现实而可能带来的各种危险谈些看法,并把这些危险同努力
的后果比较一下,以便阻止这一发展。

[正译] 分析了技术上的各种可能性后,我现在想对如果这些可能性
成为现实而可能带来的各种危险谈些看法,并把这些危险与竭力
阻止这个技术的发展所带来的各种后果作些比较。

[评析] 原译文把 to prevent this development 当成了目的状语,修饰
compare,说明 compare 的目的。但是从上下文来看,语意不通。to
prevent this development 应是定语,修饰 effort,说明是什么样的努
力在竭力阻止这一技术发展所带来的后果。

第八节　状语短语的误译

当英语原文中有几个动词,状语修饰的是一个还是几个动词往
往容易造成误译。

【例 560】He played a key role in advising the president how to foil the
conspiracy mounted against him in May of 1991 by seven of his own
ministers.

[误译] 总统于 1991 年 5 月粉碎他手下七名部长策划的阴谋时,他
的意见起了关键性的作用。

[正译] 他在建议总统如何粉碎其手下七名部长于 1991 年 5 月策划
的阴谋方面起了关键性的作用。

[评析] 原句中的状语短语 in May of 1991 前面有 played, foil 和
mounted 等好几个动词,但它所修饰的是靠近它的 mounted,而不
是其他较远的动词。

【例 561】It was a tense meeting, but in typically Arab fashion the men
who had been ready to kill one another in the morning were kissing
one another in the evening.

195

[误译] 这是一个气氛紧张的会议,但是那些早上还准备拼个你死我
　　　活的冤家,却在晚上以典型的阿拉伯方式相互亲吻了。

[正译] 这是一个气氛紧张的会议,但是那些早上还准备拼个你死我
　　　活的冤家到了晚上却相互亲吻了,这是典型的阿拉伯风格。

[评析] 原句中的状语短语 in typically Arab fashion 位于 but 引导的
　　　分句之首,它不是修饰谓语动词 were kissing,而是修饰整个 but 引
　　　导的句子,译成汉语可放在句末。

【例 562】He finds playing chess an uninteresting game, and only enters them reluctantly because he knows that at the very least he and
his friends are better than the others.

[误译] 他觉得打牌没有意思,他只是勉强地玩,因为他知道他和他
　　　的朋友们最起码要比别人强。

[正译] 他觉得打牌没有意思,他极不情愿地玩,只是因为他知道他
　　　和他的朋友们最起码要比别人强。

[评析] 如果 reluctantly 是修饰 enters,那么 only 更有理由去修饰 en-
　　　ters,因为它更靠近动词 enters。但情况不总是如此。像 only,
　　　merely, simply, probably 这些副词有时候放在动词前,但修饰的对
　　　象往往是后面的 because, if, when 等从句。

【例 563】Some people probably play chess because it is at least something to do.

[误译] 有些人可能下棋是因为这样至少有事可做。

[正译] 有些人下棋可能是因为这样至少有事可做。

[评析] 如果译成"可能下棋",与"只是勉强地参与政治"是同样的误
　　　译,本句里的 probably 虽然在动词 play 前,但是修饰的是后面的
　　　because。

【例 564】Even though one has to get up earlier and spend more time in
trains or buses one can sleep better at night, and, during week-ends
and on summer evenings, one can enjoy the fresh, clean air of the
country.

[误译] 即使你在火车上和公共汽车上不得不花很多时间,但在晚
　　　上,在周末或夏季的晚上,你可以睡得好,你可以享受到乡村新鲜、

无污染的空气。

[正译] 就算需要起得早一些,在火车上或公共汽车上多花一些时间晚上总是能睡得好一些,而且在周末和夏天的晚上,还可以尽情呼吸乡间新鲜、洁净的空气。

[评析] 原文中 sleep better at night 和 during weekends and on summer evenings 中间的连词 and 前后都有逗号隔开,说明后两个时间状语是整个并列句中第二个句子的组成部分。原译文完全忽视了这一点。错将 at night, during weekends 和 on summer evenings 全部当作 sleep better 的时间状语,使译文背离了原意。

【例 565】An occasional walk in one of the parks and a fortnight's visit to the sea every summer is all the country they want.

[误译] 每年夏季在公园一次偶然的散步和两个星期去海边的游览是他们所需要的乡村的生活。

[正译] 偶尔到某个公园里去散散步,每年夏天到海滨去玩两个星期,就是他们所需要的全部乡村生活。

[评析] 原文中的 every summer 修饰的只是 a fortnight's visit to the sea,不包括 an occasional walk in one of the parks。原译文以为 every summer 既修饰前者,也修饰后者。所以导致译文的错误。

第九节 其他结构的误译

一个词语在句中所用作的成分不同,意义也不相同。特别是一个句子中的某些词语,从形式上看既可用作这一成分,又可用作那一成分,这时必须根据上下文和全句意思作出准确的判断,否则就会产生理解错误。

【例566】Now some merchants have been exposed to the charge that they reserve their soya beans with ulterior motives.

[误译] 现在有些商人已受到受到他们储存大豆有其不可告人的目的的指责。

[正译] 现在有些商人已受到这样的指责,即他们储存大豆有其不可告人的目的。

[评析] 这句中 that 引导的从句不是修饰 charge 的定语从句,因为 that 从句里既有主语 they,又有宾语 weapons,所以 that 不可能是关系代词;它在这里是名词从句,作 charge 的同位语,说明 charge 的内容,改正译文译为"……受到这样的指责,说他们……"更加通顺达意。

【例 567】 I wrote four books in the first three years, a record never touched before.

[误译] 我在头三年写了四本书和一篇从未写过的报导。

[正译] 我在头三年写了四本书,打破了以往的记录。

[评析] 这句的 a record-never touched before 不是 wrote 的宾语,而是带有评价性质的附加语,对主句作了补充说明。相当于 and it is a record never touched before. 这里的 record 不是"报道",应解释为"记录"。这句是把附加语误解为 wrote 的宾语,此例说明附加语可能引起误解。

【例 568】 The Cossack, Nicola Kashkareff, went on board this vessel.

[误译] 哥萨克尼古拉·卡什加里夫来到船上。

[正译] 有个哥萨克名叫尼古拉·卡什加里夫来到船上。

[评析] 哥萨克是俄罗斯人的一部分,不是某一个人的名字。Nicola Kashkareff 是主语 The Cossack 的同位语,由于 the Cossack 是与人名连在一起,容易误会成这个人就叫哥萨克尼古拉·卡什加里夫。

【例 569】 There will be no heroics in a war where the safest place will be the front line, if there is one, and the most dangerous the houses of our civilian population.

[误译] 这样说并不过分:在将来的战争中,如果说有什么安全地方的话,那将是前线,而最危险的地方将是平民的房屋。

[正译] 在一场以前线(如果有什么前线的话)最为安全、以平民房屋最为危险的战争中,是谈不上什么英雄行为的。

[评析] if there is one 这个插入成分紧跟着 the front line,而距离 safest place 远一些,因此不能作原译文的理解。可是原译文在文字上又讲得通,而恰巧 heroics 又有两种解释:"英雄行为","说过

头话"。在这里如果翻译成"这样说也不过分",就完全背离了原文的意思。

【例570】Thirdly, by refusing to take refuge—as the previous chief executive officer had continually done in the preceding years—in panic-stricken stop-gap measures, we stimulated the return of confidence.

[误译] 第三,正如前任首席执行官前几年一贯所做的,我们拒绝采取因惊惶失措而安于一些补漏洞的权宜之计,因而我们促使了信誉的恢复。

[正译] 第三,我们拒绝采取前任首席执行官前几年的一贯做法,没有因为惊惶失措而安于一些补漏洞的权宜之计,因而我们促使了信誉的恢复。

[评析] as the previous Government had continually done in the preceding years 这个插入语可修饰两个动词形式,一个是动名词 refusing,另一个是不定式 to take refuge。原译把它分析为修饰 refusing,理解为上届政府也拒绝干补漏洞的事,显然这是不合原意的。因此这个短语应是修饰 to take refuge,也就是说上届政府这样干,而我们拒绝和他们一样。

第十节　分隔词语的误译

在翻译中找不出英语被分隔的和相互关联的词语之间的联系,从而造成理解错误。根据英语行文习惯把两个有关成分分开,这种语言现象称为词语的分隔;而有些词语在句中紧挨在一起,其中一个词语从语法或语义上看,有时和它前面的词语相关,有时则和它后面的词语相关,这种语言现象称为词语的关联。这两种语言现象都是理解的难点。

【例571】The strength thus developed, however, carried within it the seeds of its own decline.

[误译] 这股力量这样发展了,然而在其内部就带有衰退的因素。

[正译] 然而,这样发展起来的这股力量,在其内部就具有衰退的因

素。

[评析] 这句中的主语 strength 和谓语动词 carried 之间被定语 thus developed 和状语 however 隔开。如把作定语用的过去分词 developed 误解为谓语动词过去时,和 carried 并列,从而译为"这股力量这样发展了,然而在其内部……",那就和原文意思有出入。

【例 572】The job gives him plenty of responsibility—he is in charge of several thousand workers—and plenty of cash.

[误译] 他担任这项工作有很多责任。他在管着几千名工人和许多现金。

[正译] 他担任此项工作,责任重大,他在主管着几千名工人,报酬丰厚。

[评析] 原文中的 plenty of cash 和 plenty of responsibility 是并列成分,都是动词 give 的直接宾语。由于 he is in charge of several thousand workers 将两者间隔开,造成误译。in charge of, several thousand workers 只是补充说明 plenty of responsibility,和 plenty of cash 无关,也就是说,管的是人,不是钱。

【例 573】Even Christopher, who is not an excessively modest or silent man hesitated to face Christina with the disasters Christopher knew lay ahead.

[误译] 甚至克里斯多佛这个有点傲气喜欢大发言论的人,在要面对克里斯蒂娜时也有点踟蹰不前,因为他知道等待在前面的将是什么样的灾难。

[正译] 甚至克里斯多佛这个有点傲气喜欢大发言论的人,在把他知道要发生的灾难告诉克里斯蒂娜时,也有点踟蹰不前。

[评析] face 是作"面对"解,但是当构成 face sb with sth 搭配后,就是一个成语,意即"让某人知道某事"或"让某人面对某事",而不能把 face...with 分开来理解。

【例 574】A big company without business culture would confront the future with difficult problems, especially in the modern age.

[误译] 一个大公司若没有企业文化就会带着十分困难的问题来面对未来,尤其在当代更是如此。

[正译] 一个大公司若没有企业文化就会给未来带来难题,尤其在当代更是如此。

[评析] 如果把 confront 和 with 分隔开来按字面意思翻译,就成为"…就会带着十分困难的问题来面对世界…",就不符合原文的意思,confront sb with sth 表示"使某人面对"、"使某人面临"。例如:I am confronted with many difficulties. 我面临很多困难。

【例 575】Many sketches are in existence of peasants seated by the roadside and men and women at work in the fields.

[误译] 许多速写是关于坐在路旁的农民和在田里劳动的男男女女的存在。

[正译] 至今保存着许多速写,画的是坐在路旁的农民们和在田里劳动的男男女女。

[评析] 原句中的定语短语 of peasants seated by the roadside and men and women at work in the fields 很长,而谓语和表语 are in existence 都很短,如果将这样长的定语短语放在它所修饰的主语 sketches 后面,全句将显得头重脚轻,失去平衡,因此从修辞的效果出发,把这句的主语和它的定语分开,将定语放在 in existence 后面。不了解这种分隔现象,就容易将 of 引导的短语误解为修饰 existence 而造成错误。

【例 576】They plan to publish a work on the effects on international law of the establishment of a new nature reserve along the border.

[误译] 他们计划出版一本对有关在边境建立新的自然保护区的国际法有影响的著作。

[正译] 他们计划出版一本书,论述建立在边境建立新的自然保护区对国际法的影响。

[评析] 本句话之所以会有误译,主要是把 of the establishment of a new nature reserve along the border 这一介词短语看成了它所靠近的 law 的定语。其实,这一介词短语是 the effects 的定语。这属于一种语法成分的分隔现象。句中第一个 on 是论述的意思。第二个 on 是 effects 要求,表示"对于……的影响"。

【例 577】In addition it (English) is the language of commerce and the second language of many countries which formerly had French or German in that position.

[误译] 此外,正是这种贸易语言和许多国家的第二种语言使它以前在这个位置有法语或德语。

[正译] 另外,英语还是贸易中使用的语言和许多国家的第二语言,而在这以前,这些国家都是以法语或德语作为第二语言的。

[评析] 原文中的 it is...which 结构,似乎是可以按一个强调句型去理解,但仔细一分析,便可以看出,which 引起的从句是一个定语从句,它修饰 many countries,所以如果按强调句去译,译文便让人不知所云了。所以对强调句的识别一定要小心。主要方法就是把 it is...that 结构从原句中去掉,而后去还原整个句子,如果句子可以还原成完整的句子,成分不多不少,就是强调句,否则是主语从句或其他句型。

【例 578】 I would not change my present situation for that of my accusers, to escape all that torture can inflict upon me.

[误译] 我不会改变我的立场,因为我的告发人的现在立场就是避免受到可能加在我身上的种种苦刑。

[正译] 我不会为了逃避可能加在我身上的种种苦刑而改变我目前的立场,转而采取告发我的人的立场。

[评析] change for 是"变……为"的意思,由于中间插进了别的字,被分隔开来,容易造成误译。

【例 579】 News came through on the wireless of a rich oil field in Takang.

[误译] 从大港某一丰富油田的无线电中传来了消息。

[正译] 无线电传来了大港发现丰富油田的消息。

[评析] 这句的定语短语 of a rich oil field in Takang 不是修饰它贴近的 the wireless,而是修饰主语 news。也可把这句原文改为 News of a rich oil field in Takang came through on the wireless.

第十一节　省略词语的误译

英语用词力戒重复,常常用替代、省略和变换的表达方法避免重复;汉语用词不怕重复,常常运用实称、还原和复说的表达方法。英语词汇的音节参差不齐,结构长短不一,所以不重视用词的均衡和对偶;汉语十分讲求词语的偶式对应,特别喜欢使用四字词组和排比式词汇。英汉对译时务必要注意要它们各自的用词习惯。

【例 580】Everybody has a responsibility to the society of which he is a part and through this to mankind.

[误译] 每个人都对他所属的社会负有责任,通过这点走向人类。

[正译] 每个人都对他所属的社会负有责任,通过社会,对人类负有责任。

[评析] 原文的 this 指 society。而 through this 和 to mankind 之间,省略了主语、谓语动词和宾语 everybody has a responsibility,译成汉语应在"通过社会,对人类"后面重复"负有责任"。这句是省略主语、谓语动词和宾语可能引起的误解。汉译时要重复"社会"和"负有责任"。

【例 581】She makes a good teacher, as she has a good student.

[误译] 她成为一个好教师,因为她有一个好学生。

[正译] 她原先是个好学生,现在是个好教师。

[评析] 这句的 has 后面省略了过去分词 made,这里的 has 不作"有"解,而是助动词,has made 作"原先是"解。省略了过去分词 made 引起的误解。

【例 582】This technique has been available in Britain for years, but its versatility has never been exploited extensively as it has Germany.

[误译] 这一技术几年来在英国一直采用,但是它的多种用途还没有在德国广泛利用。

[正译] 这一技术几年来在英国一直采用,但是它的多种用途没有像德国那样广泛利用。

[评析] 这句的 as it has 后面省略谓语动词的一部分 been exploited

和状语 extensively，原意是"德国已广泛利用这种技术的多种用途，而英国还没有"，如译为"它的多种用途还没有在德国广泛利用"，那就与原意恰巧相反。这句是省略谓语动词和状语可能引起的误译。

【例 583】 I kept going back to it at odd times during the day, then at night when I was being put to bed.

[误译] 我白天不时想到它，到了晚上，我便去睡了。

[正译] 我白天不时想到它，晚上临睡时也会想到它。

[评析] 这句的 then 与 at night 之间省略了主语、谓语动词，宾语和状语 I kept going back to it，译成汉语应重复"也会想着它"。这句是省略主语、谓语动词、宾语和状语可能引起的误解。

【例 584】 Potatoes are an important source of starchy food in temperate countries and bananas in tropics.

[误译]马铃薯是温带国家淀粉食物的重要来源，香蕉则是热带地区的。

[正译]马铃薯是温带国家淀粉食物的重要来源，香蕉则是热带地区淀粉食物的重要来源。

[评析] 这句中的 bananas 和 in tropics 之间省略了 are an important source of starchy food，显而易见译成汉语时必须译出，不然就无法说明问题。至于与上面的词语发生重复对汉语来说没有什么关系。

【例 585】 This will remain true whether we are dealing with the application of psychology to advertising and political propaganda, or engineering to the mass media of communication, or of medical science to the problems of population or old age.

[误译] 无论我们说的是把心理学用之于广告宣传和政治宣传，或者工程学之于群众性宣传手段，或者医学科学之于人口或老年，情况都将是如此。

[正译] 无论我们说的是把心理学用之于广告宣传和政治宣传，或者是把工程学用之于群众性宣传手段，或者把医学科学用之于人口过多或老年学问题，情况都将是如此。

[评析] 句中的 the application 后接 of psychology to..., engineering to...和 of medical science to...,三者并列,第二个短语省略了 the application of,第三个短语省略了 the application,译为汉语时则必须译出,使意思一目了然。

【例 586】I have five young children, and now my wife has a baby girl and I do not know where the money is to come from to feed and clothe them all. We are very poor, and I fear I cannot work hard enough.

[误译] 我有五个孩子,眼下妻子又生了一个女儿,真不知道到哪里弄钱供他们吃穿,我们很穷,恐怕我也不能拼命干活了。

[正译] 我有五个孩子,眼下妻子又生了一个女儿,真不知道到哪里弄钱供他们吃穿,我们太穷了,不论怎么拼命干,恐怕也不行。

[评析] 原文最后一句如果译为"我们很穷,恐怕我也不能拼命干活了。"意思显然不通。既然很穷,更应拼命干活。误译的主要原因是没有理解原文的语法结构,只是逐词死译。最后一句实际是个省略句。如果补全,应该是 I fear I cannot work hard enough to feed and clothe them all.

　　英语中的理解问题,自然不限于语法方面,有时还涉及专业知识,文化与历史背景的知识和其他种种。不过在英汉翻译中首先总是要理解英语原文,而掌握一些英语语法知识对理解英语原文就很有必要。

第十二节　词语用法的误译

一、too

【例 587】He was too experienced not to know it.

[误译] 他太有经验,不去知道这点。

[正译] 他很有经验,不会不知道这点。

[评析] 这句的 too...not to...和上两句的 not...too...to...意义不同,too experienced not to know it = so experienced that he cannot but know it，这里的 cannot but 是双重否定的意思，可译为"不会不"或"一定会"，所以这句也可译为"他很有经验，一定会知道这点"。

【例 588】He was too near for us not to see him.

[误译] 他太近了，我们不去看他。

[正译] 他近在咫尺，我们不会没看见他。

[评析] 原文的 too near for us not to see him 相当于 so near that we cannot but see him 的意思，也可译为"他近在咫尺，我们肯定会看见他。"

【例 589】One can scarcely pay too high a price for liberty.

[误译] 人们对自由付出的代价不能太高。

[正译] 人们对自由付出的代价再高，也不过分。

[评析] 原文的 One can scarcely pay too high price for liberty. 意思是 One cannot pay too high a price for liberty. 或者表示 it is impossible for one to overpay a price，这里的 too high 意义上相当于 high enough，有"再高也不够"的意思。

【例 590】We are only too willing to do it for you.

[误译] 我们太愿意不帮你干这事。

[正译] 我们非常愿意为你干这事。

[评析] only too...to 是一个固定结构，无否定意义，它的意思是"非常"，不能同 too...to 结构相混淆。

总之，在学习中碰到上述类似情况，应多查词典，注意词的搭配，词在不同场合会有不同的意思，切勿望文生义，造成误译。

二、until

【例 591】The new rates will apply from 1st January next year. Until then the old rates, below, hold good.

[误译] 新的价格从明年 1 月 1 日开始实行，直到那时，下列旧的价格依然有效。

[正译] 新的价格从明年 1 月 1 日开始实行，那时以前，下列旧的价格依然有效。

[评析] 这句的 until then 译为"直到那时"，意义不够清楚，似乎会给

人这样的错觉,即"到了 1 月 1 日旧的价格,依然有效",而原句的意思是"1 月 1 日以前旧价依然有效,1 月 1 日开始不再有效",所以这句的 until then 应译为"那时以前"。

【例 592】Agriculture made rapid gains until 1960, but then encountered natural disasters.

[误译] 直到 1960 年,农业发展还很快,但后来遭受了自然灾害。

[正译] 1960 年之前,农业发展很快,但后来遭受了自然灾害。

[评析] 原译文把这句中的 until 理解为"直到",显然不符合原意。一般说来,主句用过去时,until 应作"直到……之前"解。

【例 593】And until recently this hostile attitude towards daydreaming was the most common one.

[误译] 直到最近这种白日做梦的敌视态度仍是人们常见的态度。

[正译] 不久前,这种对白日做梦的否定态度还是相当普遍。

[评析] 原译文把 until 误译为"直到"。until 在肯定句中,有两个基本含义:一是作"直到(为止)"解。例如:I shall go on working until next week. 直到下周我才有休息。但还有一个意思:"直到……之前"。

【例 594】Until recently I knew nothing about it.

[误译] 直到最近,我一无所知。

[正译] 直到最近我才知道。

[评析] 这句的 until recently 和前面的 until recently 不同,它与表示否定意义的 nothing 连用,应译为"直到最近……才……"。这里涉及 until 的用法问题:until 在否定句中,也即和主句中 not, no, un-等否定词连用时,表示"直到……才"。

【例 595】Until now the so-called law of the sea has been seen as a very important issue.

[误译] 直到现在大家并未把所谓海洋法看做是一件非常重要的事情。

[正译] 直到现在大家才把所谓海洋法看做是一件非常重要的事情。

[评析] 原译文如果逐词译为"直到现在……并未……",与原意恰恰相反。其实原文的意思是 the so-called law of the sea has not been

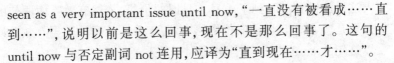

seen as a very important issue until now, "一直没有被看成……直到……"，说明以前是这么回事，现在不是那么回事了。这句的 until now 与否定副词 not 连用，应译为"直到现在……才……"。

【例 596】Until recently, scientists have been unable to devise a drill which would be capable of cutting through hard rock at great depth. (This problem has now been solved.)

[误译] 直到最近,科学家还未能设计出可以钻透坚硬岩石的钻头,达到地壳深处。

[正译] 直到最近,科学家们才设计出一种可以钻透坚硬岩石的钻头,达到地壳深处。

[评析] 原文的意思 scientists have not been able … until recently: "以前一直未能……,直到现在情况两样了"。通过原文,可看出原译文自相矛盾:既然直到最近还未设计出这种钻头,接下来怎么会说这个问题现在已解决了呢? 这里 until 用在否定句中,和表示否定意义的 unable 连用,表示"直到……才"。

三、while

有些译者在理解和翻译中有一种不良的习惯,看到一个词,总是按照自己印象最深的,最熟悉的一个释义去套。很少动动脑筋去想想这个释义是否符合上下文。不符合上下文,译出来读不通的情况下,又不去想想或查查有否更恰当的释义。

【例 597】While the leading actor on the stage captures our attention, we are aware of the importance of the supporting players and the scenery of the play itself.

[误译] 当舞台上的主角吸引了我们的注意力,我们意识到了配角和戏本身布景的重要性。

[正译] 虽然舞台上的主角吸引了我们注意力,但我们也意识到配角和戏本身布景的重要性。

[评析] while 的意思很多,可作"当……时"解,相当于 when;作"然而"解,相当于 whereas;作"只要"解,相当于 if only;还可作"虽然"解,相当于 although。有些译者一看到 while,不顾上下文意思,习

惯性地译为"当……时"。

【例598】Detente is relative and temporary, while movement is absolute and permanent.

[误译] 在运动是绝对而永久的同时,缓和是相对的,暂时的。

[正译] 缓和是相对的、暂时的,而运动是绝对的、永久的。

[评析] while 有时确实作"在……同时"解,例如 He fell asleep while studying his grammar book,应译为"他在读语法的时候睡着了"。但这句的 while 不作"在……同时"解,而作"而"解,相当于 whereas。

【例599】While such dangers clearly exist, it also seems clear that some scientists have dramatized them in order to help persuade the public of the need for radical changes in our finance.

[误译] 当这种危险已明显地存在时,有一点似乎也很清楚:某些科学家是故意夸大了它们,目的是为了说服公众觉得有必要在我们的金融方面有根本的改变。

[正译] 虽然这种危险已明显地存在,有一点似乎也很清楚:某些科学家是故意夸大了它们,目的是为了说服公众觉得有必要在我们的金融方面有根本的改变。

[评析] 本句 while 引导的从句和主句的意思是对立的,这里的 while 只能作"虽然"解。这句上下文意思也决定了 while 作"虽然"解。

四、when

【例600】When you think of the innumerable birds that one sees flying about, not to mention the equally numerous small animals like field mice and voles which you do not see, it is very rarely that one comes across a dead body, except, of course, on the roads.

[误译] 当你想到那些看得见的、到处飞翔的鸟儿,更不用说同样的、看不见的诸如野鼠、田鼠之类的动物时,除了在大路上,你很难见到动物的死尸。

[正译] 虽然你可想像到无数鸟儿在天空中飞翔,更不要说同样的、却看不见的诸如野鼠、田鼠之类的动物,但是除了在大路上外,你

很难见到动物的死尸。

[评析] 把 when 译成"当……时",句子怎么安排,怎么译,意思总不顺。问题是 when 在这里表示的并不是时间关系。when 在很多情况下,作"为……时"解,但也有"虽然"、"既然"、"尽管"、"如果"等意思。例如:She persisted in her work when she might take a good rest. 尽管她可以好好休息一下,她还是坚持工作。/When a representative exceeds his allotted time, the President shall call him to order without delay. 如果某一代表发言超过规定的时间,主席应立即敦促他遵守规则。所以在众多的意思中,when 究竟是取哪一个释义,主要是看上下文。而这句中的 when 只有译成"虽然",才符合原意。

五、or

【例 601】A dugout, or a canoe was made by hollowing out a tree trunk.

[误译] 独木舟,或者一种小舟,是通过挖空树干造成的。

[正译] 独木舟,即一种小舟,是通过挖空树干造成的。

[评析] 这句的 or 译为"或者",好像它所连接的两个部分是两个不同的东西。实际上,这里的 or 是同位用法,两者指的是同一个东西,只不过是名称不同而已,可译为"即"、"也就是"、"换言之"等。

【例 602】What decides is not explosives or wells or atom bombs, but the man who handles them.

[误译] 起决定作用的不是炸弹,或是油井,或是原子弹,而是掌握它们的人。

[正译] 起决定作用的不是炸弹,不是油井,也不是原子弹,而是掌握它们的人。

[评析] or 在肯定句中一般可译为"或者",但是在否定句中相当于 and not,因此不能译为"或者",应译为"不是"。

【例 603】The moon had no seas, lakes or rivers or water in any form. There are no forests, prairies or green fields and certainly no towns or cities.

[误译] 月球上没有海,湖或者河,或者任何形式的水,没有森林,草原或者绿色田野,肯定没有城镇或者城市。

[正译] 月球上没有海,湖和河,也没有任何形式的水,没有森林,草原和绿色田野,肯定没有城镇和城市。

[评析] 这句有四个 or 与 no 连用,但都不宜译为"或者",其中 or water in any form 中的 or 应译为"也没有",其他三个 or 可译为"和"。在否定句子中,or 可能会引起误解。试比较:He did not speak clearly or correctly. 他讲得既不清楚又不正确。这里的 or 用在 not 后面,作 and not 解,可译为"又不",即 He did not speak clearly and he did not speak correctly,相当于 He spoke neither clearly nor correctly,换句话说,两点都没做到。再如:He did not speak clearly and correctly. 他不曾讲得既清楚又正确。这里的 clearly and correctly 是一个意群,意思是不曾同时做到两点,比方说,他可能讲得正确,但不清楚。

六、as well as

【例 604】When you look up a word, notice its pronunciation as well as its meaning.

[误译] 查一个词时,不但要注意它的发音,也要注意它的意义。

[正译] 查一个词时,不但要注意它的意义,也要注意它的发音。

[评析] 这句的 as well as 作 not only...but also... 解,但它的侧重点是在它前面的 pronunciation,不能译为"也要注意它的意义"。这句说明没有正确理解 as well as 解释 not only...but also... 时的侧重点所在,以致翻译时产生错误。

【例 605】But more detached observers report failures as well as successes, and reviews of the research suggest that although the success probably predominate, the overall results of job enlargement are mixed.

[误译] 但是观察得较为公正的人说这种做法有失败的和成功的,而研究报告表明虽然成功的可能占绝大多数,但工作多样化做法的总的效果是好坏都有。

[正译]但是观察得较为公正的人说这种做法既有成功的,但也有失败的,而研究报告表明虽然成功的可能占绝大多数,但工作多样化做法的总的效果是好坏都有。

[评析] as well as 是有"和"的意思,但是根据不同的上下文,这个固定词组还有"不但……而且……","既……也(又)……"意思。例如:He takes interest in the newspaper now, the front page as well as the sports. 他对报纸发生了兴趣,不但读体育新闻,也读头版新闻。

【例 606】He had a personal as well as scientific reason to pursue his research, because his own brother had been killed in an accidental explosion.

[误译]他追求他的炸药研究,有个人和科学的原因,因为他自己的胞弟就在一次意外的爆炸中丧生。

[正译]他孜孜地进行炸药研究,不仅出于科学的原因,还出于个人的考虑,因为他自己的胞弟就在一次意外的爆炸中丧生。

[评析]原文前边表述他对科学事业的追求,后边说他搞炸药研究还有一个原因。因此将 as well as 译为"不仅出于科学的原因,还出于个人的考虑"是符合原意的。

七、and

【例 607】It is a black and white cow.

[误译]这是一头黑色母牛和白色母牛。(两头牛)

[正译]这是一头黑白相色的母牛。(一头牛)

[评析]这里的 a black and white cow 说的是一头牛,black and white 作"黑白相色"解。如果要说"一头黑色母牛和一头白色母牛",应译为 a black and a white cow,注意在 white cow 前面必须重复不定冠词 a。

【例 608】the editor and publisher of the magazine

[误译]这家杂志的编辑和发行人(两人)

[正译]这家杂志的编辑兼发行人(一人)

[评析]这里的 the editor and publisher 指同一个人,应译为"编辑兼发行人"。如果要说"编辑和发行人",应译为 the editor and the publisher of the magazine, 注意在 publish 前面重复定冠词 the。

第十三节　固定词组的误译

在阅读和翻译时, 除了正确判断词性和句子成分外, 有一种语言现象值得引起注意, 分析不当, 也会造成理解错误。这就是句子中某些词语, 从形式上看, 可以和它前面的词语有关联, 也可以和它后面的词语有关联, 但在一定上下文中, 它在意义上只可能和其中一个有关联。确定句子中词语之间在意义上的关联对正确理解极为重要, 这里涉及英语的基本功问题, 在学习翻译之前必须掌握一定数量的常用词组。英语中有些词组是不能按照其字面意思相加来理解的, 因为它们可能是成语或固定词组, 已形成特别的意思。例如把 small talk(家常话)理解为"短小的话"或"一些话"就错了。碰到意思不通、牵强时, 切不要硬译。应回过头来看看, 这个词组是否还有其他意思, 是不是成语或固定词组。

【例 609】The firemen in this part of the country went on strike.

[误译] 该国这个地区的消防员继续罢工。

[正译] 该国这个地区的消防员举行罢工。

[评析] 这句中的介词 on 在意义上和后面的 strike 有关联, 与前面的 went 无关, 因此不能译为"……继续罢工"; 又如 to go on a journey 中的 on 和 a journey 相关联, 作"去旅行"解; 不与 so 在意义上相关, 不能译为"继续赶路"; 但是在 A group of scientists were working on dyes for textiles 这句里的 on 和 were working 有关联, 不与 dyes 连在一起, to work on 作"忙于"、"从事……研究"解, 这句应译为"一批科学家当时正从事纺织品染料的研究"。动词在英语里, 可以说是一个最活跃的词类。名词和形容词, 相对说来意思比较固定, 而动词往往可以表示各种不同的含义, 用法也特别多。因此, 英译汉时, 动词处理起来弹性特别大, 需要考虑的往往是怎样选择一个能够很好地与主语搭配的动词。

【例 610】From one's own front door to home or foreign hill or sands and back again, everything is to hand.

[误译] 从自己的家门口到国内外的名山或沙滩,然后再回来,所有的东西必须在手里。

[正译] 从自己的家门口到国内外的名山或沙滩,然后再回来,一应交通工具随时可用。

[评析] 原译文把 hand 错看成名词,to hand 在这里构成一个不定式短语,也是一个固定词组,表示"近在手边"。例如:I often consult the two dictionaries that lie to hand. 我经常查阅放在手边的两本词典。原文中 everything 是上文指的车辆、交通工具,所以 everything is to hand 应译成"所有车辆随时可用"。

【例 611】 I would inevitably make mistakes at one time or another and operate on someone who didn't need surgery or sit on someone who did.

[误译] 说不定什么时候我会不可避免地出错。我会给不需要动手术的病人开刀,也可能会坐在干活的病人身上。

[正译] 说不定什么时候我会不可避免地出错。我会给不需要动手术的病人开刀,也可能会把需要动手术的病人忽略过去。

[评析] "医生坐在病人的身上"肯定是误译出了笑话。英语中有些动词词组不能从它们的字面上来推测其真正的涵义。sit on 作为一个固定词语作"忽视"、"坐在一旁不干",而不是"坐在……上面"。例如:He'd not be back till late, and they could sit up and talk. 他很晚才会回来,爷孙俩可以睡得晚点。多说一会儿话。不能因为 sit down 表示"坐下",就把 sit up 译为"坐起来"。实际上 sit up 是"熬夜不睡"的意思。

【例 612】 In country after country, talk of nonsmokers' right is in the air.

[误译] 在一个又一个国家里,不吸烟者的权利在空中说开了。

[正译] 不吸烟者的权利问题正在一个又一个国家里议论开了。

[评析] in the air 按字面意思可作"在空中"解。但这里是一个固定词组,作"流传"解。例如:There was the feeling in the air that the war would break out immediately. 人们普遍感到一场大战一触即发。in the air 作为习语时还可作"尚未决定"解,例如:My plans are still quite in the air. 我的决定还未最后决定。因此, 对某些词组, 其字面意思与上下文意思不符时, 要想一想是否是习语, 是否有其特定的意思。

【例 613】Because thanks to these elementary schools our early mechanics, especially in the New England and Middle Atlantic states, were generally literate and at home in arithmetic and in some aspects of geometry and trigonometry.

[误译] 因为由于这些小学, 我们早先的技工, 尤其是在新英格兰和大西洋沿海中部州的技工一般都懂文学, 在家里又搞算术和一些几何、三角等。

[正译] 因为正是有了这些小学, 我们早先的技工, 尤其是在新英格兰和大西洋沿海中部几个州的技工一般都会读写, 懂得算术和一些几何、三角知识。

[评析] at home 在汉语里的对应词是"在家里"。但是这个意思跟上下文的意思不相符。如果 to be at home 作"在家里"解, 那么 in arithmetic 在句中作什么成分, 又表达什么意思。当 at home 后面跟的是 in + 学科/知识时, 是固定词组, 是表示"熟悉"、"精通"的意思。literate 在这里也不表示"文学"。literate 与 literature(文学)拼写相似、发音相似, 但是意思并不相似, 不能译作"文学", literate 表示"有文化的, 有阅读和写作能力的"。小学 (the elementary schools) 不可能培养搞文学的。土木技工不可能去研究文学。上下文不符, 肯定有理解错误。

【例 614】Granddad tuned up for a minute, and then said, "This is one you'll like to remember."

[误译] 爷爷调了一分钟琴, 接着说:"这一首你会常想起的。"

[正译] 爷爷调了一会儿琴, 接着说:"这一首你会常想起的。"

[评析] for / in a minute 为固定词组, 是"一会儿"的意思, 表示模糊时间, 不表示精确的时间"一分钟", 因此不能把这一句译成"爷爷调了一分钟琴"。

【例 615】But the advantages of this law are also greater still than its cost—for it is to this law that we owe our wonderful material development, which brings improved conditions in its train.

[误译] 但是这条法则所带来的好处同样比付出的代价多,因为正是由于这条法则我们才有了了不起的物质进步,因而在其前进的列车中列车中带来了生活水平的提高。

[正译] 但是这条法则所带来的好处同样比付出的代价多,因为正是由于这条法规我们才有了了不起的物质进步,其结果是生活水平的提高。

[评析] train 是火车的意思,但是 in its train 在这里却是一个固定词组,表示"接踵而来"。例如:War often brought pestilence in its train. 战争之后往往就是瘟疫。

【例 616】 The students made these experiments in chemistry out of necessity.

[误译] 学生们不需要做这些化学实验。

[正译] 学生们出于需要才做这些化学实验。

[评析] out of 的意思很多,"从……出来","起出","脱离","在外","出于",但大多数读者受到下列词组的影响。例如:be out of sight,看不见,be out of order,不正常。out of 在这里则表示原因,作"出于"讲。

【例 617】 The evening will come before you know it.

[误译] 在你知道这件事之前,夜晚将来临。

[正译] 晚上很快就会到来。

[评析] before you know it 是一个固定词组,意思是"很快"。

【例 618】 He gave me three apples. They were good and ripe.

[误译] 他给我三只苹果,它们又好又熟。

[正译] 他给我三只苹果,它们熟透了。

[评析] good and 是一个固定词组,不能拆开来看,把 and 看做连接两个形容词。例如:He is good and hungry. 他非常饿。

第十四节 成语的误译

成语的含义大部分是由原词义引申、转化而成,其意义与原词义多有一定联系,但单词大多一词多义。单词组成词组之后,词组的含义往往只与它的某一意义相近,所以仍不能简单按原单词含义推定。即使单词词义固定,结合成词组以后,也往往会有所变化。成语的正确意思难以把握。像汉语一样,英语中有大量成语,在语言中占有相当重要的位置,有的见词明义,有的比较含蓄,有的出自典故,有的不止一个意思,有的和它的各个成分的表面意义有很大距离,甚至毫不相干,必须根据语境来确定其意义。所以在翻译实践中,对习语的理解也会遇到相当大的困难。

【例 619】Hairless Yunus has a few marbles missing because he is a
　　　wrestler.

[误译] 秃头尤诺斯丢掉了几块大理石,因为他是个角力士。

[正译] 秃头尤诺斯是个角力士,他缺心眼。

[评析] 当 marble 用作复数时有"理智,常识"等含义,如 to lose one's
　　　marbles,"失去理智"。原句如果按 marble 的字面意思译成"大理
　　　石"则译文便成了"秃头尤诺斯丢掉了几块大理石,因为他是个角
　　　力士。"这样的汉译文就令人不不知所云。有些单词组成词组之
　　　后,意义显著变化。还有些词组,意思与原单词词义已毫不相关。
　　　如果按原词义推断,就会出现误译。所以,对不熟悉的词组、成语,
　　　一定要查一查,千万不可推测,想当然地翻译。

【例 620】Not without reason Mr. Dulles is called a bull in the Indo-
　　　China shop.

[误译] 难怪人们说杜勒斯先生被称为一只闯进印度支那店的公牛。

[正译] 难怪人们说杜勒斯先生在印度支那问题上是"一只闯进瓷器
　　　店的公牛",蛮不讲理。

[评析] 这句话借用 A bull in a china shop 这一成语(意即"公牛闯进
　　　瓷器店"或"肆意捣乱"),把成语中的 china 一词换成 Indo-China。
　　　但如果译者不了解成语并对新的句子进行分析,也是很难吃透原
　　　文的意思的。

【例 621】These men who lost their senses tried to make hell while the
　　　sun shines.

[误译] 这些失去理智的人要趁天好时蛮干一番。

[正译] 这些失去理智的人要趁着末日来临之前蛮干一番。

[评析] 这句英语也是巧改成语 to make hay while the sun shines(趁天晴晒干草),而表达了另外的意思。

第十五节 比较意义的固定词组

同样,英语中有些词组,可以从其字面的相加意思来理解,但同样是这个词组,有时则有它的特别含义或另外的意思。因此,主要还应通过上下文来确定其含义。

【例 622】 Compare this with what happens in the mass production of poultry: there are battery farms, for example, where thousands of chickens live crowded together in one building and are fed on food which is little better than rubbish.

[误译] 把这个与大规模养鸡的情况相比:例如在层架式鸡场里,成千上万只鸡挤在一幢房子里,吃的是稍微比垃圾好一点的东西。

[正译] 把这个与大规模养鸡的情况相比:例如在层架式鸡场里,成千上万只鸡挤在一幢房子里,吃的简直就是垃圾。

[评析] better than 是比较级,有"比……好"的意思,a little better than 可译成"比……稍许好一些"。但是,这句用的是 little better than,是一个固定的词组搭配,作"几乎等于"、"无异于"解。所以不能粗略一看,就把它当作一般的词组理解。要注意有固定意义的词组和只有字面意义的词组的区别。

【例 623】 It is evident that the responsibility of the citizen involves more than just paying taxes to buy defense hardware.

[误译] 很明显,公民的责任是要超过交税,去购买国防武器。

[正译] 很明显,公民的责任不仅仅是在于纳税,让国家购买国防武器。

[评析] more than 看上去是一个比较结构,实际上是一个固定词组,作"不仅仅是"解。例如:I discovered that more than desire and feeling were necessary to write. 我发现要写作,需要的不仅仅是愿望和感情。有时 do more than + v.结构也表示这个意思,例如:

Universities across the nation have decided to do more than talk about the rise in student cheating. 全国各地的大学已决定不仅仅只谈论学生作弊上升。

【例 624】Such work requires more than indomitable will.

[误译] 这项工作所需要的是比坚忍不拔的意志多。

[正译] 这项工作不仅仅需要坚忍不拔的意志。

[评析] 这句的 more than...也作 not only 解, 可译为"不仅仅"。

【例 625】He is not fond of playing chess any more than you are. (= He is no more fond of playing chess than you are.)

[误译] 他不比你更喜欢下棋。

[正译] 他同你一样不喜欢下棋。

[评析] "他不比你更喜欢下棋"的意思是"他喜欢下棋,但不比你更喜欢",有肯定含义,即两人都喜欢下棋,这并不符合原义。原文的意思则是"他不喜欢下棋,如同你不喜欢下棋一样",原句相当于 He is not fond of playing chess just as you are not fond of playing chess,因而译为"他同你一样不喜欢下棋"是正确的,意思是"两个人都不喜欢下棋"。如果要表达"不比你更喜欢下棋",这种意思,英语应用 He is not more fond of playing chess than you are, 或者 He is as fond of playing chess as you are.

【例 626】For example, they do not compensate for gross social inequality, and thus do not tell how able an underprivileged youngster might have been had he grown up under more favorable circumstances.

[误译] 例如,测试并不弥补明显的社会不公;因此它们不能说明一个物质条件差的年轻人,如果在更好的环境下成长的话,会有多大才干。

[正译] 例如,测试并不弥补明显的社会不公;因此它们不能说明一个物质条件差的年轻人,如果在较好的环境下成长的话,会有多大才干。

[评析] 对一个具体的比较级是译成"比较"还是"更"就要看上下文意思。这句上下文很清楚,如果说更好的环境,意味着原来环境已

经比较好了,但原文意思是原先的物质条件是差的。所以这里的 more favorable circumstances 应是"较好的环境",而不是"更好的环境"。例如:Sarah is more ugly than Mary. 这句话有两个意思:一是 Sarah 比 Mary 要难看一些,但并不意味着 Mary 是丑的。另一个意思是 Sarah 比 Mary 更难看,说明两人都丑。可见比较级在中文中可以表达"比较"、"更"两个不同的意思,而英语中只有一个形式。adj + er 也有类似情况,例如:

【例 627】As a result of those immediate measures, and aided by the tremendous effort which they evoked from the these people, we weathered the storm and moved on into calmer waters and a period of economic expansion and financial investments.

[误译] 由于及时采取了措施,由于这些人在这些措施下,做出了巨大的努力为我们提供了帮助,我们经受了风暴,进入了一个更平静的海面,进入了一个经济发展与金融投资的时期。

[正译] 由于及时采取了措施,由于这些人在这些措施下,做出了巨大的努力为我们提供了帮助,我们经受了风暴,进入了一个比较平静的海面,进入了一个经济发展与金融投资的时期。

[评析] 这句如译成"更平静"就不符合原意,因为前面说了刚刚经历过暴风雨,只能说是进入了比较平静的海面。

【例 628】I had always felt a vast distance separating me from the boss. And now I felt closer to him, though still distant.

[误译] 过去我一直感到我和老板之间相隔千里,现在我觉得离他更近了,虽然我们之间还有一定距离。

[正译] 过去我一直感到我和老板之间相隔千里,现在我觉得离他比较近了,虽然我们之间还有一定距离。

[评析] 原先和老板之间有很大的距离,现在应是较近了些,而不是更近了。

【例 629】It was a curious exchange, less a debate than a quarrel between two aggressive men, each of them determined to impress the audience as more peaceful than the other.

[误译] 这是一次奇妙的交谈,是两个好斗的人之间的一场辩论比一

次吵嘴少，双方竭力想使听众觉得自己比对方更爱和平。

[正译] 这是一次奇妙的交谈，与其说是两个好斗的人之间的一场辩论，不如说是一次吵嘴，双方竭力想使听众觉得自己比对方更爱和平。

[评析] 这句前半句的 less...than... 不能译为"比……少"，也可用汉语"与其说……不如说……"来译，但 less...than... 在意义上同 more...than... 相反，例如，more A than B：less B than A，这里的 less a debate than a quarrel：more a quarrel than a debate。由于这句的 less...than... 肯定 than 后面的 quarrel，译成汉语"与其说……不如说……"，不必互换位置。

【例 630】He was less hurt than frightened.

[误译] 他的受伤比惊慌少。

[正译] 他与其说是受伤，不如说是受惊。

[评析] 这句的 less hurt than frightened 换一种说法就是 more frightened than hurt，可译为"与其说……不如说……"。

【例 631】(When word came that the Pentagon planned to shut down a number of obsolete military basis, communities across the US launched pre-emptive strikes against the plan.) The issue had less to do with military utility than with economic survival.

[误译] 这个问题关系到基地的军事使用价值要比关系到基地所在地的经济生存少。

[正译] 这个问题并非关系到基地的军事使用价值，而是关系到基地附近的经济生存。

[评析] less...than 结构一般是表达比较关系，但有时，特别是 less...than... 后面的语法成分是同一词性、同一结构时，往往表示"不是……而是……"的意思。此时的 less...than... 和 more...than... 表达的意思基本一样，只是词序不同：less B than A：more A than B。例如：A skyscraper is less the product of architectural virtuosity than of economic necessity. 摩天大楼与其说是建筑艺术的精湛之作，倒不如说是经济上万般无奈的产物。

【例 632】How the government dealt with that unfolding crisis is a sto-

ry not so much of a failed policy as an administration unprepared for
the aftermath of a war.

[误译] 该政府处理那场不断蔓延的危机的经过,作为一个对一场战
争所带来的结果毫无准备的政府,并不是一项政策的失败。

[正译] 该政府处理那场不断蔓延的危机的经过并不说明政策失败,
而是说明该政府对一场战争所带来的结果缺乏准备。

[评析] 把 as an administration unprepared for... 译成"作为一个……
政府",孤立地看没有错,但是这句的 as 是和前面的 not so much
连在一起的。作为一个固定的词组, not so much...as(but)相当
于 less...than 作"不是……而是……"或"与其说……倒不如说
……"解。

【例 633】This is as much the by-product of his marketing strategy as it
is a deliberate move by the two sides to mend relations.

[误译] 这是他的营销策略的一个副产品,因为它是双方为改善关系
而深思熟虑之后走出的一步。

[正译] 这既是双方为改善关系而深思熟虑之后走出的一步,也是他
的营销策略的一个副产品。

[评析] as much...as 是一个固定的搭配,而原译文却把 as it is a deliberate move 当成一个单独的连词从句,译成了"因为……"。as
much...as 作为一个固定词组,其基本意思是:"既……也……",
"不仅……而且","是……不是"。

【例 634】The oceans do not so much divide the world as unite it.

[误译] 海洋把世界分隔开来没有像把它连接起来多。

[正译] 与其说海洋把世界分隔开来,不如说把它连接起来。

[评析] 如果把这句中的 not so much...as... 逐词译为"海洋把世界
分隔开来没有像把它连接起来多",那就没有正确理解这里的 not
so much...as... 是意义上相互关联的一个固定词组, as 前后嵌入
了 divide the world 和 unite it 两个相应成分,可用汉语"与其说
……不如说……"来译。

第六章　与词义有关的误译

　　除了正确地分析原文的语法结构以外,还必须准确地把握词义。翻译句子首先是对词汇的理解和表达,而英语词汇的多义性又决定了词义理解及其翻译的困难性。所以在分析理解一个词汇的意思时,要同整个句子、整个段落甚至整篇文章联系起来进行通盘考虑。这样才能达到语义确切,句子通顺,文章优美。如果孤立地去理解一个词,往往会出现误译。词的含义是复杂的,它不仅有直接的、表面的、一般的意思,还有引申的、内涵的、特定的含义。一个词的确切含义往往需要由具体的上下文来决定。正如一位语言学家所说的那样:"在新的上下文里使用的每一个词都是新词。"分析一些错译的实例,可以看出,有的译者不求甚解,望文生义,凭主观想象进行翻译。还有一种译者。虽然查了字典,但并不考虑上下文的具体内容,也不认真琢磨有关词语的内在含义;而是将词典上的释义生硬地搬到译文中去。

【例 635】We expressed our gratitude for the outstanding and challenging speech of Mr Smith.

[误译] 我们对史密斯先生杰出而又有挑战性的演说表示感谢。

[正译] 我们对史密斯先生非常出色而又发人深省的演说表示感谢。

[评析] challenging 在这里是现在分词作定语,说明 speech。challenge 一词本意为"挑战",还有"检查"、"引起"、"发人深省"等意义,联系全句它有表示感谢的意思,应译为"发人深省"。

【例 636】He put forward some new ideas to challenge the interest of all concerned.

[误译] 他提出了一些新见解,挑战有关人士的兴趣。

[正译] 他提出了一些新见解,引起了有关人士的兴趣。

[评析] challenge 一词的基本含义是"挑战"。但如果望文生义把 challenge 译成"挑战",则"挑战兴趣"是说不通的。此处只有译出

其深层含义"引起"为好。

【例 637】 None of them challenged the validity of those resolutions.

[误译] 没有一个人挑战那些决议的有效性。

[正译] 没有一个人对那些决议的有效性提出异议。

[评析] challenge 的核心意义是"挑战",但是可以根据上下文语境引申为"产生怀疑"、"重新考虑"、"否认"等等意思。下列例句都需要对 challenge 进行重新审视及推理,译成不同的引申意义。Recent discoveries have challenged their old notions. 新近的发现使他们对旧的想法产生怀疑。/I challenge my own conclusion. 我重新考虑我的结论。/Can he produce evidence in proof to challenge the fact? 他能拿出证据来否认这一事实吗?

　　当然分析词义时一定要通晓词语的搭配,上下文联系,语法特征,如词性、词的单复数、可数不可数、表层词义及深层含义乃至引申含义等去考虑。

【例 638】(... They were unarmed and unprotected, ... knowing perfectly well the special kind of hell ahead.) Still, they went, plugging gamely along.

[误译]……然而,他们像做游戏一样的堵住漏洞,继续向前。

[正译]……然而他们仍然毫不畏惧地奋力向前驶去。

[评析] 原译者完全不考虑上下文的内容。望词生义,硬把"做游戏"和"堵漏洞"拉在一起,使译文完全走了样。这句里的 plug 是"苦干"的意思,gamely 作"雄赳赳地"解,和"做游戏"毫无关系。

【例 639】 Any man who was a man could travel alone.

[误译] 无论是谁,只要是人,就可以单独旅行。

[正译] 任何有胆量的男子汉都可以单独旅行。

[评析] 原译违背了根据上下文来确定词义这一原则。把原文中的第二个 man 完全孤立于全句之外,把原句的意思改得面目全非。第二个 man,显然不是泛指男人,更不是泛指别于动物的人,而是指有勇气的硬汉子。

第一节　一词多义的误译

　　无论哪种语言,都有一词多义的问题。英语尤其如此,在多数情况下一个英语单词往往有好几个,甚至几十个意思,错综复杂。例如 turn 便有二十多个定义,除"转动"以外,还可表示"转折"、"剧目'、"举动"、"值班"、"性情"、"特征"等等,而且这些意思之间有的并无多大关联。同一单词也会因词性不同而产生不问含义,例如名词 spring 常作"春天"、"泉水"、"弹簧"解,而动词 spring 则是"跳跃"的意思。同一名词还会因其可数与不可数,或抽象与具体之分,而产生不同含义。例如 value 作不可数抽象名词用时,意为"价值",但作可数名词用时,其复数形式 values 则意为"准则"。所有这些必然给翻译带来困难。词义对上下文的依赖性较大。如果只记住某个单词的一、两个基本意义,便不分场合,不加区别地套译原文,往往会使译文生硬难懂,甚至歪曲原义。即使是由极简单的词语或词组构成的句子,也必须根据上下文所构成的语言环境确定词义才能弄懂句子的完整意思。例如:Fire!　由于上下文不同,也许是上级下了命令:"开火!"也许是另一个意思:"失火啦!"同样一个 Let me see. 有时是"给我看看",有时是"让我想一想","等一等",所以在大多数情况下都得看上下文所构成的语言环境确定词义。译者必须十分谨慎,要对原文的词义做深入细致的分析,才能准确无误地译出原意。

【例 640】This was the last place the explorers would leave, for it lay riches and natural resources.

[误译] 这是那些探险家最后离开的地方,因为那里蕴藏着财富和自然资源。

[正译] 这是那些探险家最不愿意离开的地方,因为那里蕴藏着财富和自然资源。

[评析] 一般只知道 last 一词有"最后一个"的意思,例如:He is the last to come. 他最后一个来。但是不要忘了英语单词的多义性,由于 last 一词多义,还有其他含义。在本句子里,原句中 last 不是"最后的"意思,而表示"最不适合"或"最不配的"。例如:That is the last thing I should do. 那样的事我才不会干呢。

【例 641】The draft resolution urges the United Nations to send its peace-keeping troops to the region in accordance with the resolution adopted at a special meeting last May.

[误译] 决议草案敦促联合国遵照今年五月特别会议通过的决议，派遣维持和平部队到该地区。

[正译] 决议草案催促联合国按照去年五月特别会议通过的决议，派遣维持和平部队到那个地区去。

[评析] 问题出在 last 这个词上。从时间概念来讲，last 表示"最近过去"的意思，所以 last May 究竟是指"去年五月"，还是"今年五月"，要取决于说这句话的时间。如果是在六月份说的，那么应译成"今年五月"；如果是在四月份说的，译为"去年五月"。本例句摘自联合国大会的一次发言，发言时间是八月份，所以译文应是"今年五月"。

【例 642】The alloys are quite late arrivals for engineers to use.

[误译] 该合金是供工程师们使用的很晚到达的东西。

[正译] 该合金是工程师们使用的新型工程材料。

[评析] 此句英语有两个词是多义词：late 和 arrival 根据上下文，late 只能选用"最近的"一义；arrival 选择"到达的人或物"为宜，但到底是"人"还是"物"，由于与前面的 alloys 相呼应，所以推断出它代表"物"，又根据它与 for engineers to use 有着密切联系，可判定是"工程材料"。如果把这句英语译为"该合金是供工程师们使用的很晚到达的东西"，就误译了原文的意思，至少是意义不明，令人费解。

【例 643】Such gigantic efforts, involving an entire nation's economic and technological resources and utilizing the skills of thousands of scientists and engineers, are widely publicized and become identified as the real purpose of scientific investigation.

[误译] 这样巨大的努力，牵涉到整个国家的经济资源和技术资源，以及利用千千万万科学家与工程师的技能得到了广泛的宣传，并被看成是科学研究的真正目的。

[正译] 这样一些牵涉到整个国家的经济资源和技术资源,以及运用千千万万科学家与工程师技能的巨大成就,并被看成是科学研究的真正目的。

[评析] 许多人一看到 effort 就理解为"努力"。实际上 effort 在许多情况下的释义:成就、成果。是"努力"的意思还是"成就"的意思,从词的用法上看不出,因为作这两个意思解时,都可以是单数或。但是从上下文来看,从它的前面一句提到的 the launching of a manned space vehicle, or the creation of a nuclear weapon(发射有人驾驶的宇宙飞船或制造原子武器)来分析,这里的 effort 应是"成就"的意思。

【例 644】Unhappily, this plentiful general literature about interviewing pays little attention to the journalistic interview.

[误译] 不幸的是,有关面试的许多大量普及性文学不大涉及新闻面试。

[正译] 不幸的是,有关面谈的许多大量一般性文献专著较少涉及新闻采访这一领域。

[评析] literature 是可作"文学"解,但还有一个意思:"关于某一学科或专题的文献"。从这个句子的意思来看,interview 应是"文献",而不是"文学"。interviewing 译成"面试"也不妥。面试主要指企业录取雇员和学校录取学生的口头考核。因此宜用面谈来概括。至于 the journalistic interview 译成"新闻面试"更不对了。和 journalistic 搭配,应译为"新闻采访"。

【例 645】You must remember that we are here to serve the society that we are building a New Society. The bureaucracy bas this rare opportunity to prove it's worth to build a progressive nation.

[误译] 你们必须记住,我们是为社会服务的,我们正在建设一个新社会,这是官僚主义显示其才能,建设一个进步国家的好机会。

[正译] 你们必须记住,我们是为社会服务的,我们正在建设一个新社会,这是全体政府官员显示其才干,建设一个进步国家的好机会。

[评析] bureaucracy 既有"官僚政治、官僚制度"的意思,但还有"全体

政府官员"的意思。如果把它译成"官僚主义",那就与整个句子的
意思不相符。翻译应考虑到整个上下文的逻辑性。

【例646】 There is a definite link between smoking and heart disease
and lung cancer. But this doesn't make you too uncomfortable because you are in good company.

[误译] 抽烟和心脏病以及肺癌的确有联系。但这并不能使人们感
到太大的不舒服,因为你是在一个好的公司里。

[正译] 抽烟和心脏病以及肺癌的确有联系。但这并不能使人们感
到太大的不舒服,因为和你一样抽烟的人很多。

[评析] company 用作可数名词做"公司"、"连队"等解,而用作不可
数名词则是"伙伴"、"伴侣"等意思。句中的 good company 中没有
任何冠词,是不可数名词,故译作"和你一样抽烟的人很多"。如果
按照自己印象最深的、最熟悉的释义去套,就会把后半句译成:"因
为你是在一个好的公司里",这样的意思就和前半句的意思毫不相
干。

【例647】 Samantha has had problems with Elizabeth and Jonathan but
he tried hard to remain in touch with their parents.

[误译] 萨曼塔与伊丽莎白和乔纳森之间已有问题,但他仍竭尽全力
与他们的父母保持接触。

[正译] 萨曼塔与伊丽莎白和乔纳森之间早有纠纷,但他仍竭尽全力
与他们的父母保持接触。

[评析] problem 本意是"问题"、"麻烦",在此句中选用它们都不合
适。译为"纠纷"、"纠葛"较好。

【例648】 From life to death is man's reach.

[误译] 从生到死是人所能达到的。

[正译] 人生历程就是从生到死。

[评析] 此句中的 reach 是个多义词,根据上下文,取其"历程"一义。
所以全句译为"人生历程就是从生到死"。

【例649】 The new principal has no previous experience of school government.

[误译] 这位新校长以前没有学校政府的经验。

[正译] 这位新校长缺乏学校管理的经验。

[评析] government 如果作为一个无语境的词,则具有"政府"、"政治"、"管理"及"支配"等多种语义。对大多数译者来说,一看到 government 会迅速在心理词典中想到其对应词"政府"。因为 government 作"政府"解出现的频率似乎远远高于其他语义。实际上, government 作"管理"解,因为在此它是不可数名词。作"政府"解时为可数名词,其前面应有冠词。之所以出现了误译是因为 government 所处的篇章语境对它作"管理"解的语义所起的抑制作用太弱。在语境效果的作用非常突出的情况下,通常不大可能出现误译现象,

【例 650】 The essence of the mistake was the failure to carry out the principle.

[误译] 错误的实质在于执行该原则的失败。

[正译] 错误的实质在于没有执行该原则。

[评析] failure 作抽象名词时可译为"失败",如 failure is the mother of success,可译为"失败是成功之母",但这句里的 failure 后面接动词不定式 to carry out,用作动作名词,相当于 to fail to carry out,一般可译为"不"、"没有",不直译为"失败"。

【例 651】 Contemporaries were in little doubt about the two crucial economic factors :first , the ripeness of the globalization in economy, and second, the preponderance of the Western economy for good or ill.

[误译] 现代的人对于这样两个关键的经济问题是深信不疑的:一是经济全球化已是瓜熟蒂落,一是西方经济具有压倒优势,且不论其是好是坏。

[正译] 当时人们对于这样两个关键的经济问题是深信不疑的:一是经济全球化已是瓜熟蒂落,一是西方经济具有压倒优势,且不论其是好是坏。

[评析] contemporary 表示"当代的"、"现代的"。如果文中谈的是几十年、几百年前的事,这个"当代"就指几十年、几百年前的"那个时代"。这一点如果不搞清楚,会造成全句理解上的错误:这里的

contemporaries是指上个世纪的人,而不是现代的人。一般情况下,只要句子的意思清楚明白,便没有必要分析每一个单词意义。但如果汉译文句子意思模糊不清,上下文意不连贯时,便应看看是不是有这一方面的问题。

【例652】Last December, the Post first reported that the research was being made in each of those cities, but they refused to confirm the story.

[误译] 去年12月,邮件首先报道研究工作已在那些城市进行,但他们拒绝证实这个故事。

[正译] 去年12月,《邮报》首先报道研究工作已在那些城市进行,但他拒绝证实这条消息。

[评析] 本句需要确定story的词义。story一词有"故事"、"内情"、"身世"、"消息"等意思,在句中是名词,联系句中提到《邮报》的报道,这里story应译为"消息"。Post是确定story词义的关键词,由于Post大写,就应该意识到它是个专有名词,再联系到其后的谓语动词reported"报道",根据这样的语境便能理解story的确切含义。

【例653】The exceptions provided in paragraph(a)arc subject to the following additional provisions.

[误译] 甲款的例外规定还有待于制定下述补充规定。

[正译] 甲款的例外规定应受下列补充规定的约束。

[评析] 在通常情况下,be subject to是"有待于"的意思,但是我们不能见到be subject to就"对号入坐",将它译为"有待于"。它还有许多别的意思,如be subject to colds便是"易患感冒"。be subject to the law of the land则是"受国家法律的管辖"。因此,我们在翻译时要根据上下文对词义做出正确的选择。

【例654】The porch stairs were rotting away. Every time he set his foot on them he felt them give under his weight.

[误译] 门廊的木台阶腐朽了,每当他踩在上面,就觉得那些木板在他的重量下让步。

[正译] 门廊的木台阶渐渐朽了,每逢他踩在上面,就觉得那些木板

经不住他身体的压力,往下塌。

[评析] give 一词在这里是动词不定式作宾补,其汉语对应词是"给予",在词典中还有许多其他意思,其中一个意思是"陷下"、"塌下"。我们从 under his weight 可以判定这里的意思是"身体太重把楼板压塌"。一个人的词语能力是有限的。在翻译中我们可能碰到不认识的词,但较多的是多义词。在这种情况下,我们千万不能想当然,按照自己印象最深,或最熟悉的词义去套。而应利用上下文意思来分析、确定词义。

【例 655】 It seems to me that the time is ripe for the Department of Employment and the Department of Education to get together with the universities and produce a revised educational system which will make a more economic use of the wealth of talent, application and industry currently being wasted on certificates, diplomas and degrees that no one wants to know about.

[误译] 我认为时机已成熟。就业部门和教育部门应同大学携起手来,修正我们的教育制度,使之能把学生的才能、申请及工业都更好地运用于经济方面。而这些才能、申请和工业现在都浪费在无人感兴趣的证书、文凭和学位上。

[正译] 我认为时机已成熟。就业部门和教育部门应同大学携起手来,修正我们的教育制度,使之能比较合理地使用学生的才能、勤奋和刻苦。而现在他们这些才能和努力都浪费在无人感兴趣的证书、文凭和学位上。

[评析] 原译文将 talent, application and industry 译成才能、申请和工业,是对这些词的理解有问题。application 是有"申请"的意思,例如:a letter of application 求职信。但从上下文来看,这句中的 application 显然不作"申请"解,而应是另一个释义:"勤奋刻苦"。例如:If you show application in your studies, you will succeed. 如果你刻苦用功,你就会成功。根据上下文,这里的 industry 应作"勤劳"解。industry 除了作"工业"解,还有一个常用的意思:"勤劳"。例如:A country's greatest wealth is the industry of its people. 一个国家的最大财富就是人民的勤劳。economic 也有误译。

economic 如同 economy,有两个常用的意思,一是"经济的",另一个是"节省的",相当于 economical。根据原文的意思:现在把学生的才干都浪费在追求学位和文凭上,所以 economic 在这里表示"节约的"、"合理的"。例如:Economy is one powerful motive for camping, since after the initial outlay upon equipment, or through hiring it, the total expense can be far less than the cost of hotels. 省钱是野营旅行的一个强大动力,因为开始时付出一笔装备购置费之后,总的花费远比住旅馆的费用少。如果译为"经济是野营旅行的一个强大动力"就不符合原意。所以根据上下文来确定词义是翻译中很重要的原则。

显然,一个词在一句中只能有一个确切的意义,这就是词义的排他性。在翻译实践中,我们必须对词的概念范围加以分析,确定词的语境、地位和作用,从语法上、逻辑上对词义做出恰如其分的判断。

第二节 抽象与具体

英语抽象名词是表示状态或其他抽象概念的名词。英语抽象名词的汉译常常要化抽象为具体,需要增词翻译或者改换说法。例如:tension, complacency, unemployment 这类的抽象名词,译成汉语时应分别在"紧张"后面加上"局势","自满"后面增加"情绪","失业"后面补充"现象",等等。例如:dependence 依赖性;commercialization 商业化;jealousy 嫉妒心理;irregularity 越轨行为;abstraction 抽象化;arrogance 傲慢态度;lightheartedness 轻松愉快的心情等等。

【例 656】The civilization of China is the civilization of longest continuous existence.

[误译] 中华文明是存在最长、从未间断过的一个文明。

[正译] 中华文明是历史最长、其间又从未间断过的一个文明。

[评析] 这里的抽象名词 existence 如果译成"存在",就很不明确。所以要增词翻译,选用"历史"和"从未中断过的一个文明",比较具体易懂。

【例 657】Washington wants to maintain an American presence in that region.

[误译] 华盛顿想在那个地区维持美国的存在。

[正译] 华盛顿想在那个地区维持美国的军事力量。

[评析] presence 有许多释义,作为一个政治术语多被译为"存在"。但在某个地区驻扎部队是"存在",设立领事馆、开办教堂、学校等也叫"存在"。至于"存在"指什么具体内容,应该根据上下文来判断。应该根据上下文提供的信息,译出比较具体的指称。如果上下文中有美国派驻部队的信息,那么这句话就可译为:"华盛顿想在那个地区维持美国的军事力量";如上下文中有美国设立领事馆的信息,这句话可译为"华盛顿想在那个地区维持美国的外交机构";如上下文中出现美国派遣传教士或建立教堂的信息,这句话则应译为:"华盛顿想在那个地区维持美国的宗教机构。"等等。

【例 658】 (In other words, he was not ready to join the team, but if they wanted to call him from time to time, his expertise would be available.) Why such an extraordinary leap, literally overnight, from overt antagonism to qualified accessibility?

[误译] 为什么几乎一夜之间就发生这样一个不寻常的飞跃,从公然对抗变为合格接近了呢?

[正译] 为什么几乎一夜之间就发生这样一个不寻常的飞跃,从公然对抗变为半推半就了呢?

[评析] 英语中有一种比较特殊的表达法,即往往用较抽象的词来表达一个具体的事物。由于抽象名词的词义一般隐晦含混,只有分析上下文的意思,把握抽象名词中蕴含的具体意义,才能译得正确。这句中的 accessibility 是抽象名词,其意义是"可接近"、"可得到"。但根据上下文,accessibility 是指 his expertise would be available(他是愿意提供他的专业知识的)。qualified 在这里不作"合格的"解,应是另外一个意思:"有限制的"、"有保留的"。而"有保留地提供、有保留地得到他的知识",就是"半推半就参加尼克松的竞选"。对抽象名词要分析,设法化抽象为具体,用意义清晰的词语来代意义含混的词语。

【例 659】 The upper society then had not lost its exclusiveness nor its brilliance.

[误译] 当时的上流社会仍焕发着奇光异彩，没有失去它的排外性。

[正译] 当时的上流社会仍焕发着奇光异彩，而且依然壁垒森严，不容下层人涉足。

[评析] exclusiveness 这个抽象名词不好翻译，如果原样直译，译成"没有失去它的排外性"就让人不知所云了。exclusiveness 在本句中的意思是"排他性"、"独家享有"，在这里应当化抽象为具体，将其译为"壁垒森严，不容下层人涉足"。

【例 660】So I bought at my own expense the thinnest vestments I could find, also a heavy one with a warm top coat, because I knew I would encounter extremes of weather.

[误译] 所以我就自己出钱买了一套我能物色到的最薄的衣服，还买了一套厚衣服，带有一件暖和的大衣，因为我知道我会碰到天气的极端。

[正译] 所以我就自己出钱买了一套我能物色到的最薄的衣服，还买了一套厚衣服，带有一件暖和的大衣，因为我知道我会碰到最冷和最热的天气。

[评析] extremes 这个抽象词很难译，如果不采取化抽象为具体的方法，译成"碰到天气的极端"，就让人不知所云了。

第三节　增词翻译

增词翻译是指英汉互译时增词而不增义。一般来说，英语译成汉语时的增词就意味着汉语译成英语时要减词，反之亦然。英译汉中的增词翻译涉及许多方面的问题，这里只讨论其中最主要也是翻译实践中最容易出现误译的问题。原文的逻辑是清楚的，但翻译时句子经过改组或套用成语，有时会造成逻辑不通的文字。用词遣字要注意避免引起误解。英语用词有时很简略，我们要注意照字翻译会不会引起误解，必要时得加些字。例如：the bombardment to cover the landing 掩护登陆的轰炸，最好译作"为了掩护登陆而进行的轰炸"。to show favorable reactions 做出有利的反应，到底对谁有利？

好像不太明确,这一般都是文章中的主人公的立场,因此可译为"做出有利于我的反应"。

【例 661】Men and nations working apart created these problems, men and nations working together must solve them.

[误译] 人们和国家离心离德产生了这些问题:人们和国家同心同德必定能解决这些问题。

[正译] 人与人之间以及国与国之间离心离德产生了这些问题:人与人之间以及国与国之间同心同德必定能解决这些问题。

[评析] 英语复数名词译成汉语,如果不增译一些词,就会引起误解。这句中 men 和 nations 都是复数名词。如果简单地译成"人们"和"国家"不符合原意,而且还容易误解为人们同国家之间离心离德或同心同德。原句中的 men 指"人与人之间",nations 指"国家与国家之间",因此在"人们"和"国家"后面应分别补充"之间"。故此,应在"人"和"国家"之后加上"之间",使句子不仅准确地表达了 men 和 nations 两个词在句中的深层含义,而且读起来也通顺。

【例 662】He wanted to learn, to know, to teach.

[误译] 他渴望博学广闻,喜欢追根穷源,并且好为人师。

[正译] 想学习,增长知识,也愿意把自己的知识教给别人。

[评析] 这一句话虽然不长,但不好译。若直译成"他想学习、知道事情和教学",意思不明晰。因此按照原文的意思,增词翻译。但增词要恰如其分。改正译文增词适当,并未超出原文的内容。原译文的译法增词过了头。

【例 663】He seaized the chance for peace between them.

[误译] 他抓住了他们和解的机会

[正译] 他抓住了实现他们和解的机会

[评析] 译作"实现他们和好的机会",加了"实现"二字。英语中有许多抽象名词译成汉语时都需根据上下文增加一些词尽量使之具体化,即把英语之"虚"化为汉语之"实"。

【例 664】I like your policies of first come, first served.

[误译] 我喜欢你们的先到先接待政策。

[正译] 我喜欢你们执行的先到先接待政策。

235

[评析] 改正译文译作"我喜欢你们执行的先到先接待政策",加了
　　　"执行"二字。在定语里加了一个动词,这符合汉语的表达方式。

【例665】Deflation has now reached unprecedented level.

[误译] 通货紧缩现在已经到了空前的水平。

[正译] 通货紧缩已经发展到了空前严重的地步。

[评析]"到了空前的水平"是逐词死译,不符合汉语的表达习惯,为
　　　避免意义含混,这里需要增词改译为"空前严重的地步"。

【例666】The strength of our financial services sector is well-known.

[误译] 我们的金融服务业的实力是众所周知的。

[正译] 我们的金融服务业以其实力雄厚而著称。

[评析] 为补足语气,连接上下文,同时为避免意义含混,本句增词
　　　"雄厚"。

【例667】Deaths and fasts are provoking bombings, gun battles, riots
　　　and public concerns.

[误译] 死亡和绝食正在引发爆炸事件、枪战及骚乱,以及公众的关
　　　注。

[正译] 死亡和绝食正在引发爆炸事件、枪战及骚乱,从而也引起了
　　　公众的普遍关注。

[评析] 因"引发"不能与"公众关注"搭配使用,所以得增译动词"引
　　　起"。

【例668】His fury was exaggerated.

[误译] 他狂怒得夸张了。

[正译] 他大发雷霆,未免小题大作。

[评析] 这句中 exaggerate 一词可以引申出较广的含义,不能照字面
　　　理解为"被夸张了",而应译为"他大发雷霆,未免小题大作"。

【例669】You may well be surprised.

[误译] 你可能会很惊奇。

[正译] 你感到惊奇,可能是颇有道理的。

[评析]"你可能会很惊奇"是逐词死译,没有体会到原文的实质含义。
　　　"你感到惊奇,可能是颇有道理的"改换说法,将原文的意思译得比
　　　较到位。

第四节　拆分翻译

英语的思维方式与汉语有较大的不同,英译汉时时常需要重新安排句子结构。超出句子负荷力的句子,最好拆开来翻译,分成几个短句。

【例 670】Law enforcement cannot responsibly stand aloof.

[误译] 执法部门不能负责任地对此不闻不问。

[正译] 执法部门如果负责任,就不应该对此不闻不问。

[评析] 本句如果按照英语原文逐字死译,汉译文就有逻辑矛盾,让人不知所云,本句一定要拆开来翻译,才能将原文的真实意义译出。

【例 671】They were then friendly to me and my opinions.

[误译] 他们当时对我和我的看法都是友好的。

[正译] 他们当时对我是友好的,对我的看法是支持的。

[评析] 英文用了 friendly 一字双挑,用之于人,意思是"友好的";用之于事,意思是"支持的"。译成中文时若依照原文句式,就会造成误译。这时需要拆开来译。

【例 672】Administrative measures and words soon poured out the president's office.

[误译] 不久,总裁办公室便发出了大量措施和命令。

[正译] 不久,总裁办公室便制定大量措施,发出了许多命令。

[评析] poured 在这里可以译成"大量发出",但"发出"管得命令,却管不了"措施"。因此只得打破原文形式,拆开来译。有时在原文里两个主语可以共用一个动词,或一个动词可以有两个并列的宾语,而在译文里却不能这样搭配。这就需要根据有关的主语或宾语,选用不同的动词,分别处理了。

第五节　词语搭配

词语的搭配,对翻译中英文的人来说尤其重要,因为中英文在词语的搭配上有同有异。例如有的词与另一个词常常结合在一起,成为一个固定词组。我们要熟悉它的含义,或在有疑问时去查阅一下词典,千万不要照字面揣测。例如 balance 作名词用时,是"天平"、"均衡"的意思。但是 be in the balance 却是"主意未定",(成败)"未决",而不是已经"定下来"的意思。hold in balance 表示悬置未定。而 hold the balance 却是"掌握决定权"的意思。汉语译文中出现词不搭配的现象是由于有些译者将原文语言词组按各词的字面意义进行翻译,结果这些词在译文语言中不能构成词组或意义与原文不同,不但费解而且有时竟不知所云。

【例 673】 That is the official kind of strike.

[误译] 这是一种官方的罢工。

[正译] 这是工会组织的罢工。

[评析] "官方的罢工"定语与其主语词不搭配。official strike 指的是由工会组织或批准的罢工。

【例 674】 Kino hurrying towards the house, felt a surge of exhilaration.

[误译] 基诺朝着他的屋子匆匆地走去,感到一阵涌起的兴奋。

[正译] 基诺加快步伐,兴致勃勃地朝自己的家走去。

[评析] "涌起的"和"兴奋"在汉语中不能搭配使用。

【例 675】 The delta and the narrow Nile Valley to the south make up only 3 percent of Egypt's land but are home to 96 percent of her population.

[误译] 三角洲和南边狭窄的尼罗河河谷只占埃及土地的百分之三,却是百分之九十六的人口的家园。

[正译] 三角洲和南边狭窄的尼罗河河谷只占埃及土地的百分之三,却有百分之九十六的人口住在这里。

[评析] 英语可以说 are home to . . . of her population,但是汉语却没有"是……人口的家园"的表达方式,"是……人口"与"家园"在汉语中不能搭配。这里需要改换主谓搭配意译出其义。

【例 676】 As an early agricultural marketing center, it handled wheat, wool, fruits, and wine.

[误译] 这里是早期的一个农业贸易中心,处理过小麦、羊毛、水果和

酒类。

[正译] 这里是早期的一个农业贸易中心,经营过小麦、羊毛、水果和
　　酒类。

[评析] 本句的动词 handle 的汉语对应词是"处理","买卖",但是前
　　面的主语是以指 an early agricultural center,后面的宾语是 wheat,
　　wool, fruits, and wine,因此, handle 译作"经营"比较恰当。

【例 677】It is very necessary for you to have a sound sleep.

[误译] 你非常需要熟睡。

[正译] 充足的睡眠对你非常需要。

[评析] sound 是个多义词,它的词类就有名词、动词、形容词三种。
　　sound 在本句中是形容词。作为形容词,它的意义也随着搭配关
　　系不同而变化。如 sound body 健全的身体, sound policy 审慎的政
　　策, sound walls 坚固的墙壁, sound fruit 完好的水果,等等。这里
　　它和 sleep 搭配,意为熟睡、充足的睡眠。

【例 678】Nothing came of the enemy's efforts to break through.

[误译] 敌人企图突围,但什么都没来。

[正译] 敌人企图突围,但毫无结果。

[评析] come 一词往往随着搭配的词不同而产生不同的意思。come
　　of 在这里是"是……的结果。"

【例 679】He once again imparted to us his great knowledge, experience
　　and wisdom.

[误译] 他又一次传授了他渊博的学识、丰富的经验和无穷的智慧。

[正译] 我们又一次领受了他渊博的学识、丰富的经验和无穷的智
　　慧。

[评析] great 的释义很多。great 在本句中修饰着三个名词,随着搭
　　配关系的不同,意义也发生变化。汉语中词与词之间也有搭配问
　　题,因此英译汉时要照顾到两种语言的要求。

【例 680】They seemed to have little to eat but bread and some small
　　potatoes they had raised and then placed in a hole in the dirt floor
　　under the bed to keep them from freezing.

[误译] 他们除了面包和一些小土豆外,似乎没有什么东西可吃。这

种土豆是他们自己种的,并放在床下积满灰的地板的一个洞内,以
防冻坏。

[正译] 他们似乎除了面包和一些小土豆外,很少有吃的东西。这些
土豆是他们以前种的,然后放在床下泥地的小洞内,以防冻坏。

[评析] the dirt floor,不是"积满灰的地板"、"肮脏的地板"或者"脏
地"。dirt 有"灰尘"、"肮脏"的意思,但也作"泥土"解。而这里的
上下文很清楚:放在 a hole in the dirt floor 是为了 keep them from
freezing。只有放在泥土的洞内才能防冻伤。dirt 和 floor 搭配,只
能作泥地解,要说肮脏的地板或满是灰尘的地板应用形容词
dirty。之所以有各种错译,就是因为不看上下文,不理解句子的意
思,想当然地翻译。

第六节　词义的褒贬

英汉词汇都有褒贬之分,有些词有其两面性,他们有贬义,有时
也可能不带贬义,是中性词;有褒义,有时也可能不带褒义。例如英
语的 ambitious,用于黑社会或色情行业是贬义,用于正当而又颇有
成就的行业是褒义,用于一般性的商业活动是中性。其中的褒贬含
义相当微妙。在翻译 He is bright and ambitious. 时,根据不同的语
境,可以译为"他很聪明,野心勃勃。"或者译为"他很聪明,有抱负。"
又如:They incited him to go into further investigation. 根据不同的上
下文,可以将这句译为"他们扇动他再作进一步调查。"或者"他们鼓
励他再作进一步调查。"

【例 681】She tried going through the first pages, but Irwin Shaw, for
all his lucidity, could not hold her interest.

[误译] 她试着翻翻第一页,可是作家欧文·萧写得过于浅白直露,难
以引起她的兴趣。

[正译] 她翻了翻前几页,虽然欧文·萧的文笔明白晓畅,可她还是看
不进去。

[评析] Irwin Shaw 是美国当代名作家。lucidity(明白,明朗)在原文
是褒义,应为"明白易懂",原译文"浅白直露"含有贬义。原译文没

有正确理解"for all..."（尽管，虽然）的意思。

【例682】We had been conferring with our allies on the crucial question of whether and when the island should be invaded.

[误译] 我们已经同我们的盟国商谈了是否入侵该岛及何时入侵的紧要问题。

[正译] 我们已经同我们的盟国商谈了是否进攻该岛及何时进攻的紧要问题。

[评析] invasion, invaded 一般指"入侵"，是贬义；但也可以用作"进攻"，无贬义。这句主语是 we, 谈自己一方当然不会使 invasion, invaded 带有贬义。

第七节　中文语法

我们用中文写作时，自行造句，常常由于文字根底较浅 或粗心大意而造成语病。翻译时，出现语病的可能性更大，这是可以理解的。翻译是以英文句子为原文，照着英文意思和形式造中文句子；中英文语法不同，表现方法不同，英语句子往往又是冗长、复杂，或者是生疏的句型，因此很容易译出病句。或是照顾了这一头，照顾不了那一头；或是弄拧了关系，摆错了位置；或者语无伦次，令读者不知所云。

【例683】And now they persisted in their fury, undaunted by the punishment and indifferent to the repentance of their comrades.

[误译] 目前他们仍然满腔怒火，惩罚吓不倒他们，对于他们同伴的悔过表现无动于衷。

[正译] 目前他们仍然满腔怒火，不怕惩罚，对于他们同伴的悔过表现无动于衷。

[评析] 整个一句话的主语 they（他们），他们"满腔怒火"，"不怕惩罚"，"无动于衷"。"不怕惩罚"若改为"惩罚吓不倒他们"，"他们"从主格变为宾格，语法就乱了。

【例684】The rabble was slaughtered till the passion and the light waned.

[误译] 乱民们遭到屠杀,直到天色和热劲衰退以后才告结束。

[正译] 乱民们遭到屠杀,直到天色快黑,杀人者的热劲过去以后,屠杀才告结束。

[评析] 这一句话是被动语态。从文义看,the passion 显然不是乱民们的热劲,而是杀人者的热劲。第二种译法有语病,造成相反的意思。

【例 685】 When the news reached him, perturbed more by the disgrace of his own men than by the success of his business rivals, he resorted to a new measure.

[误译] 当他听到这个消息时,使他感到不安的与其说是竞争对手的胜利,毋宁说是他自己的部下的不光彩的表现,于是他采取了新措施。

[正译] 当他听到这个消息时,他感到不安的与其说是竞争对手的胜利,毋宁说是他自己的部下的不光彩的表现,于是他采取了新措施。

[评析] 这里不能加这个"使"字,否则全句便没有主语,而且语态上也不统一:一会儿"使他如何如何",一会儿又"采取了什么什么"。

【例 686】 He had endeared himself to the higher and the lower orders by his affection for the chase, the banquet, and the other favorite pastimes.

[误译] 由于他喜欢狩猎、宴饮和喜爱其他娱乐而取得了好感。

[正译] 他由于喜欢狩猎、宴饮和喜爱其他娱乐而取得了好感。

[评析] "他由于"和"由于他"大不一样。有了"他由于",全句才有了主语;若改为"由于他",便没有动作的执行者即句子的主语了。
有时中文语法倒是不错,但是文理不太通顺。究其原因,汉译文没有真正理解原文的思想,只是紧跟原文的形式,逐词死译,达不到英汉交流的目的。

【例 687】 At this, he flung himself back in his chair with a gesture of incredulous astonishment.

[误译] 对于这一点,他颓然使自己跌入座椅中,带有一种惶惑不解的吃惊姿态。

[正译] 说到这里,他猛地往椅背上一靠,做出一种惶惑不解的吃惊
姿态。

[评析] at this, 从上下文看, 是"说到这里"的意思。flung himself
back in his chair 若译成"颓然使自己跌入座椅中",到底是怎样的
动作呢? 这两处误译都是由于没有弄清楚英文意思,译成中文后
又不作仔细推敲造成的。with 译为"带有",译得太死板。

【例 688】Once again, he wished to weaken the text, in the end an
electronic mail telegram only fairly satisfactory from my point of
view was dispatched.

[误译] 他再一次要求把电文的语气放低一点,因此最后发出的只是
相当满足我的意见的电子邮件。

[正译] 他再一次要求把电文的语气放低一点,因此最后发出的只是
我认为还算可以的电子邮件。

[评析] only fairly satisfactory 只是还算满意。从上下文看,应译为
"只是还算符合要求",因为作者的语气显然是不满意的。from my
point of view 从我的观点看来, 或"我认为"。这两者合并起来说,
若译成"只是相当满足我的意见",意思颇为费解。

【例 689】Their language was almost unrestrained by any motives of
prudence.

[误译] 他们的言论几乎不受任何深思熟虑的动机的约束。

[正译] 他们几乎爱讲什么就讲什么,全然不考虑什么慎重不慎重的
问题。

[评析] 紧跟原文形式译出的汉译文往往是拗口而又费解的句子,原
文的思想内容和生动风格都不复存在。

第八节 词序误译

英语、汉语都讲究词序。英语中的顺序不能照搬成汉语的词序。

【例 690】It is said that Marco Polo personally visited six Sumatran
kingdoms.

[误译] 据说马可波罗曾亲自访问过六个苏门答腊岛上的王国。

[正译] 据说马可波罗曾亲自访问过苏门答腊岛上的六个王国。

[评析] 原译文的译法表达的意思是:这些王国在六个苏门答腊岛上,他都访问了。这不符合原文的意思。

【例 691】All the activities of the men were exposed.

[误译] 所有这些人的活动都被揭露出来了。

[正译] 这些人的所有活动都被揭露出来了。

[评析] 误译指的是"所有间谍",毫无例外,而不是间谍的"所有活动"。这不是原文的意思, all 在原文中修饰的是 the activities, 而非 the spies。

【例 692】They are top newspaper editors from African countries.

[误译] 他们是来自非洲国家的第一流报纸的编辑。

[正译] 他们是来自非洲国家的第一流的报纸编辑。

[评析] 这句的形容词 top 不是修饰紧跟在它后面的名词 newspaper, 而是修饰 newspaper editors 这个词组,组成的一个复合名词。然而, 在 top secret information (绝密情报)中, top 修饰 secret, top secret 一起修饰 information, 而不是 top 修饰 information。

【例 693】Big city mayors throughout the country are looking carefully at the crisis besetting the nation's most populous district.

[误译] 整个国家各个城市的市长大人们正在密切注视笼罩这个国家的人口最稠密地区的危机。

[正译] 整个国家各大城市的市长正在密切注视笼罩这个国家的人口最稠密地区的危机。

[评析] 这句的形容词 big 显然并不修饰 mayors, 而是修饰 city, 而且是 big city 一起修饰 mayors, 意思是"大城市市长"。

【例 694】The ambassador was a skillful English-speaking diplomat.

[误译] 这位大使是个英语讲得很熟练的外交家。

[正译] 这位大使是个能讲英语的熟练的外交家。

[评析] 这句的形容词 skillful 不是修饰 English-speaking, 而是修饰 diplomat, 因为形容词一般只修饰名词,不能修饰形容词,只有副词才可以修饰形容词。

【例 695】A further continuing and thus far insurmountable problem has been descending in technological innovation in the industry.

[误译] 技术改进的减少始终是今后继续存在,因而是远远不可解决的一个问题。

[正译] 技术改进的减少始终是今后继续存在、而目前无法解决的一个问题。

[评析] 这句的副词 far 从形式上看也可修饰它后面的形容词 insurmountable,但意义上与它前面的 thus 有关,这里的 thus far 是个固定词组,作 to the point 解,可译为"目前"或"至今"。

【例 696】At Beijing University later he studied biology.

[误译] 在北京大学他后来学习生物。

[正译] 他后来在北京大学学习生物。

[评析] 这句的副词 later 不是修饰它后面的 studied,而是修饰它前面的 at Beijing University。

【例 697】No other man ever stooped to flatter her so much.

[误译] 任何人对她也不会像他那么曲意奉承。

[正译] 任何人也不会像他对她那么曲意奉承。

[评析] 这句话译成中文时容易搞乱关系:到底是对"她"还是对"他"曲意奉承。原文的是意思清楚的。

第九节 词义引申

单词的词义并不总是能在词典中一查就得。即使是最详尽的词典,其释义也不是完备无遗的,它只是提供最基本的释义,让使用者去运用、引申、衍化。只要符合这个词的基本意义,尽可以千变万化,以使文从字顺,丰富多彩,生动活泼。分析词义时一定要通晓词语表层词义及深层含义乃至引申含义等去考虑。英文常用词,绝大部分为多义词,极为复杂。词典给出了众多的释义,是我们选择的依据。但需结合上下文的文意仔细推敲选择

【例 698】The board of directors has been seized of the question since December 1986.

[误译] 自一九八六年十二月以来,董事会一直被这一问题所纠缠。

[正译] 董事会从一九八六年十二月以来就一直受理这个问题。

[评析] 英语词汇用在不同场合,可以有不同的引申意义,引申意义有贬、褒之分。本句的 seize 根据上下文是褒义的引申,因而应译为"受理"。

【例 699】 This book consists of my recollections of a man with whom I was thrown into close contact at long intervals.

[误译] 这本书包含我对一个至交的回忆,但是我同他要隔很长一段时间才能见一次面。

[正译] 这本书追叙我偶然结识一个人。我和他虽然比较接近,但是每次见面都要相隔很长一段时间。

[评析] 判断词的引申意义还要考虑原文作者的意图。人们一般用 come into contact 或 establish contact 来表示"建立联系",而作者偏偏使用动词 throw,而且是被动语态,可见是有其用心的。略加分析,我们不难发现,作者使用 throw,一词,是为了向读者表明他与书中主人公只是萍水相逢,因此译文不能用"至交",而是"偶然结识"。这样才正确表达了作者的意图。

【例 700】 The financial implications of this resolution remain to be defined.

[误译] 这一决议的财政含义仍然要被确定。

[正译] 本决议所涉及的财政问题尚待确定。

[评析] 本句里的 implication 一词由动词 implicate 变来,而 implicate 既可以是 to imply(包含)的意思,又可以是 to involve(涉及)的意思,如果将 implication 译为"含义"就与上下文不符。

第十节　辨清词性

英语中的一个词,往往可以分别属于几种不同的词类。词性不同,在句中的作用也必然不同。正确判断词性对理解词语的意义起着决定的作用。英语中的一个词,往往可以分别属于几个词类。例如 discontent,意思都是"不满",但它可以用作名词、动词、形容词。有些词的词类更多,作不同词性时,意思也有所不同。如 like 可以用作动词、名词、形容词、副词、介词、连词。用作动词表示"喜欢";用作名词表示"同样的人或事";用作介词表示"像"、"如"等。词性不同,在句中的作用也不同,因而意思也必然不同。例如:Workers can fish,如把 can 看做助动词,作"能够"解,把 fish 看成原形动词,作"捕鱼"、"钓鱼"解,全句意思就为"工人们能够捕鱼"。但是如把 can 看成谓语动词,作"把……装罐"解,把 fish 看做名词,作"鱼"解,全句就译为"工人们把鱼制成罐头"。有些词虽然从其形式上能判断它们的词性,但在句中的功能不同,意思也会发生变化。如-ed 可以构成过去分词,也可以构成过去时、过去完成时;-ing 可以构成现在分词、动名词,也可以构成现在或过去进行时。在 Flying airplanes can be dangerous,如把 flying 看做动名词,句子意思就是:驾驶飞机很危险。但是如把 flying 看做现在分词,修饰 airplanes,句子就译为:正在飞行的飞机很危险。因此正确判断词性对于理解词语的意义乃至全句的意义起着决定性的作用。

　　一个词,由于其词性不同,在句中的位置可以是不同的,与其搭配的词也可以是不同的。例如,like 在主语后,就是动词:I like her;在形容词后,就是名词:We share the same likes;在谓语后就是介词:You must do like this,等等。因此,利用其语法特征,往往可以确定词性,继而确定词义。

【例 701】His parents were dead against the trip.

[误译] 他的双亲为了反对这次旅行死了。

[正译] 他的双亲坚决反对这次旅行。

[评析] 如果把这句中的 dead 看做形容词,势必把全句误译为"他的双亲为了反对这次旅行死了"。其实这里的 dead 是副词,修饰介词短语 against the trip,不作"死"解,相当于 completely,意思是"完全地",这里可译为"坚决"。又如 This substance could kill deadly bacteria.英语形容词 + ly 一般构成副词,但 deadly 是个例外,它是形容词,作"致命的"解,修饰 bacteria,全句译为"这种药物能杀死致命的细菌。"

【例 702】Such a feat requires a perfect adjustment and timing of all the apparatus employed.

[误译] 要做到这点,所有使用的仪器的调节和时间必须精确无误。

[正译] 要做到这点,所有使用的仪器的调节和定时必须精确无误。

[评析] 动名词 timing 和名词 time 的含义不同:名词 time 可译为"时间";但动名词 timing 作"确定时间"解。又如 doctoring and nursing,不能译为"医生和护士",应译为"医疗和护理"。

【例 703】 Drive carefully on that road in bad weather, it's very winding.

[误译] 气候恶劣的情况下,在那条路上开车要小心,因为风非常大。

[正译] 那条路弯弯曲曲的,天气不好的时候开车可得小心。

[评析] 本句 winding 一词由 wind 变化而来,但不是名词 wind,而是动词 wind,而且在意义上同"风"根本没有一点关系。严格地讲,这两个 wind 是两个同形异义词,一个是我们所熟悉的"风",读作[wind],另一个则是"蜿蜒",读作[waind]。"刮风"是 windy,不是 winding。

【例 704】 The volume of trade has increased tremendously to the advantage of both countries

[误译] 贸易额增加得很大,这使两国都有好处。

[正译] 两国间的贸易有很大的增加,这使双方都受益。

[评析] 为了使译文通顺,有时可以转换词类。在这里,动词 increase 被译成了名词,副词 tremendously 译成了形容词,名词 advantage 译成了动词,都是出于译文表达的需要。

【例 705】 Here I had social life at all levels but privacy when I chose.

[误译] 在这里,我除了没有自己选择的私人生活以外,有各方面的社交生活。

[正译] 在这里,我有各方面的社交生活,但需要时也有自己选择的私人生活。

[评析] but 可以作连词,也可以作介词(还可以作副词)。从形式上看,这句中的 but 用作连词和介词都讲得通。如果用作连词,but 后面省略了 I had,意思如改正译文;如果用作介词,but 作"除了(没有)……以外"解,译文变为"……我除了没有自己选择的私人生活以外,有各方面的社交生活"。这样的疑问逻辑上有问题,能

有各方面的社交生活,就应该有自己选择的私人生活。这句的 but 是连词,后面省略了 I had。

【例 706】Under the law of competition, the factories of factoriesthousands is forced into the strictest economies, among which the rates paid to labor figure prominently.

[误译] 在竞争的法则下,上万人的工厂不得不实行一些最严厉的节约措施,其中主要的钱付给工人了。

[正译] 在竞争的法则下,上万人的工厂不得不实行一些最严厉的节约措施,其中付给工人的那部分费用占很大一部分。

[评析] 把 figure 看做名词,作"人物"解,在结构上有两点说不通。其一是,如果这里的 figure 作"人物"解,应是可数名词,而句中的 figure 既不是复数,前面又没有冠词,没有可数名词的语法特征。其二是,如把 figure 看做名词,就是把句中 paid 看做谓语动词了。但主句用的是现在时,定语从句里为什么用"过去时"呢? 而且 pay 的用法是:sb pay sb, 或者 sth is paid to sb, 而没有 sth pay to sb 的用法。因此句中的 paid 不具备谓语动词的条件。实际上, paid 是一个过去分词,修饰 rates。真正的谓语动词是 figure。figure 可用作动词,有"占重要位置"解的意思。例如: Agriculture figures prominently in the economy of Africa. 农业在非洲经济中占很重要的位置。

【例 707】He thought that directly directors of the company confidence in the chief executive officer declined, the financial structure would be in danger.

[误译] 他认为董事对首席执行官信心的直接下降,其财政结构就会出现危机。

[正译] 他认为一旦董事对首席执行官的信心下降,公司的财政结构就会出现危机。

[评析] 把 directly 看成副词,修饰动词 declined,似乎意思也过得去。但这样分析后,语句就出了问题:后面一句 her financial structure would be in danger 和前面一句之间就缺少了连词联系,成了病句。实际上这里的 directly 正是连词,而不是副词,它相当于 as soon as, 作"一……就"解。例如：Directly the teacher came in everyone was quiet. 老师一走进教室，大家就都安静了下来。

【例 708】All humanity in the long run would benefit through having the influence of the advanced culture extended and scattered peoples united.

[误译] 从长远来看，如果能把先进文化的影响扩展并分散到世界各地，人们团结起来，那么人类最终会从中受益的。

[正译] 从长远来看，如果能把先进文化的影响扩展开来，使分散的人们团结在起来，那么人类最终会从中受益的。

[评析] 按照原译 united 是一个谓语动词。但是作"团结"、"联合"解时，unite 一般是及物动词，也就是说，从结构上看，句子应当是 scattered Germanic peoples were united under one rule。但这里没有 were，因此 united 不像谓语动词。实际上，仔细分析全句，就会看到，全句是一个 have sth done 的结构。united 和 extended 一样，都是这个结构中的过去分词：having the habitat… extended 和 having scattered Germanic peoples united。句中的 scattered 虽是过去分词，但只是修饰 Germanic peoples。

　　分析句子结构和词的本身用法对判断词性起着关键作用。词性的分析，离不开句子结构的分析。是句子结构决定了某个词的词性。

第十一节　翻　译　腔

　　翻译腔有种种表现：用词造句生硬，呆板，重复，不自然，或把简单的句子译得很绕口，有时又喜欢套用固定格式，"因为……所以"、"虽然……但是"、"当……的时候"、"有鉴于……"、"就……而言"、"正如我们看到的那样"一大套，或者在很长的定语之前硬加上"那种"二字，千句一型，千篇一律，把英语原文译成得苍白僵硬，淡而无味的汉译文。这样的译文不自然、不流畅，但能看懂，读起来略感别扭。主要是由于不符合译文语言的语言习惯。我们在翻译时要力戒翻译腔，译文带有洋味，恐怕是难免。外国人写的文章用词造句，所用的形象、比喻、成语以至整个文章的风格都跟中国人写的不一样。

但是,舍弃合适而流畅的中文不用,而硬要仿照英文格式翻译出既不符合汉语规范,这样不符合中国人的表达习惯。译者应讲求全句的平衡、协调,追求流畅、自然、简洁的汉译文。产生翻译腔的根本原因是不同语言表达方式不同。人们用语言表达一种思想,必须使用一些词语。用某些词语来表达某种思想,必须符合语言的习惯,才能为人们所接受。在语内交流中只使用一种语言,对交流双方,即信息发出人和信息接受人来说都是本族语。受过一些教育,有一定文化的人,都不会说出或写出不合乎语言习惯的话。但在语间交流过程中,必须接触两种语言:原文语言和译文语言。同一个意思,原文语言的表达方式往往和译文语言不同。如汉语叫"百货商店",英语则叫department store。说"部门商店"不符合汉语习惯。同样,说 a hundred-goods store 也不符合英语习惯。这两种说法均不能为使用该语言的读者所接受。因此,翻译时必须作一些调整,将原文语言的表达方式换用符合译文语言习惯的表达方式,才能为译文语言读者所接受。否则,就会出现翻译症。下面例句译文读起来别扭,原因就在译者完全按原文语言表达方式进行翻译。

【例 709】Mr Nicholas invited me to join him at dinner in his villa. "Let us make it a family affair," he said.

[误译] 尼古拉斯先生请我到他的别墅和他一同进餐。他说,"让我们像一个家庭那样来吃饭。"

[正译] 尼古拉斯先生请我到他的别墅和他一同进餐。他说,"让我们来一次家常便饭。"

[评析] "像一个家庭那样来吃饭",就是翻译腔,说话呆板,不自然,文绉绉的,但翻译得并不恰当。

【例 710】It is a small, old-fashioned but important port.

[误译] 它是一个小的、老式的但很重要的港口。

[正译] 它是一个老式的小港,但很重要。

[评析] 原译文的译法字、句都没有错,也符合中文文法,但读起来不顺口,不自然,相比之下改正译文干净利索。

【例 711】The telephone announced that the supervision of the building must see me at once and was on his way. He arrived in unusual per-

251

turbation.

[误译] 电话里宣称,施工监理必须马上来同我会见,而且已在途中。他在一种不平常的张惶状态下来到。

[正译] 有电话来,说施工监理马上要来见我,而且已在途中。大使来时,神色很为不安。

[评析] "宣称","马上来同我会见","在一种不平常的张惶状态下来到",这些话很不自然,是典型的翻译腔。

【例 712】 We were told that the new general manager was going to speak to us.

[误译] 我们被告知说新来的总经理要跟我们讲话。

[正译] 我们听说新来的总经理要跟我们讲话。

[评析] we were told 本可以译成中文中相同的意思:"我们得知"、或"我们听说"、"有人告诉我们","我们获悉"。原译文也许是想用一种新的表现方法,但是很少有人能接受这种表达方式。

【例 713】 He is so arrogant that no one will keep company with him.

[误译] 他是如此狂妄自大,以致谁也不愿意与他交往。

[正译] 他很狂妄自大,谁也不愿意与他交往。

[评析] so...that 在字典里及语法书里都释为"如此……以致"、"如此……使得",我们可未能过多地应用这个公式,弄成不中不西的译文。

【例 714】 The study found that non-smoking wives of men who smoke cigarettes face a much greater than normal danger of developing lung cancer. The more cigarettes smoked by the husband, the greater the threat faced by his non-smoking wife.

[误译] 这项研究发现抽烟男子的不抽烟妻子患肺癌的危险比一般人大得多,丈夫烟抽得越多,其不抽烟妻子面临的威胁越大。

[正译] 这项研究表明,妻子不抽烟丈夫抽烟,妻子得肺癌的危险性比一般人大得多。丈夫抽的烟越多,妻子受到的威胁也就越大。

[评析] 原文中有 non-smoking wives of men who smoke cigarettes,译文就用了"抽烟男子的不抽烟妻子"这种不符合汉语表达习惯的词句,使人看了很不舒服。应该根据原文含义,按译文语言的习惯重

新表达。这正是翻译的技巧所在。也只有这样才不至于出现翻译腔。

【例 715】He is too wise not to understand such things.

[误译] 他太聪明了,以致不能不懂这样的事情。

[正译] 他很聪明,能懂得这样的事情。

[评析] too...to 表示"太…以至不", too...not to 表示"太……以至不能不",这是字典里的释义,译者要根据这种意思灵活翻译。要尽量避免译得生硬呆板,翻译腔十足。

【例 716】It noted that being overweight has been linked to sickness and death from such diseases as high blood pressure, diabetes and heart disease.

[误译] 它指出,过胖与疾病及诸如高血压和糖尿病引起的死亡有关。

[正译] 报告指出,肥胖容易引起疾病,容易导致由高血压、糖尿病和心脏病等引起的死亡。

[评析] 原译者的译文完全按原文句子结构,而且用了不符合汉语习惯的长定语。使读者十分费解。一个词语或句子可有多种译法。意思虽然相同,但有合乎中文习惯的,有不合中文习惯的。中文的语法修辞就是一种语言实际。进行再认识时,要善于联系语言实际,从多种译法中选用中国人喜闻乐见的形式,就会增加译文的感染力。要摆脱翻译腔就是思索时越过文字,进入实境,想一想中国人习惯的说法是什么,改变思维习惯是做好翻译工作的首要条件。例如:the most favorable situation 最有利的形势→大好形势/the best opportunity 最好的机会→大好时机

第十二节　望文生义

望文生义是翻译中最大的敌人。所谓望文生义就是对句子中某个词语,或某一个结构不仔细辨认,不仔细分析,而是想当然,或凭着一知半解,对生疏、不认识的词语和结构妄加推测,由于词的拼法或句子结构十分相近,而把此词错当成那词,把此结构错当成那结构,

结果造成误译。

一、派生词的误译

英语中有很多词都是从某一词根派生出来的。例如 exhaustible, exhausting, exhaustion, exhaustive, exhaustibility, exhaustively 等等,都是以 exhaust 派生出来的。但是派生出来的词,意思并不总是相同的,例如:exhaustible 作"可耗尽的"解,exhausting 则主要作"使人筋疲力尽的"解,exhaustive 则主要指"详尽彻底的"。因此不能望文生义,想当然。发现意思不对头,就要查上下文。

【例 717】Hers (the world she described) is the drawing-room, and people talking, and by the many mirrors of their talk revealing their characters.

[误译] 她的世界是画室和画室中闲聊的人们,他们的谈话犹如一面面镜子反映出他们各自的性格特征。

[正译] 她的世界是客厅和客厅中闲聊的人们,他们的谈话犹如一面面镜子反映出他们各自的性格特征。

[评析] 把 drawing-room 译成"画室"是典型的望文生义。drawing 是作"绘画"解,drawing paper, drawing table, drawing board 都分别作"画图纸"、"绘图台"、"画图板"解。但不能因此就推理 drawing-room 是画室。实际上,drawing-room 和画室根本没有联系。它表示客厅、起居室等。

【例 718】A shy, retiring man known to his own Columbia University students as a dull lecturer, he had the brilliance of mind that made him the teacher of his time, respected by presidents and philosophers alike.

[误译] 他是一个怕羞,即将退休的人。在他的哥伦比亚大学的学生们看来,他是一个令人乏味的教师。然而他极其聪明,智慧过人,这使他成为当时那个教师,深受各大学校长和哲学家的尊敬。

[正译] 他是一个怕羞,性情孤独的人。在他的哥伦比亚大学的学生们看来,他是一个令人乏味的老师。然而他极其聪明,智慧过人,这使他成为当时最杰出的教师,深受各大学校长和学者们的尊敬。

[评析] retire 和 retirement 都有"退休"的意思,但是,不能因此就推断此处的 retiring 是"将要退休的"意思。当 retiring 和人搭配时根本没有退休的意思,而是"沉默寡言"的意思。句中的 the 一般是起限定作用。但不能以此类推,每个 the 都是限定词。本句的 the 是起强调作用,修饰人和事物时有"最典型","最理想"、"最重要"等意思。所以原句如果把 retiring man 译成"即将退休的人",把 make him the teacher 译成"使他成为那时老师",整个句子的意思就相差太大了。所以,这里的 the teacher of his time,应译为"当时最杰出的教师"。

【例 719】Secondly we embarked on a reasoned policy to ensure steady economic growth.

[误译] 第二,我们采取了合理的政策,以保证经济的稳步发展。

[正译] 第二,我们采取了经过深思熟虑的政策,以保证经济的稳步发展。

[评析] 这句中的 a reasoned policy 既不能译为"合理的政策",也不能译为"推理的政策"。现在分词 reasoning 作"推理的"解,reasonable 作"合理的"解。这里的 reasoned 是过去分词,作"经过思考的"、"经过研究的"解,所以译为"经过深思熟虑的"。

【例 720】They didn't hear the two people coming down the gully path, Dad and the pretty girl with the hard, bright face like a china doll's.

[误译] 他们没听见沟底小道上走来两个人,是老爸和他那漂亮的女人。她的脸蛋又冷又艳,活像一个中国娃娃。

[正译] 他们没听见沟底小道上走来两个人,是老爸和他那漂亮的女人。她的脸蛋又冷又艳,活像一个瓷娃娃。

[评析] China, Chinese 都和中国有关,但不能由此推想 china 也作"中国"解。当 China 大写时,是作"中国"解,例如:China tea 中国茶/Chinatown 中国城;但是小写 china 根本没有中国的意思,而是作"瓷器"解,例如:china shop 瓷器店/blue china 青瓷。

【例 721】Light industrialism itself has actually gone through many successive stages of development.

[误译] 轻工业本身实际上已经历了发展的许多成功阶段。

[正译] 轻工业本身的发展实际上已连续经历了许多阶段。

[评析] succeed 是动词"成功", success 是名词"成功", successful 是形容词, 作"成功的"解, 因此就推断 successive 也作"成功的"解。实际上 successive 和成功根本没有关系, 它的基本意思是"连续的"。在翻译中, 类似的被误译词还有 respective (各自的), considerate (体贴的), exhaustive (彻底的), 往往被想当然地译为"尊敬的"、"考虑的"和"疲劳的"。

【例 722】 This seems mostly effectively done by supporting a certain amount of research not related to immediate goals but of possible consequence in the future.

[误译] 这一点看来可非常有效地被解决, 通过支持与目前目标无关的科研, 但在将来有可能的后果。

[正译] 给某些与眼前目标无关但将来可能产生影响的科研的支持, 看来通常能有效地解决这一问题。

[评析] 原文的 of possible consequence in the future 修饰的是 research, 是 not related to immediate goals 的并列成分, 而不是 of research 的并列成分。对 mostly 也有理解错误。mostly 与 most 的意思是不一样的, 例如: In general, the tests work most effectively when the qualities to be measured can be most precisely defined and least effectively when what is to be measured or predicted can not be well defined. 一般地说, 当所要测定的特征能很精确地界定时, 测试最为有效; 而当要测定或预测的东西不能明确地界定时, 测试的效果则最差。两个句子的 most effectively 和 mostly effectively 的意思是不同的。most 是副词, 作"最"、"非常"、"十分"解, most effectively 表示"最为有效"。mostly 虽然也是副词, 但是没有"最"、"非常"的意思, 而表示"主要地", "通常地"。mostly 也不是修饰 effectively, 而是修饰 seems。原译文是把 mostly 当成了 most 的意思, 认为 mostly 和 most 表达的意思一样。这类错误相当多, 把 nearly (几乎) 当作 near (接近); 把 mighty (非常) 当作 high (高); 把 hardly (几乎不) 当作 hard (努力地)。

【例 723】Power can be transmitted over a great distance with practically negligible loss if it is carried by electric current.

[误译] 实际上损耗极微地损耗把它送到很远的地方去。

[正译] 用电流输送动力,几乎能以微不足道的损耗把它送到很远的地方去。

[评析] practical 表示"实际上",而 practically,在很多情况下是"几乎"的意思。

二、错看近形词

英语中有许多词,两词之间只相差一两个字母。由于粗枝大叶和学识不足而将原文本来正确,甚至简单的词汇搞错。例如:ingenuously(坦率地),ingeniously(巧妙地);illegible(难以辨认的)eligible(符合条件的);literacy(识字),literary(文学上的);等等。把 ordinance 误当 ordnance 而译为"大炮",把 eager 误作 eagle 译为"鹰"等等低级错误,就有点说不过去。这些词拼写极其相近,往往使译者错看。因此在翻译中仔细认真很重要,意思稍有不对,应核查原文,加以辨认。

【例 724】The soldiers, while requiring far to luxurious logistical support, put up a nice fight; he was fresh well-fed, and unscarred by battle.

[误译] 这些士兵虽然需要过于奢侈的后勤支持,但是进行了顽强的战斗,他们精神饱满,营养充足,并没被战争所吓倒。

[正译] 这些士兵虽然需要过于奢侈的后勤支持,但是进行了顽强的战斗,他们精神饱满,营养充足,还没受到战争的创伤。

[评析] 原译文把 unscarred 和 unscared 两个词混淆了。尽管两个词只差一个字母 r,但意思完全不同,unscarred 表示"未留下伤痕",而 unscared 表示"未被吓倒"。之所以看错,原因之一是粗心,另一原因,文章的内容诱导译者的错误:unscared by battle"未被战争吓倒",和原文意思能对上。因此很容易把 unscarred 错看成 unscared。

【例 725】Each day is a holiday, and ordinary holidays when they come are grudged as enforced interruptions in an absorbing vocation.

[误译] 每一天都是节假日,而当真正的假日来到时,却遭到他们抱怨,认为它们强行打断了他们正在享受的假期。

[正译] 每一天都是节假日,而当真正的假日来到时,却遭到他们抱怨,认为它们强行打断了他们的有趣工作。

[评析] vocation 是"工作"的意思,vacation 表示"假日",两词只差一个字母,而这两词的不同意义在这个句子中又似乎都讲得通。尤其句中有 ordinary holidays,这样很容易把 absorbing vocation 看成 absorbing vacation,和 ordinary holidays 形成同义对照。

【例 726】The development of literacy, the acquisition of information, and the problem-solving of beginners differ in degree rather than in kind from the mental activities of experts.

[误译] 初学者文学上的发展,信息的获取以及问题的解决与专家的思维活动只是程度上的不同,本质上是一样的。

[正译] 初学者文化能力的提高,信息的获取以及问题的解决与专家的思维活动只是程度上的不同,本质上是一样的。

[评析] 显然,原译是把 literacy 看成是 literary。虽然两词也只有一个字母不同,但前者是指"文化、识字能力",而后者则作"文学上的"解;前者是名词,后者是形容词。作"文学"解的名词是 literature,而不是 literary。

【例 727】But most probably it will all depend upon campers themselves:how many heath fires they cause; how much litter they leave.

[误译] 但是很可能一切要取决于野营者自己:他们造成多少有益健康的大火,又留下了多么少的东西。

[正译] 但是很可能一切要取决于野营者自己:他们造成多少的野火,又丢下了多少的垃圾。

[评析] heath 是作"荒野"解,heath fire 即野火。原译文把 heath 当成 health 了。但是"有益健康的大火"文理上不通,这时就要考虑是否误看、误译的地方。同样 litter 不是 little,litter 是名词,表示"废弃物"。how much little 从语法上讲不通。

英语中有些词的拼法很相似到两个词之间只差一两个字母,特别是它们的不同意义在句中又似乎都讲得通时,容易张冠李戴,造成误译。

【例728】He ingenuously denies such influence but in fact he unquestionably continues to be one of the half dozen most important men in this research institute.

[误译] 他巧妙地否认他的影响,但事实上,他无疑仍旧是这个研究所六、七位最重要的人物之一。

[正译] 他公然否认他的影响,但事实上,他无疑仍旧是这个研究所六、七位最重要的人物之一。

[评析]这句中的 ingenuously 很容易被错认为 ingeniously,两者只在中间相差一个字母:前者在 inge-后面是 nu-,而后者是 ni-,两词的其他字母都完全相同。ingenuously 作"坦率地"、"公然"解,ingeniously 则可作"巧妙地"解。如果把这句上半句译为"他巧妙地否认他的影响……",意义上也说得过去,正因为如此,误译了还自以为是对的。

【例729】His handwriting was considerately legible.

[误译] 他的字迹总是相当清楚易懂。

[正译] 他写的字清楚易认,让人一看就懂。

[评析] 原译文把这句中的 considerately 误以为 considerably,因而误译为"他的字迹总是相当清楚易懂",这里的 considerately 表示"替人着想地"。由于这种误译比较隐蔽,一定要认真阅读原文,仔细辨别词义,切忌不求甚解。

【例730】He has often counseled the president on the formulation of crucial decisions in domestic and foreign affairs

[误译] 他在总统形成国内外事务重大决策过程中,常参与意见。

[正译] 他在总统制订国内外事务重大决策的过程中,常参与意见。

[评析] formulation 很容易和 formation 混淆,如果把这句译为"他在总统形成国内外事务重大决策过程中……",似乎意思也可以,但是原译文把 formulation 误认为 formation 了。formation 的动词形式是 to form,表示"形成",而 formulation 的动词形式是 to formulate,表示"制订"。

第十三节　多枝共干

在英汉翻译中,修饰方面的误译占了很大的比例。这是因为在英语中,无论是副词还是介词短语,它既可以就近修饰某一个成分,也可以分隔修饰较远的一个成分,甚至可以同时修饰两个,或两个以上的成分。尤其是介词短语,它既可以作为定语,修饰句子的主语或宾语等,也可作为状语,修饰句子的谓语。因此,不仔细分析句子结构和上下文意义,往往会造成误译。句子的上下文意思是一个词语受好几个修饰语修饰,或好几个词语共同受一个修饰语修饰。但是由于分析不透,只注意到最明显、最直接的一个修饰关系,而忽视了其他修饰关系,结果出了错。英语句子中有两个或几个动词共受一个状语的修饰,共有一个主语或宾语;或者两个或几个状语共同修饰一个动词,两个或几个主语或宾语共有一个动词;以及其他类型等等。我们把这种语言现象比做几根树枝长在同一根树干上,称之为多枝共干式结构。

【例731】Intense light and heat in the open contrasted with the coolness of shaded avenues and the interiors of buildings.

[误译] 强烈的光线和露天场所的炎热,同林阴道上的凉爽和建筑物内部形成了对比。

[正译] 露天场所的强烈光线和酷热,同林阴道上和建筑物内部的凉爽形成了对比。

[评析] 这样译法当然和原文的意思有出入。从语法分析上究其错误的原因,在于误把句中的后置定语短语 in the open 看做只修饰它前面贴近的名词 heat,而忽略了它也修饰和 heat 并列的 light;其次,误把前置定语 intense 看做只修饰它后面最近的名词 light,而忽略了它既修饰 light 又修饰 heat;在后半句里,也误把 coolness 看做只受后置定语短语 of shaded avenues 的修饰,而没有注意到 the interiors of buildings 的前面省略了 of,其实 coolness 也受 of the interiors of buildings 的修饰。这句中,定语 in the open 和 intense

共同修饰两个名词 light 和 heat, 名词 coolness 受两个定语 of shaded avenues 和（of）the interiors of buildings 的共同修饰。intense light and heat, 与其译为"强烈的光线和炎热"，不如在 heat 前重复 intense, 改为"强烈的光线和酷热"，这样把 intense 修饰 heat 的意思更清楚地表达出来了，所以汉语译文中有时需在第二（或第三）个名词前重复修饰它的定语。

英语句子中一个前置定语修饰几个名词的多枝共干式结构。就一个前置定语修饰两个或几个名词来说，英汉两种语言基本相同，所以理解与翻译都较容易。然而，就两个或几个前置定语修饰一个名词来说，英汉两种语言并不完全相同。例如：

【例 732】the commercial and cultural districts

[误译] 商业和文化区

[正译] 商业区和文化区

[评析] 在英语这个词组中，commercial 和 cultural 共同修饰 districts, 如果按照原文逐词译为"商业和文化区"，译文不够清楚，可能使人误解为"商业和文化"属一个区。其实原文词组也可以说在 commercial 后面省略了 district, 相当于 the commercial district and the cultural district, 实际上是说两种不同类型的地区。按照汉语习惯，应在"商业"后面重复"区"字。英语倾向于省略，汉语习惯于重复，这便是两种语言结构中的一个重要差别，它在英语"多枝共干"式结构的汉译中也有明显的表现。

【例 733】anti-globalization and cutural revival movements

[误译] 反全球化与文化振兴运动

[正译] 反全球化运动与文化振兴运动

[评析] 首先，有些译者对名词 labour 在这里用作什么成分容易搞错，往往会逐词译为"反全球化与文化振兴运动"。这样译法令人费解，它既可能使人把"反全球化"误解为和"文化振兴运动"并列，又可能使人误解为"劳反全球化与文化振兴"属于同一运动。这里的 anti-globalization 其实虽是名词，但用作定语，和 cutural revival 并列，共同修饰 movements。原文相当于 anti-globalization movement 与 cutural revival movement, 说的是"劳工运动"与"民族解放

运动"两个运动,译成汉语应在"劳工"后面重复"运动",译为"劳工运动与民族解放运动"。anti-globalization and cutural revival movements,不能译为"反全球化与文化振兴",应在"反全球化"后面重复"运动",译为"反全球化运动与文化振兴运动",因为它们是两个范畴不同的运动。

【例 734】I trust simplicity and avoidance of fancy frilling will be sedulously sought for.

[误译] 我相信简单化,避免花哨一定会尽力做到的。

[正译] 我相信,大家一定会力求简单,避免花哨的。

[评析] trust 之后省略了一个 that,就容易引起误解。I trust 是管全句的。

【例 735】For new machines or techniques are not merely a product, but a source of fresh creative idea.

[误译] 因为新的机器,新的技术不仅是一种产品,而且是新的创造性思想的源泉。

[正译] 因为新的机器、新的技术不仅是新的创造性的思想的结果,而且是新的创造性思想的源泉。

[评析] 本句中 of fresh creative idea 不仅是 a source 的定语,而且也是 a product 的定语。如果只按 a source 的定语去译,这样的译文就错了。

【例 736】Very proud of their native ancestry and passionately patriotic, they also imbibed the eighteenth century European Culture.

[误译] 他们以土生土长和具有强烈爱国心而自豪,但他们也吸收了十八世纪的欧洲文化。

[正译] 他们以土生土长而自豪,并且也具有强烈的爱国心,但他们也吸收了十八世纪的欧洲文化。

[评析] very proud of 只修饰到 their native ancestry,但也容易误解为一直修饰到 patriotic。这就产生了误译。如果 Very proud of 一直修饰到 patriotic,原句就应为:very proud of their native ancestry and of their passionately patriotic.

【例 737】It would be foolish not to try to understand what is passing in

other people's minds, and what are the springs of action to which
they are responded.

[误译] 如果不想了解别人做出反应时心里想的是什么和他们行动
的动机是什么,那是愚蠢的。

[正译] 如果不想了解别人心里想的是什么,或是不想了解使他们所
以做出反应的动机是什么,那是愚蠢的。

[评析] 原文的 to which they are responded 只跟 action,与 minds 无
关。原译文误判了语法结构。

【例 738】 It is not easy to get the information about that school which
is at once up-to-date, concise and accurate.

[误译] 要立即得到有关这个学校最新的和简明准确的信息是不容
易的。

[正译] 要得到有关这个学校既是最新的,又是简明准确的信息是不
容易的。

[评析] 原文中的 at once...and...是一个固定词组,原译文错误理
解 at once, at once 在此不是"立即"的意思,and 也不是"和"、"以
及"的意思。这一结构连在一起用,是"同时"的意思。一般可以译
为"既……又……"。例如:This book is at once interesting and in-
structive. 这本书既有趣又有益。

【例 739】 Intense light and heat in the open contrasted with the coolness of shaded avenues and the interiors of buildings.

[误译] 强烈的光线和露天场所的炎热跟林阴道上的凉爽和建筑物
内部形成了对照。

[正译] 露天场所那种强烈的光线和酷热跟林阴道上和建筑物内部
的凉爽形成了对照。

[评析] 原句中的定语 intense 不但修饰 light,也修饰 heat,in the
open 不但修饰 heat,还修饰 light;名词 coolness 不但为 of shaded
avenues 所修饰,而且也为(of)the interiors of buildings 所修饰。
这种"多枝共干"式结构很容易引起误解而造成翻译上的错误。

【例 740】 He made little progress in English and Latin compositions.

[误译] 他的英语和拉丁文作文进步都不大。

[正译] 他的英语作文和拉丁文作文进步都不大。

[评析] 如果译成:"他的英语和拉丁文作文进步都不大。"语法上没有错。但意思和原文不相符。是否是多枝共干关系,对上下文的分析很重要。而误译较多的是往往没有注意多枝共干关系。

【例 741】(My patients seemed to like me—not only the nice old ladies...who lived near the park...) but the cabbies, porters and dead beats in the mews and hack streets of Bayswater...

[误译] ……还有马车夫、搬运工和住在贝斯沃特后街和小巷里的穷人们。

[正译] ……还有住在湾水区横街陋巷里的马车夫、搬运工和无业游民。

[评析] 原文中的 cabbies, porters 和 dead beats 显然都属于"穷人"一类,和住在(海德)公园附近的"有教养的老太太,恰成对照。in the mews and back streets of Bayswater 不仅修饰 dead beats 而且修饰 cabbies 和 porters,是一种多枝共干式结构(后置式定语修饰前面的几个名词),原译者没有正确理解这种修饰关系,误以为后置式定语只修饰与之最贴近的一个名词,因而造成误译。

【例 742】 Andrew was a good speaker and student of political philosophy.

[误译] 安德鲁是一个杰出的演说家,又是一个政治哲学系的学生。

[正译] 安德鲁擅长演说,又刻苦学习政治哲学。

[评析] 原译文没有注意到 good 不但修饰 speaker,而且还修饰 student。很清楚,如果 good 仅仅修饰 speaker,不修饰 student 的话,在 student 前应有不定冠词 a。这是一个前置定语修饰两个名词的"多枝共干"结构。

【例 743】 To determine the consequences of sleep deficit, researchers have put subjects through a set of psychological and performance tests requiring them, for instance, to add columns of numbers or recall a passage read to them only minutes earlier.

[误译] 为了确定睡眠不足所带来的后果,研究人员对测试对象进行了一系列的心理表现测试,例如,要求他们做一些数字加法,或让

他们回忆几分钟前读给他们听的材料。

[正译] 为了确定睡眠不足所带来的后果,研究人员对测试对象进行了一系列的心理测试和表现测试,例如,要求他们做一些数字加法,或让他们回忆几分钟前读给他们听的材料。

[评析] "心理表现测试"与"心理测试和表现测试"是两个不同的概念。前者是说一个测试,后者是说两个测试。当然,若没有上下文,这两种译法都可接受。如 the commercial and cultural district,既可译成"商业文化区",也可译成"商业区和文化区"。但这里上下文很清楚;psychological and performance tests 相当于 psychological tests and performance tests。不仅 and 是这种情况,用 or 也有这种情况。例如:The X-ray or post-mortem examination reveals many broken bones. 爱克司光检查或死后检查表明有许多骨头已经折断。

【例 744】 Over the years, tools and technology themselves as a source of fundamental innovation have largely been ignored by historians and philosophers of science.

[误译] 多年来,工具和技术本身作为根本性创新的源泉在很大程度上被历史学家和科学思想家忽视了。

[正译] 多年来,工具和技术本身作为根本性创新的源泉在很大程度上被科学史学家和科学思想家忽视了。

[评析] 这是一个后置定语修饰两个名词的"多枝共干"结构。也就是说句中的 of science 不仅仅修饰靠近的 philosophers,还应同时修饰较远的 historians。

【例 745】 For new machines or techniques are not merely a product, but a source, of fresh creative idea.

[误译] 因为新的机器、新的技术不仅是一种产品,而且是新的创造性思想的源泉。

[正译] 因为新的机器、新的技术不仅是新的创造性思想的结果,而且还是新的创造性思想的源泉。

[评析] 原译文只注意到最明显、最直接的一个修饰关系,而没有注意 of fresh creative idea 不仅修饰 a source,还应修饰 a product,结

果出现了误译。

【例 746】He has never mixed with them or spoken to them on equal terms, but has demanded and generally received a respect due to his position and superior intelligence.

[误译] 他从来没有和他们打成一片, 也从来没有以平等的地位和他们交谈过, 可是由于他的地位和高超的才智, 他要求他们尊敬他, 而且一般来说他总是得到他们的尊敬。

[正译] 他从来不以平等的地位和他们交往, 也不以平等的地位与他们交谈, 可是由于他的地位和高超的才智, 他要求他们尊敬他, 而且一般来说他总是得到他们的尊敬。

[评析] 本句中的 on equal terms 是就近修饰 spoken, 还是同时也修饰前面的 mixed? 在没有上下文的情况下原译也说得过去。但是, 原文中的 he 并不是从不和普通百姓交往, 而是从不以平等的地位和他们交往。后半句 but has demanded... 也说明这一点。所以 on equal terms 也应修饰 mixed。由此可见, 确定多枝共干的关系, 主要靠上下文。

【例 747】He said before the mugging, he went where he wanted, when he wanted, without fear.

[误译] 他说在他被抢劫之前, 他想去哪儿就去哪儿, 想去的时候也不害怕。

[正译] 他说在他被抢劫之前, 他想去哪儿就去哪儿, 想什么时候去就什么时候去, 从不提心吊胆。

[评析] 原译文在两个意思上与原文有出入, 一是 when he wanted 与 where he wanted 是并行结构, 多枝共干于 he went; 二是介词短语 without fear, 不仅修饰 when he wanted, 也修饰 where he wanted。

【例 748】And even those legislative lions who roar against the president on Capitol Hill tend to usually lower their voices and follow their prepared speeches when they walk through the White House door.

[误译] 甚至在国会上对总统咆哮如雷, 不可一世的议员们也常压低嗓音, 当进入白宫大门时, 也只按事先准备的稿子讲话。

[正译] 甚至在国会上对总统咆哮如雷,不可一世的议员们一跨进白宫大门也往往把嗓音压低,并按事先准备好的稿子讲话。

[评析] 原译文认为 when they walk through the White House door 这个状语从句仅仅修饰 follow their prepared speeches。但是从意思上来分析,这个状语从句还应修饰 lower their voices。确切地说是修饰 tend,那么它引出的两个不定式短语当然都受这个状语从句修饰。

【例 749】 The modern school that hails technology argues that such masters as Galileo, Newton, Maxwell, Einstein, and inventors such as Edison attached great importance to, and derived great benefit from craft information and technological devices of different kinds that were usable in scientific experiments.

[误译] 认为技术起重大作用的现代学派说像伽利略、牛顿、马克斯韦尔、爱因斯坦这些大师,像爱迪生这样的发明家都非常注重行业信息以及可用在科学实验中的各种技术工具,并从中获得很大的益处。

[正译] 认为技术起重大作用的现代学派说像伽利略、牛顿、马克斯韦尔、爱因斯坦这些大师,像爱迪生这样的发明家都非常注重可用于他们科学实验中的各种工艺信息和各种技术工具,并从中获得很大的益处。

[评析] 从形式上来看, of different kinds 似乎只修饰 technological devices,因为 devices 是复数,和 of different kinds 是一致的。但是要看到前面的 craft information 实际上也受 of different kinds 修饰。因为 information 是不可数名词,不是一般的单数名词,因此也可和 of different kinds 搭配。另外, that were usable in scientific experiments 也不应只修饰靠近的 technological devices of different kinds,而应包括 craft information。根据上下文,工艺信息和技术工具都属于技术,对科学实验都相当重要。

【例 750】 Other animals were trapped in tar pits, like the elephants, sabre-toothed cats, and numerous other creatures that are found at Rancho la Brea, which is now just a suburb of Los Angeles.

[误译] 还有些别的动物陷入焦油坑内无法脱身,诸如大象、剑齿虎以及在兰桥拉布雷亚(现在洛杉矶的一个郊区)发现的很多别的动物。

[正译] 还有些别的动物陷入焦油坑内无法脱身,诸如在兰桥拉布雷亚(现为洛杉矶的一个郊区)发现的大象、剑齿虎和许多其他动物。

[评析] 本句中的 that are found at Rancho la Brea,这个定语从句被误认为只修饰 numerous other creatures。实际上它还应修饰前面的 elephants, sabre-toothed cats,这不仅从上下文意思中可以作出判断,还可以从 elephants, sabre-toothed cats, and numerous other creatures 合用一个定冠词 the 看出。一般说来,定语从句或其他修饰语的修饰范围应从有定冠词的那个名词开始。

【例 751】How well the predictions will be validated by later performance depends upon the amount, reliability, and appropriateness of the information used and on the skill and wisdom with which it is interpreted.

[误译] 这些预测在多大程度上为后来的表现所证实,这取决于所采用的信息的数量、可靠性和所采用的信息的适宜性,以及技能和解释这些信息的才智。

[正译] 这些预测在多大程度上为后来的表现所证实,这取决于所采用的信息的数量、可靠性和适宜性,以及解释这些信息的技能和才智。

[评析] of the information used 从 the amount 开始修饰;with which it is interpreted 也是从 the skill 开始修饰。如视其分别只修饰 appropriateness 与 wisdom,译成"数量、可靠性和所采用的信息的适宜性"与"技能和解释这些信息的才智"就不符合原意。

【例 752】The standardized educational or psychological tests that are widely used to aid in selecting, classifying, assigning, or promoting students, employees, and military personnel have been the target of recent attacks in books, magazines, the daily press, and even in Congress.

[误译] 教育方面或心理方面的标准化测试已被广泛用来帮助选择、

分类、分配或提拔学生,雇员和军事人员。这种测试最近成为书、杂志、报纸,甚至国会的攻击对象。

[正译] 广泛用来帮助对学生、雇员、军事人员进行选拔、分类、分配任务或提拔的教育或心理方面的标准化测试最近受到了书报杂志,甚至国会的抨击。

[评析] students, employees, and military personnel 不仅是 promoting 的宾语,还应是 selecting, classifying, assigning 的宾语,而原译没有反映出这层关系。所以在组织中文句子,考虑如何表达时,应注意这一点。

第十四节 意群修饰

一个中心词受几个修饰语修饰,前有前置定语,后有后置定语。一般是按自然顺序译的;先译前置定语,后译后置定语,前置定语有好几个,就从右到左译下去。但是由于这些修饰语的层次、性质不同,与中心词的意义关系也不同,若不顾意群关系,按自然顺序译,往往出现错误。

【例 753】The commission of certain acts such as armed attacks, naval blockades, support lent to armed gangs of terrorists was considered as a form of aggression.

[误译] 从事某些行为如武装进攻、海上封锁、向恐怖分子的武装集团提供援助,都被认为是一种侵略。

[正译] 从事某些行为如武装进攻、海上封锁、向武装的恐怖分子集团提供援助,都被认为是一种侵略。

[评析] 在 armed gangs of terrorists 中, gangs of terrorists 是个意群,由 of + terrorists 构成的定语修饰 gangs,而 armed 则是修饰 gangs of terrorists 这整个词组。原译文错误地把 of terrorists 当作修饰 armed gangs,因而误译为"恐怖分子的武装集团"。

【例 754】There is a small boat anchorage.

[误译] 有个泊小船的抛锚地。

[正译] 有个泊船的小抛锚地。

[评析] 如果不注意 boat anchorage 是一个意群, small 是指 anchorage, 就会造成原译文那样的误译。

【例 755】The method of scientific investigation is nothing but the expression of the necessary mode of working of the human mind.

[误译] 科学研究的方法不过是表达必要的人类思维活动方式。

[正译] 科学研究的方法不过是人类思维活动表达的必要方式。

[评析] the expression of the necessary mode of working of the human
mind 这样复杂的结构, 不小心, 就容易误译。当把握不住意群时,
只要根据修饰语按逆序先译, 前置修饰语按顺序后译的原则就不
会产生误译, 在本句中 working of the human mind 是一个意群,
the expression of the necessary mode 是一个意群。

【例 756】What is called "modern civilization" is not the result of a balance development of all man's nature, but of accumulated knowledge applied to practical life.

[误译] 所谓"现代文明"并非是全人类的天性平衡发展的结果, 而是
把积累的知识应用于实际生活的产物。

[正译] 所谓"现代文明"并非是人的全部天性均衡发展的结果, 而是
把积累的知识应用于实际生活的产物。

[评析] all man 不是一个意群, 因为英语里只讲 all men, 没有 all man
的说法。这里的 man 是指 mankind, man's nature 可以是一个意
群:人类的天性, 人类的本性。all 是修饰 nature 的:所有天性。所
以为避免译文表达中的修饰关系不清, 可以把所有格名词 man's
先译出, 再译 all 和 nature, 因为 all nature 是一个意群。

【例 757】He showed that that average individual's sleep cycle is punc-
tuated with peculiar bursts of eye-movements, some drifting and
slow, others jerky and rapid.

[误译] 他证明了人的平均睡眠周期中不时伴有一阵阵独特的眼球
活动, 有的活动飘忽而缓慢, 有的则呈快速跳动状。

[正译] 他证明了正常人的睡眠周期中不时伴有一阵阵独特的眼球
活动, 有的活动飘忽而缓慢, 有的则呈快速跳动状。

[评析] 虽然这里的 average individual's sleep 和上面 all man's nature

表层结构一样,但深层结构不同。因为 average sleep 不是一个意群,不能译为平均睡眠。相反, average individual 应是一个意群:"正常人"、"一般人"。所以,主要要看上下文,若没有上下文 old man's bicycle 既可译成"一位老头的自行车",也可译为"一男式旧自行车"。

【例 758】Hitler realized, as the confidential German papers and subsequent events make clear, that Charnberlain's action was a godsend to him.

[误译] 正如秘密德国文件和随后发生的事件所表明的,希特勒很明白张伯伦的行动对他来说是一个天赐良机。

[正译] 从德国的秘密文件和以后的事态演变看来,希特勒很明白张伯伦的行动对他来说是一个天赐良机。

[评析] confidential 有"秘密的"意思,但是 confidential German 并不是一个意群,confidential papers 才是一个意群:秘密文件。所以一般说来,在几个修饰语中,如有一个表人名、机构名、地名的修饰语,就应首先译出,这样就会形成正确的意群。

【例 759】Its recognition could significantly contribute to the new company economic structure if it leads to a wide acceptance of the need for structural adjustment in the short-, medium-, and long-term.

[误译] 如果这一认识会使更多的人同意经济都需要进行短期、中期和长期的结构调整,那么就会大大有助于新的公司经济结构的建立。

[正译] 如果这一认识会使更多的人同意各国经济都需要进行短期、中期和长期的结构调整,那么就会大大有助于公司经济新结构的建立。

[评析] "新的经济结构"会使人联想到"旧的结构"。其实这里的 new 并不修饰 company,它们不是一个意群。new 是修饰 order,因此 new structure 是一个意群。也就是说,表实义内容的修饰语先译出,让表示新旧、颜色、程度、形状等修饰语靠近被修饰的词语。例如 a reasonably advanced technological society,如译成比较发达的技术社会,就不正确。因为 technological society 并不是一个意

群,应当把 technological 首先译出:一个在技术上相当发达的社会。

第十五节　汉语措词

英语十分倾向于用被动语态,而汉语正好相反,不常用被动语态,在英译汉时要注意转换。

【例 760】The method of scientific investigation is simply the mode by which all phenomena are reasoned about and given precise and exact explanations.

[误译] 科学研究的方法就是所有现象受到这种方式的思索和得到精确而严谨的解释。

[正译] 科学研究的方法就是对一切现象进行思索并给以精确而严谨解释的方法。

[评析] 在英译汉中,除了长句外,被动句也比较难译,很容易出现误译。如果改变说法,用中文主动句来译英语被动句,就不易出错。这个从句中的主语 all phenomena 有两个被动式谓语:are reasoned about, are given precise and exact explanations,但是 by which (= by the mode) 并不是被动式 by 短语。如按主动态,句子就为 by the mode we reason about all phenomena and give them precise and exact explanations 如果按照这个结构翻译,既通顺又准确。

【例 761】Her (China) presence is felt, more than ever, all over the world, assuming historic dimensions in the world political situation.

[误译] 她的存在比以往任何时候都在全世界被感到了,承认了它在世界政治形势中占有历史性的重要地位。

[正译] 全世界比以往任何时候都更加感到中国的存在,它在世界政治形势中占有历史性的重要地位。

[评析] 只要上下文的连贯和原文的强调没有影响,应尽可能把英语的被动句转化为主动句。其中有两个主要方法。一是把原文中的状语,尤其是地点状语用来作译文的主语。例如:Many outstanding officials have been trained in West Point. 西点军校培养出了许

多优秀的军官。二是翻译成汉语无主句,尤其当原文中含有
must, should 等情态动词时。例如:The problem must be dealt
with at the appropriate time with appropriate means. 必须在适当的
时候以适当的手段解决这个问题。

【例 762】To preserve the fiction, the writers kept a steady stream of
visitors driving from Islamabad to Nathia Gali to pay their respects
to the indisposed traveler.

[误译] 为保存这一小说,这些人还组织了一批又一批访客,从伊斯
兰堡驱车,至纳蒂亚加利去探望这位身体欠佳的贵宾。

[正译] 这些人为了不露破绽,还组织了一批又一批访客,从伊斯兰
堡驱车,至纳蒂亚加利去探望这位身体欠佳的贵宾。

[评析] 首先 fiction 在这里不作"小说"解,而是"虚构"、"虚假"的意
思。根据上下文,这里是指设下的骗局,或布置的假象。但是,To
preserve the fiction,译成"保护假象",也不好理解。这也就牵涉到
英汉两种语言不同的表达习惯。有时候原文是肯定的表达形式,
用否定的形式来译出,就更接近中文的表达习惯。译成"为了不露
破绽"就很好地表达了 To preserve the fiction 的内在含义。

【例 763】Asia was passed over by the industrial revolution.

[误译] 亚洲被工业革命忽视了。

[正译] 工业革命没有光顾亚洲。

[评析] 如果不改变说法,逐词死译为"亚洲被工业革命忽视了",意
思就不明晰,翻译不准确。

【例 764】Even Christopher, who is not an excessively modest or silent
man, hesitated to face Christina with the disasters Christopher knew
lay ahead.

[误译] 甚至克里斯多佛这个不是过分谦虚或安静的人在把他知道
要发生的灾难告诉克里斯蒂娜时,也有点踟躇不前。

[正译] 甚至克里斯多佛这个有点傲气,喜欢乱发言论的人在把他知
道要发生的灾难告诉克里斯蒂娜时,也有点踟躇不前。

[评析] "不是过分谦虚"过分拘泥于原文的形式,反而表达不清意
思。英语中有些句子以否定形式出现,如果难于用汉语表达,换个

273

说法,用肯定形式来翻译,意思就会顺畅。

【例 765】 The animal protection organization has not so far justified the hopes which the people who love animals set on it.

[误译] 到目前为止这个动物保护组织还没有为热爱动物的人所寄予的希望辩护。

[正译] 到目前为止,这个动物保护组织辜负了热爱动物的人所寄予的希望。

[评析] 如果照搬原文结构,按照原译文的译法,读者就很难理解汉译文意思,改正译文把否定句改为肯定的说法,使得译文简洁易懂。

【例 766】 The thought of returning to his native land has never deserted him.

[误译] 归国念头没有离开过他。

[正译] 归国的念头一直在他心中萦绕。

[评析] 原句以否定形式出现,如果照样翻译,汉译文就很难理解。用肯定形式来翻译,既没有改变原文的意思,又符合汉语的表达习惯。

第十六节　改换说法

英语和汉语是两种完全不同的语言。英语中除了句子的修饰方法,表达重点之外,在其他方面也有独特的表达方式,如被动结构,无生命非人称主语,抽象虚化表达,否定结构,代词用法等等。对英语中这些独特的表达习惯只有改换说法,才能准确地把意思表达出来。

【例 767】 She modelled between roles.

[误译] 她在两个角色之间当模特。

[正译] 她在不演戏的时候就去当模特儿。

[评析] 原文如果不改变表达方式,生硬地译为“在两个角色之间当模特”,词不达意,会让读者感到不知所云。

【例 768】 I have read your articles. I expected to meet an older man.

[误译] 我拜读过大作。我盼望遇到一个更老的人。

[正译] 我拜读过大作。没有想到你这么年轻有为。

[评析] 原译文的译法不通顺,不符合汉语的表达习惯,应变换说法,
　　以使汉译文更加达意。

【例769】Every time I come back from business trip it makes a new
　　man of me.

[误译] 每次出差回来,这儿都使我成为一个新人

[正译] 每次出差回来,这儿都叫我感到耳目一新,精神一爽。

[评析]"这儿都使我成为一个新人"的译法很别扭,汉语不这样表
　　达,改换说法,译出其深层次的意思"这儿都叫我感到耳目一新"。

【例770】But the master of the house was his mother. She was twice
　　man her son was.

[误译] 这个房子的主人是他母亲,他母亲是他的两倍。

[正译] 在这个家里是他母亲当家,他连他母亲的一半也顶不上。

[评析] 本句如果译为"他母亲是他的两倍"或者"他母亲赛过他两个
　　人"等,意思都含混不清。应根据对其深层意思的理解译为"可是
　　这个家里是他母亲说了算",或者译为"他母亲当家",原文还可译
　　为:"他那样的人,两个也比不过他母亲。"

【例771】When she and he met again, each had been married to anoth-
　　er.

[误译] 他和她又见面了,他们各自与另一个人结婚了。

[正译] 他们再次相逢时,一个已经娶妻,一个也已经出嫁。

[评析] 如果将这句的主语译成"他和她"就显得不顺畅,改译为"他
　　们"就比较上口;后半句如译成"他们各自与另一个人结婚了"则意
　　思不够清楚,改换说法,将二人的情况分译。

【例772】I will go and attend the reception, if only to make some new
　　friends.

[误译] 只是为了交几个新朋友,我会去参加招待会的。

[正译] 我会去参加招待会的,那怕交几个新朋友也好

[评析] if only 在本句不能翻译为"只是为了……",这个译法很令人
　　费解,改换说法为"那怕……",汉译文意思便清晰了。

第十七节 转移修辞

【例 773】So I swam and, presumably because of the long absence of foreigners from here, before an undeservedly large and enthusiastic audience.

[误译] 于是我就下水游泳了。大概这儿的人很久没有见过外国人了,所以我游泳时旁边有一群不值得的热心观众。

[正译] 于是我就下水游泳了。大概这儿的人很久没有见过外国人了,所以我游泳时河边站了一大群热心的观众,而单凭我的技术是引不来这么多人的。

[评析] undeservedly 位于 large 之前,副词修饰形容词,似乎语法上很顺。但这只是英语中的一种表达法。这种副词状语,用来表示说话人对事物的看法和态度。它们虽然出现在某个词前面,说明的却是说话人的态度。因此,只有换一下说法,才能把意思确切表达出来。undeservedly 虽然出现在 large and enthusiastic audience 之前,说的却是对自己游泳的评价。

【例 774】He also concluded that insight into prehistoric cultures should ideally proceed from knowledge of living cultures.

[误译] 他还得出这样的结论:要对史前各种文化有深刻的认识,应从了解现存的种种文化理想地入手。

[正译] 他还得出这样的结论:要对史前各种文化有深刻的认识,应从了解现存的种种文化着手,这是最理想的方法。

[评析] 如果照原来修饰顺序翻译:“应从了解现存的种种文化理想地入手”就误译了。ideally 虽然出现在 proceed from knowledge of living cultures 之前,但是用来表示说话人对该行为的看法和态度。

【例 775】Tobacco addicts remain hopelessly blind to signs that say NO SMOKING.

[误译] 瘾君子对那些“禁止吸烟”的标志毫无希望地理也不理。

[正译] 瘾君子对那些“禁止吸烟”的标志视若无睹,已达到无可救药的地步。

［评析］如果照原来修饰顺序翻译，就是没有了解 hopelessly 的作用。hopelessly 虽然是副词状语，修饰 remain blind，说明的却是说话人的态度。

【例 776】It was sharply different from the West, where an evening was hurried from phase to phase toward its close, in a continually disappointed anticipation or else in sheer nervous dread of the moment itself.

［误译］这种情况和我在西部所见到的截然不同。那里，晚间社交活动总是匆匆而过直到结束，要么是以一种不断失望的心情期盼着，要么每时每刻紧张得害怕。

［正译］这种情况和我在西部所见到的截然不同。那里，晚间社交活动总是匆匆而过直到结束，每一阶段，参加者不断地期望着，又不断失望，要不然就是心情十分紧张，每时每刻都担惊受怕。

［评析］"以不断失望的心情期盼着"这话令人费解。这里涉及英语的另一表达法：移位修辞法。即表明 A 特性的修饰语被移去说明不具有这种特性的 B。例如：an exhausting hill, a sleepless night, gray peace, exhausting, sleepless 是指人的状况，现在直接修饰"山"和"夜"。gray 指天色，这里用来修饰抽象概念"宁静"。有时候可以按字面修饰译出。例如 an exhausting hill 可以译为"累人的小山"、a sleepless night 可以译为"不眠之夜"、gray peace 可以译为"灰色的宁静"。但是有时候必须要调整，改换说法，否则难以表达其含义。这里的 disappointed anticipation 和 nervous dread, disappointed 和 nervous 都是描写人物心情的，因此在翻译时，不能去直接修饰 anticipation 和 dread, 而是要和人联系上。又如：Darrow had whispered throwing a reassuring arm round my shoulder. 达罗用一只胳膊搭在我肩头上悄声安慰我说。/And then I went upstairs to the library and studied investments and securities for a conscientious hour. 然后我上楼去了书房，用了一小时认真研究了投资及证券。

英语教材书目

1. 新世纪博士生综合英语(配有磁带 5 盘)　　　　　24 元
2. 新世纪英语专业听力教程 1(配有磁带 5 盘)　　　　17 元
3. 新世纪英语专业听力教程 2(配有磁带 5 盘)　　　　16 元
4. 新世纪英语专业听力教程 3(配有磁带 5 盘)　　　　13 元
5. 新世纪英语专业听力教程 4(配有磁带 4 盘)　　　　13 元
6. 高级英文写作教程：实用写作　　　　　　　　　　13 元
7. 高级英文写作教程：论文写作　　　　　　　　　　17 元
8. 高级英文词汇教程　　　　　　　　　　　　　　　25 元
9. 英语文体翻译教程　　　　　　　　　　　　　　　26 元
10. 英汉汉英翻译教程　　　　　　　　　　　　　　　10 元
11. 新编英汉汉英翻译教程：翻译技巧与误译评析　　　14 元
12. 英语学习背景知识：美国加拿大（第三版）　　　　17 元
13. 英语学习背景知识：英国澳大利亚（第三版）　　　10 元
14. 英语学习背景知识：欧洲概观　　　　　　　　　　20 元
15. 最新大学英语六级统考词汇手册　　　　　　　　　19 元
16. 美国法治面面观　　　　　　　　　　　　　　　　20 元
17. 文本与他者：福克纳解读　　　　　　　　　　　　35 元
18. 性别·种族·文化：托妮·莫里森与二十世纪美国黑人文学 15 元